American Men of Letters.

EDITED BY

CHARLES DUDLEY WARNER.

Engraved by J.C.Buttre.

J. Fenimore Cooper

American Men of Letters.

JAMES FENIMORE COOPER.

BY

THOMAS R. LOUNSBURY,

PROFESSOR OF ENGLISH IN THE SHEFFIELD SCIENTIFIC SCHOOL,
YALE COLLEGE.

BOSTON:
HOUGHTON, MIFFLIN AND COMPANY.
New York: 11 East Seventeenth Street.
The Riverside Press, Cambridge.
1883.

Copyright, 1882,
By THOMAS R. LOUNSBURY.

All rights reserved.

The Riverside Press, Cambridge:
Electrotyped and Printed by H. O. Houghton & Co.

PREFATORY NOTE.

WHEN Cooper lay on his death-bed he enjoined his family to permit no authorized account of his life to be prepared. A wish even, that was uttered at such a time, would have had the weight of a command; and from that day to this pious affection has carried out in the spirit as well as to the letter the desire of the dying man. No biography of Cooper has, in consequence, ever appeared. Nor is it unjust to say that the sketches of his career, which are found either in magazines or cyclopædias, are not only unsatisfactory on account of their incompleteness, but are all in greater or less degree untrustworthy in their details.

It is a necessary result of this dying injunction that the direct and authoritative sources of information contained in family papers are closed to the biographer. Still it is believed that no facts of importance in the record of an eventful and extraordinary career have been omitted or have even been passed over slightingly. A large part of the matter contained in this volume has never been given to the public in any form: and for that reason among others no pains have been spared to make this narrative absolutely accurate, so far as it goes. Correction of any errors, if such are found, will be gratefully welcomed.

JAMES FENIMORE COOPER.

CHAPTER I.

1789–1820.

In one of the interior counties of New York, less than one hundred and fifty miles in a direct line from the commercial capital of the Union, lies the village of Cooperstown. The place is not and probably never will be an important one; but in its situation and surroundings nature has given it much that wealth cannot furnish or art create. It stands on the southeastern shore of Otsego Lake, just at the point where the Susquehanna pours out from it on its long journey to the Chesapeake. The river runs here in a rapid current through a narrow valley, shut in by parallel ranges of lofty hills. The lake, not more than nine miles in length, is twelve hundred feet above tide-water. Low and wooded points of land and sweeping bays give to its shores the attraction of continuous diversity. About it, on every side, stand hills, which slope gradually or rise sharply to heights varying from two to five hundred feet. Lake, forest, and stream unite to form a scene of quiet but picturesque beauty, that hardly needs the additional charm of romantic association which has been imparted to it.

Though it was here that the days of Cooper's childhood were passed, it was not here that he was born. When that event took place the village had hardly even an existence on paper. Cooper's father, a resident of Burlington, New Jersey, had come, shortly after the close of the Revolutionary War, into the possession of vast tracts of land, embracing many thousands of acres, along the head-waters of the Susquehanna. In 1786 he began the settlement of the spot, and in 1788 laid out the plot of the village which bears his name, and built for himself a dwelling-house. On the 10th of November, 1790, his whole family — consisting, with the servants, of fifteen persons — reached the place. The future novelist was then a little less than thirteen months old, for he had been born at Burlington on the 15th of September of the year before. His father had determined to make the new settlement his permanent home. He accordingly began in 1796, and in 1799 completed, the erection of a mansion which bore the name of Otsego Hall. It was then and remained for a long time afterward the largest private residence in that portion of the State. When in 1834 it came into the hands of the son, it still continued to be the principal dwelling in the flourishing village that had grown up about it.

On his father's side Cooper was of Quaker descent. The original emigrant ancestor had come over in 1679, and had made extensive purchases of land in the province of New Jersey. In that colony or in Pennsylvania his descendants for a long time remained. Cooper himself was the first one, of the direct line certainly, that ever even revisited the mother-country. These facts are of slight importance in themselves. In the general disbelief, however, which fifty years ago prevailed in Great Britain, that anything good could come out of this western Nazareth, Cooper was immediately furnished with an English nativity as soon as he had won reputation. The same process that gave to Irving a birthplace in Devonshire, furnished one also to him in the Isle of Man. When this fiction was exploded, the fact of emigration was pushed merely a little further back. It was transferred to the father, who was represented as having gone from Buckinghamshire to America. This latter assertion is still to be found in authorities that are generally trustworthy. But the original one served a useful purpose during its day. This assumed birthplace in the Isle of Man enabled the English journalists that were offended with Cooper's strictures upon their country to speak of him, as at one time they often did, as an English renegade.

His mother's maiden name was Elizabeth Fenimore, and the family to which she belonged was of Swedish descent. Cooper himself was the eleventh of twelve children. Most of his brothers and sisters died long before him, five of them in infancy. His own name was at first simply James Cooper, and in this way he wrote it until 1826. But in April of that year the Legislature of New York passed an act changing the family name to Fenimore-Cooper. This was done in accordance with the wish of his grandmother, whose descendants in the direct male line had died out. But he seldom employed the hyphen in writing, and finally gave up the use of it altogether.

The early childhood of Cooper was mainly passed in the wilderness at the very time when the first wave of civilization was beginning to break against its hills. There was everything in what he saw and heard to impress the mind of the growing boy. He was on the

border, if indeed he could not justly be said to be in
the midst of mighty and seemingly interminable woods
which stretched for hundreds of miles to the westward.
Isolated clearings alone broke this vast expanse of foli-
age, which, covering the valleys and clinging to the sides
and crowning the summits of the hills, seemed to rise
and fall like the waves of the sea. The settler's axe
had as yet scarcely dispelled the perpetual twilight of
the primeval forest. The little lake lay enclosed in a
border of gigantic trees. Over its waters hung the in-
terlacing branches of mighty oaks and beeches and
pines. Its surface was frequented by flocks of wild,
aquatic birds, — the duck, the gull, and the loon. In this
lofty valley among the hills were also to be found, then
as now, in fullest perfection, the clear atmosphere, the
cloudless skies, and the brilliant light of midsummer
suns, that characterize everywhere the American highlands. More even than the beauty and majesty of nature that lay open to the sight was the mystery that
constantly appealed to the imagination in what might
lie hidden in the depths of a wilderness that swept far
beyond glance of eye or reach of foot. This, indeed,
may have affected the feelings of only a few, but there
were numerous interests and anxieties which all had in
common. The little village had early gone through
many of the trials which mark the history of most of
the settlements in regions to which few travelers found
their way and commerce seldom came. Remote from
sources of supply, and difficult of access, it had known
the time when its population, scanty as it was, suffered
from the scarcity of food. Sullivan's successful expedi-
tion against the Six Nations did not suffice to keep it
from the alarm of savage attack that never came.

The immense forest shutting in the hamlet on every side had terrors to some as real as were its attractions to others. Its recesses were still the refuge of the deer; but they were also the haunt of the wildcat, the wolf, and the bear. All these characteristics of his early home made deep impression upon a nature fond of adventure, and keenly susceptible to the charm of scenery. When afterward in the first flush of his fame Cooper set out to revive the memory of the days of the pioneers, he said that he might have chosen for his subject happier periods, more interesting events, and possibly more beauteous scenes, but he could not have taken any that would lie so close to his heart. The man, indeed, never forgot what had been dear to the boy; and to the spot where his earliest years were spent he returned to pass the latter part of his life.

The original settlement, moreover, was composed of a more than usually singular mixture of the motley crowd that always throngs to the American frontier. The shock of convulsions in lands far distant reached even to the highland valley shut in by the Otsego hills. Representatives of almost every nationality in Christendom and believers in almost every creed, found in it an asylum or a home. Into this secluded haven drifted men whose lives had been wrecked in the political storms that were then shaking Europe. Frenchmen, Dutchmen, Germans, and Poles, came and tarried for a longer or shorter time. Here Talleyrand, then an exile, spent several days with Cooper's father, and, true to national instinct, wrote, according to local tradition, complimentary verses, still preserved, on Cooper's sister. An ex-captain of the British army was one of the original merchants of the place. An ex-governor of Martinique was for a time the village grocer. But the prevailing element in the population were the men of New England, born levelers of the forest, the greatest wielders of the axe the world has ever known. Over the somewhat wild and turbulent democracy, made up of materials so diverse, the original proprietor reigned a sort of feudal lord, rather by moral qualities than by any conceded right.

Cooper's early instruction was received in the village school, carried on in a building erected in 1795, and rejoicing in the somewhat pretentious name of the Academy. The country at that time, however, furnished few facilities for higher education anywhere; on the frontier there were necessarily none. Accordingly Cooper was early sent to Albany. There he entered the family of the rector of St. Peter's Church, and became, with three or four other boys, one of his private pupils. This gentleman, the son of an English clergyman, and himself a graduate of an English university, had made his ways to these western wilds with a fair amount of classical learning, with thorough methods of study, and as it afterwards turned out, Cooper tells us, with another man's wife. This did not, however, prevent him from insisting upon the immense superiority of the mother-country in morals as well as manners. A man of ability and marked character, he clearly exerted over the impressionable mind of his pupil a greater influence than the latter ever realized. He was in many respects, indeed, a typical Englishman of the educated class of that time. He had the profoundest contempt for republics and republican institutions. The American Revolution he looked upon as only a little less monstrous than the French, which was the sum of all iniquities.

Connection with any other church than his own was to be shunned, not at all because it was unchristian, but because it was ungentlemanly and low. But whatever his opinions and prejudices were, in the almost absolute dearth then existing in this country of even respectable scholarship, the opportunity to be under his instruction was a singular advantage. Unfortunately it did not continue as long as it was desirable. In 1802 he died. It had been the intention to fit Cooper to enter the junior class of Yale College; that project had now to be abandoned. Accordingly he became, at the beginning of the second term of its freshman year, a member of the class which was graduated in 1806. He was then but a mere boy of thirteen, and with the exception of the poet Hillhouse, two weeks his junior, was the youngest student in the college.

Cooper himself informs us that he played all his first year, and implies that he did little study during those which followed. To a certain extent the comparative excellence of his preparation turned out a disadvantage; the rigid training he had received enabled him to accomplish without effort what his fellow-students found difficult. Scholarship was at so low an ebb that the ability to scan Latin was looked upon as a high accomplishment; and he himself asserts that the class to which he belonged was the first in Yale College that had ever tried it. This may be questioned; but we need not feel any distrust of his declaration, that little learning of any kind found its way into his head. Least of all will he be inclined to doubt it whom extended experience in the class-room has taught to view with profoundest respect the infinite capability of the human mind to resist the introduction of knowledge.

Far better than study, Cooper liked to take solitary walks about the wooded hills surrounding New Haven, and the shores of the bay upon which it lies. These nursed the fondness for outdoor life and scenery which his early associations had inspired. In these communings with nature, he was unconsciously storing his mind with impressions and images, in the representation and delineation of which he was afterward to attain surpassing excellence. But the study of scenery, however desirable in itself, cannot easily be included in a college curriculum. No proficiency in it can well compensate for failure in studies of perhaps less intrinsic importance. The neglect of these latter had no tendency to recommend him to the regard of those in authority. Positive faults were in course of time added to negative. A frolic in which he was engaged during his third year was attended by consequences more serious than disfavor. It led to his dismissal. The father took the boy's side, and the usual struggle followed between the parents and those who, according to a pretty well worn-out educational theory, stand to the student in place of parents. In this particular case the latter triumphed, and Cooper left Yale. In spite of his dismissal he retained pleasant recollections of some of his old instructors; and with one of them, Professor Silliman, he kept up in later years friendly personal relations and occasional correspondence.

It had been a misfortune for the future author to lose the severe if somewhat wooden drill of his preparatory instructor. It was an additional misfortune to lose the education, scanty and defective as it then was, which was imparted by the college. It might not and probably would not have contributed anything to Cooper's intellectual development in the way of accuracy of thought or of statement. It would not in all probability have added materially to his stock of knowledge. But with all its inefficiency and inadequacy, it would very certainly have had the effect of teaching him to aim far more than he did at perfection of form. He possibly gained more than he lost by being transferred at so early an age to other scenes. But the lack of certain qualities in his writings, which educated men are perhaps the only ones to notice, can be traced pretty directly to this lack of preliminary intellectual drill.

His academical career having been thus suddenly cut short, he entered in a little while upon one better suited to his adventurous nature. Boys are sent to sea, he tells us in one of his later novels, for the cure of their ethical ailings. This renovating influence of ocean life he had at any rate a speedy opportunity to try. It was decided that he should enter the navy. The position of his father, who had been for several years a representative in Congress, and was a leading member of the Federalist party, naturally held out assurances that the son would receive all the advancement to which he would be legitimately entitled. At that time no naval school existed. It was the custom, in consequence, for boys purposing to fit themselves for the position of officers to serve a sort of apprenticeship in the merchant marine. Accordingly in the autumn of 1806, Cooper was placed on board a vessel that was to sail from the port of New York with a freight of flour to Cowes and a market. The ship was named the Sterling, and was commanded by Captain John Johnston, of Wiscasset, Maine, who was also part owner. Cooper's position and prospects were well known ; but he was employed regularly before the mast and was never admitted to the cabin. The vessel cleared from the port of New York on the 16th of October. The passage was a long and stormy one; forty days went by before land was seen after it had once been left behind. The ship reached the other side just at the time when the British Channel was alive with vessels of war in consequence of one of the periodical anticipations of invasions from France. It went to London, and stayed for some time there discharging its cargo and taking in new. Cooper embraced the opportunity to see all the sights he could of the great metropolis. " He had a rum time of it in his sailor rig," said afterward one of his shipmates, " but hoisted in a wonderful deal of gibberish, according to his own account of the cruise."

The Sterling sailed with freight in January, 1807, for the Straits of Gibraltar. It took on board a cargo of barilla at Aguilas and Almeria, and returned to England, reaching the Thames in May. Both going and coming the voyage was a stormy one, and during it several of the incidents occurred that Cooper worked up afterward into powerful passages in his sea novels. In London the vessel lay several weeks, discharging its cargo and taking in more, which this time consisted of dry goods. Towards the end of July, it left London for America, and reached Philadelphia on the 18th of September, after another long and stormy passage of fifty-two days.

This was Cooper's introduction to sea life. During the year he had spent in the merchant vessel he had seen a good deal of hard service. His preparatory studies having been completed after a fashion, he now regularly entered the navy. His commission as midshipman bears date the 1st of January, 1808. On the 24th of the following February he was ordered to report to the commanding naval officer at New York. But the records of the government give little information as to the duties to which he was assigned during the years he remained in its service. The knowledge we have of his movements comes mainly from what he himself incidentally discloses in published works or letters of a later period. The facts we learn from all sources together, are but few. He served for a while on board the Vesuvius in 1808. During that year it seemed as if the United States and Great Britain were about to drift into war. Preparations of various kinds were made; and one of the things ordered was the dispatch to Lake Ontario of a party, of which Cooper was one, under the command of Lieutenant Woolsey. The intention was to build a brig of sixteen guns to command that inland water; and the port of Oswego, then a mere hamlet of some twenty houses, was the place selected for its construction. Around it lay a wilderness, thirty or forty miles in depth. Here the party spent the following winter, and during it the Oneida, as the brig was called, was finished. Early in the spring of 1809 it was launched. By that time, however, the war-cloud had blown over, and the vessel was not then used for the purpose for which it had been constructed. More permanent results, however, were accomplished than the building of a ship. The knowledge and experience which Cooper then gained was something beyond and above what belonged to his profession. It is to his residence on the shores of that inland sea that we owe the vivid picture drawn of Lake Ontario in " The Pathfinder " and of the wilderness which then surrounded it on every side.

After the completion of the Oneida, Cooper accompanied Lieutenant Woolsey on a visit to Niagara Falls. The navy records show that on the 10th of June, 1809, he was left by his commander in charge of the gunboats on Lake Champlain. They further reveal the fact that on the 27th of September of this same year he was granted a furlough to make a European voyage. This project for some reason was given up, as on the 13th of November, 1809, he was ordered to the Wasp, then under the command of Lawrence, who afterwards fell in the engagement between the Shannon and the Chesapeake. To this officer, like himself a native of Burlington, he was very warmly attached. The next notice of him contained in the official records is to the effect that on the 9th of May, 1810, permission was granted him to go on furlough for twelve months. Whether he availed himself of it is not known. An event soon occurred, however, that put an end to his naval career as effectively as one had previously been put to his collegiate. An attachment had sprung up some time before between him and a Miss DeLancey. On the 1st of January, 1811, the couple were married at Mamaroneck, Westchester County, New York. Cooper was then a little more than twenty-one years old; the bride lacked very little of being nineteen.

His wife belonged to a Huguenot family, which towards the end of the seventeenth century had fled from France, and had finally settled in Westchester. During the Revolutionary War the DeLanceys had taken the side of the crown against the colonies. Several of them held positions in the British army. John Peter DeLancey, whose daughter Cooper had married, had been himself a captain in that service. After the recognition of American independence he went to England, but, having resigned his commission, returned in 1789 to this country, and spent the remainder of his life at his home in Mamaroneck. The fact that his kinsmen by marriage had belonged to the defeated party in the Revolutionary struggle led Cooper in his writings to treat the Tories, as they were called, with a fairness and generosity which in that day few were disposed to show, at least in print. This tenderness is plainly to be seen in " The Spy," written at the beginning of his career; it is still more marked in " Wyandotte," produced in the latter part of it, when circumstances had made him profoundly dissatisfied with much that he saw about him. One of the last, though least heated, of the many controversies in which he was. engaged was in regard to the conduct on a particular occasion of General Oliver De-Lancey, a cousin of his wife's father. This officer was charged unjustly, as Cooper believed, with the brutal treatment of the American General Woodhull, who had fallen into his hands. The discussion in regard to this point was carried on in the " New York Home Journal" in the early part of 1848.

It seldom falls to the lot of the biographer to record a home life more serene and happy than that which fell to the share of the man whose literary life is the stormiest to be found in the history of American men of letters. Cooper, like many persons of fiery temperament and strong will, was very easily managed through his affections. In theory he maintained the headship of man in the household in the extremest form. He gives in several of his works no uncertain indication of his views on that point. This only serves to make more conspicuous the fact, which forces itself repeatedly upon the attention, that his movements were largely, if not mainly, controlled by his wife. This becomes noticeable at the very beginning of their union. She was unwilling to undergo the long and frequent separations from her husband that the profession of a naval officer would demand. Accordingly, he abandoned the idea of continuing in it. The acceptance of his resignation bears date the 6th of May, 1811. He had then been regularly in the service a little less than three years and a half.

After quitting the navy Cooper led for a long time a somewhat unsettled life. For about a year and a half he resided at Heathcote Hall, Mamaroneck, the residence of his wife's father. He then rented a small cottage in the neighborhood, and in this remained about a year. His early home, however, was the spot to which his heart turned. To Cooperstown, in consequence, he went back in 1814, taking up his residence at a place outside the village limits, called Fenimore. He purposed to devote his attention to agriculture, and accordingly began at this spot the building of a large stone farm house. While it was in process of construction his wife, anxious to be near her own family, persuaded him to go back to Westchester. Thither in 1817 he went, leaving his dwelling at Fenimore unfinished, and in 1823 it was completely destroyed by fire. In Westchester, a few months after his return, he took up his residence, in the town of Scarsdale, on what was called the Angevine farm, from the name of a French family that had occupied it for several generations. The site of his dwelling was a commanding one, and gave from the south front an extensive view of the country about it and of Long Island Sound. It remained his home until the literary profession, upon which he unexpectedly entered, forced him to leave it for New York city.

Great changes had occurred during these years, or were occurring, in his personal surroundings. His father had died in 1809, and his mother in 1817. Before 1820 five daughters had been born to him. The first of these did not live to the age of two years; but the others all reached maturity. The second, Susan Augusta, herself an authoress, became in his later years his secretary and amanuensis, and would naturally have written his life, had not his unfortunate dying injunction stood in the way. A son, Fenimore, born at Angevine, in 1821, died early, and his youngest child, Paul, now a lawyer at Albany, was not born until after his removal to New York city. Surrounded by his growing family, he led for the two or three years following 1817 a life that gave no indication of what was to be his career. His thoughts were principally directed to improving the little estate that had come into his possession. He planted trees, he built fences, he drained swamps, he planned a lawn. The one thing which he did not do was to write.

CHAPTER II.

1820–1822.

COOPER had now reached the age of thirty. Up to this time he had written nothing, nor had he prepared or collected any material for future use. No thought of taking up authorship as a profession had entered his mind. Even the physical labor involved in the mere act of writing was itself distasteful. Unexpectedly, however, he now began a course of literary production that was to continue without abatement during the little more than thirty years which constituted the remainder of his life.

Seldom has a first work been due more entirely to accident than that which he composed at the outset of his career. In his home at Angevine he was one day reading to his wife a novel descriptive of English society. It did not please him, and he suddenly laid down the book and said, "I believe I could write a better story myself." Challenged to make good his boast, he sat down to perform the task, and wrote out a few pages of the tale he had formed in his mind. The encouragement of his wife determined him to go on and complete it, and when completed the advice of friends decided him to publish it. Accordingly, on the 10th of November, 1820, a novel in two volumes, entitled "Precaution," made its appearance in New York. In this purely haphazard way did the most prolific of American authors begin his literary life.

The work was brought out in a bad shape, and its typographical defects were unconsciously exaggerated by Cooper in a revised edition of it, which was published after his return from Europe. In the preface to the latter he said that no novel of modern times had ever been worse printed than was this story as it originally appeared. The manuscript, he admitted, was bad ; but the proof-reading could only be described as execrable. Periods turned up in the middle of sentences, while the places where they should have been knew them not. Passages, in consequence, were rendered obscure, and even entire paragraphs became unintelligible. A careful reading of the edition of 1820 will show something to suggest, but little to justify, these sweeping assertions. But the work has never been much read even by the admirers of the author ; and it is a curious illustration of this fact, that the personal friend, who delivered the funeral discourse upon his life and writings, avoided the discussion of it with such care that he was betrayed into exposing the lack of interest he sought to hide. Bryant confessed he had not read " Precaution." He had merely dipped into the first edition of it, and had been puzzled and repelled by the profusion of commas and other pauses. The non-committalism of cautious criticism could hardly hope to go farther. Punctuation has had its terrors and its triumphs ; but this victory over the editor of a daily newspaper must be deemed its proudest recorded achievement. The poet went on to say that to a casual inspection the revised edition, which Cooper afterward brought out, seemed almost another work. The inspection which could come to such a conclusion must have been of that exceedingly casual kind which contents itself with contemplating the outside of

2

a book, and disdains to open it. As a matter of fact the changes made hardly extended beyond the correction of some points of punctuation and of some grammatical forms; it was in a few instances only that the construction of the sentences underwent transformation. Not an incident was altered, not a sentiment modified.

Such ignorance on the part of a contemporary and personal friend, if it proves nothing else, shows certainly the little hold this novel has had upon the public taste. Nevertheless, the first work of any well-known author must always have a certain interest belonging to it, entirely independent of any value the work may have in itself. In this case, moreover, the character of the tale and the circumstances attending its production are of no slight importance, when taken in connection with the literary history of the times. It was accident that led to the selection of the subject; but as things then were, Cooper was not unlikely, in any event, to have chosen it or one very similar. The intellectual dependence of America upon England at that period is something that it is now hard to understand. Political supremacy had been cast off, but the supremacy of opinion remained absolutely unshaken. Of creative literature there was then very little of any value produced: and to that little a foreign stamp was necessary, to give currency outside of the petty circle in which it originated. There was slight encouragement for the author to write; there was still less for the publisher to print. It was indeed a positive injury ordinarily to the commercial credit of a bookseller to bring out a volume of poetry or of prose fiction which had been written by an American; for it was almost certain to fail to pay expenses. A sort of critical literature was struggling, or rather gasping, for a life that was hardly worth living; for its most marked characteristic was its servile deference to English judgment and dread of English censure. It requires a painful and penitential examination of the reviews of the period to comprehend the utter abasement of mind with which the men of that day accepted the foreign estimate upon works written here, which had been read by themselves, but which it was clear had not been read by the critics whose opinions they echoed. Even the meekness with which they submitted to the most depreciatory estimate of themselves was outdone by the anxiety with which they hurried to assure the world that they, the most cultivated of the American race, did not presume to have so high an opinion of the writings of some one of their countrymen as had been expressed by enthusiasts, whose patriotism had proved too much for their discernment. Never was any class so eager to free itself from charges that imputed to it the presumption of holding independent views of its own. Out of the intellectual character of many of those who at that day pretended to be the representatives of the highest education in this country, it almost seemed that the element of manliness had been wholly eliminated; and that along with its sturdy democracy, whom no obstacles thwarted and no dangers daunted, the New World was also to give birth to a race of literary cowards and parasites. With such a state of feeling prevalent, a work of fiction that concerned America might seem to have small chance of success with Americans themselves. It would not, therefore, have been strange, under any circumstances, that in beginning his career as an author Cooper should have chosen to write a tale of English social life. The fact that he knew personally nothing about what he was describing was in itself no insuperable objection. That ignorance was then and has since been shared by many novelists on both sides of the water, who have treated of the same subject. Relying upon English precedent, he might in fact feel that he was peculiarly fitted for the task. He had cruised a few times up and down the British channel, he had caught limited views of British manners and customs by walking on several occasions the length of Fleet Street and the Strand. Knowledge of America equivalent to this would then have been regarded in England as an ample equipment for an accurate treatise upon the social life of this country, and even upon its existing political condition and probable future.

But much more than the choice of a foreign subject did the pretense of foreign authorship prove the servility of feeling prevailing at that time among the educated classes. This was in the first place, to be sure, the result of the freak that led Cooper originally to begin writing a novel; but it was a freak that would never have been carried out, after publication had been decided upon, had he not been fully aware of the fact that the least recommendation of a book to his countrymen would be the knowledge that it was composed by one of themselves. "Precaution" was not merely a tale of English social life, it purported to be written by an Englishman; and it was so thoroughly conformed to its imaginary model that it not only reëchoed the cant of English expression, but likewise the expression of English cant. To talk about dissenters and the establishment was natural and proper enough in a work written ostensibly by the citizen of a country in which there was a state church. But Cooper went much farther than this in the reflections and moral observations which are scattered up and down the pages of this novel. These represent fairly views widely held at the time in America, and may not impossibly express the personal opinions he himself then entertained. He speaks in one place, in his assumed character of an Englishman, of the solidity and purity of our ethics as giving a superior tone to our moral feelings as contrasted with the French. He goes out of his way to compliment George III. One of the personages in the novel was tempted to admit something to his credit that he did not deserve. The love of truth, however, finally prevailed. But it was not because the man himself had any innate love of truth, but because " he had been too much round the person of our beloved monarch not to retain all the impressions of his youth." Passages such as these are remarkable when we consider the sentiments in regard to England that Cooper subsequently came to express. If they do not show with certainty his opinions at that time, they do show the school in which he had been brought up : they mark clearly the extent and violence of the reaction which in after years carried him to the opposite extreme.

In its plan and development " Precaution " was a compromise between the purely fashionable novel and that collection of moral disquisitions of which Hannah More's Cœlebs was the great exemplar, and still remained the most popular representative. As in most tales of high life, nobody of low condition plays a prominent part in the story, save for the purpose of setting off the dukes, earls, baronets, generals, and colonels that throng its pages. A novelist in his first production never limits his creative activity in any respect; and

Cooper, moreover, knew the public well enough to be aware that a fictitious narrative which aimed to describe aristocratic society might perhaps succeed without much literary merit, but would be certain to fail without an abundance of lords. The leading characters, however, whether of higher or lower degree, are planned upon the moral model. They either preach or furnish awful examples. It would certainly be most unfair to an author to judge him, as in this case, by a work which he had begun without any view to publication, and which he afterward learned to think and to speak of slightingly. Still, though, compared with many of his writings, " Precaution " is a novel of little worth, it is, in some respects, a better guide to the knowledge of the man than his better productions. The latter give evidence of his powers ; in this are shown certain limitations of his nature and beliefs. Peculiarities, both of thought and feeling, which in his other writings are merely suggested, are here clearly revealed. Some of them will appear strange to those whose conception of his character is derived from facts connected with his later life, or whose acquaintance with his works is limited to those most celebrated.

Cooper was, by nature, a man of deep religious feeling. This disposition had been strengthened by his training. But there is something more than deep religious feeling exhibited in his first novel. There runs through it a vein of pietistic narrowness, which seems particularly unsuited to the man whom popular imagination, investing him somewhat with the characteristics of his own creations, has depicted as a ranger of the forests and a rover of the seas. Yet the existence of this vein is plainly apparent, though all his surroundings would seem to have been unfavorable to its birth and development. He shared, to its fullest extent, in the jealousy which at that time, far more than now, prevailed between the Middle States and New England. He was strongly attached to the Episcopal Church, and he had, or fancied he had, a keen dislike to the Puritans and their manners and creeds. To these " religionists," as he was wont to call them, he attributed a great deal that was ungraceful in American life, and a good deal that was disgraceful. But the Puritan element is an irrepressible and undying one in English character. It can be found centuries before it became the designation of a religious body. It can be traced, under various and varying appellations, through every period of English history. It is not the name of a sect, it is not the mark of a creed ; it is the characteristic of a race. It is, therefore, never long put under ban before it comes back, and takes its turn in ruling manners and society. The revolt against it in the eighteenth century had stripped from religion everything in the shape of sentiment, and left it merely a business. The reaction which brought the Puritan element again to the front was so intensified by hostility to what were called French principles that the minor literature of the latter half of the reign of George III. exhibits a cant of intolerance from which many of its greatest writers were rarely great enough to be wholly free. This influence is clearly visible in the earliest work of Cooper. There is no charge, probably, he would have denied sooner or disliked more, but in his nature he was essentially a Puritan of the Puritans. Their faults and their virtues, their inconsistencies and their contradictions, were his. Their earnestness, their intensity, their narrowness, their

intolerance, their pugnacity, their serious way of looking at human duties and responsibilities, all these elements corresponded with elements in his own character.
His, also, were their lofty ideas of personal purity and
of personal obligation, extending not merely to the acts
of the life, but to the thoughts of the heart. Like them,
moreover, he was always disposed to appeal directly to
the authority of the Supreme Being. Like them, he had
perfect confidence in the absolute knowledge he possessed of what that Being thought and wished. Like
them, he considered any controverted question as settled,
if he could once bring to bear upon the point in dispute
a text beginning, " Thus saith the Lord." No rational
creature, certainly, would think of contesting a view of
the Creator, or acting contrary to a command coming
unmistakably from Him. But at this very point the difficulty begins ; and in nothing did Cooper more resemble
the Puritans than in his incapacity to see that there was
any difficulty at all. It never occurred to him that there
might possibly be a vast difference between what the
Lord actually said and what James Fenimore Cooper
thought the Lord said. It is hardly necessary to add,
however, that this characteristic of mind has its advantages as well as disadvantages.

It was not unnatural, accordingly, that " Precaution "
should exemplify in many cases that narrowness of
view which seeks to shape narrow rules for the conduct
of life. For its sympathy with this, one of the most
distinguishing and disagreeable features of Puritanism,
the novel has an interest which could never be aroused
by it as a work of art. Extreme sentiments are often
expressed by the author in his own person, though they
are usually put into the mouths of various actors in the

story. Their especial representative is a certain Mrs. Wilson, who was clearly a great favorite of her creator, though to the immense majority of men she would seem as disagreeably strong-minded as most of Cooper's female characters are disagreeably weak-minded. This lady is the widow of a general officer, who, the reader comes heartily to feel, has, most fortunately for himself, fallen in the Peninsular war. From her supreme height of morality she sweeps the whole horizon of human frailties and faults, and looks down with a relentless eye upon the misguided creatures who are struggling with temptations to which she is superior, or are under the sway of beliefs whose folly or falsity she has long since penetrated. In her, indeed, there is no weak compromise with human feelings. The lesson meant to be taught by the novel is the necessity of taking precaution in regard to marriage. One point insisted upon again and again is the requirement of piety in the husband. It is the duty of a Christian mother to guard against a connection with any one but a Christian for her daughters : for throughout the whole work the sovereign right of the parent over the child is not merely implied, it is directly asserted. " No really pious woman," says Mrs. Wilson, " can be happy unless her husband is in what she deems the road to future happiness herself." When she is met by the remark that the carrying out of this idea would give a deadly blow to matrimony, she rises to the occasion by replying that "no man who dispassionately examines the subject will be other than a Christian, and rather than remain bachelors they would take even that trouble." Nor in this was the author apparently expressing an opinion which he did not himself hold in theory, however little he might have regarded it in practice. He takes up the same subject in another place, when speaking in his own person. "Would our daughters," he says, " admire a handsome deist, if properly impressed with the horror of his doctrines, sooner than they would now admire a handsome Mohammedan?" On the matter of Sunday observance the narrowest tenets of Puritanism were preached, and the usual ignorance was manifested that there were two sides to the question. Some of the incidents connected with this subject are curious. One of the better characters in the novel asks his wife to ride out on that day, and she reluctantly consents. This brings at once upon the stage the inevitable Mrs. Wilson, who always stands ready to point a moral, though she can hardly be said to adorn the tale. She draws from the transaction the lesson that it is a warning against marrying a person with a difference of views. In this particular instance the respect of the man for religion had been injurious to his wife, because "had he been an open deist, she would have shrunk from the act in his company on suspicion of its sinfulness." It is justice to add that many of these extreme opinions, at least in the extreme form stated in this work, the author came finally to outgrow if in fact he held them seriously then.

There are certain other peculiarities of Cooper's beliefs that "Precaution" exemplifies. He has been constantly criticised for the unvarying and uninteresting uniformity of his female characters. This is hardly just; but it is just in the sense that there was only one type which he ever held up to admiration. Others were introduced, but they were never the kind of women whom he delighted to honor. Of female purity he had the highest ideal. Deference for the female sex as a sex he felt sincerely and expressed strongly. Along with this he seemed to have the most contemptible opinion of the ability of the female individual to take care of herself. On the other hand, if she had the requisite ability, the greater became his contempt; for helplessness, in his eyes, was apparently her chiefest charm. The Emily Moseley of his first novel is the prototype of a long line of heroines, whose combination of propriety and incapacity places them at the farthest possible remove from the heroic. She is worthy of special mention here, only because in this novel he describes in detail the desirable qualities, which in the others are simply implied. He furnishes us, moreover, with the precise training to which she had been subjected by her aunt, Mrs. Wilson. Accordingly, we learn both what, in Cooper's eyes, it was incumbent for a woman to be, and what she ought to go through in order to be that woman. A few sentences taken at random will show the character of this heroine. She was artless, but intelligent; she was cheerful, but pious; she was familiar with all the attainments suitable to her sex and years. Her time was dedicated to work which had a tendency to qualify her for the duties of this life and fit her for the life hereafter. She seldom opened a book unless in search of information. She never read one that contained a sentiment dangerous to her morals, or inculcated an opinion improper for her sex. She never permitted a gentleman to ride with her, to walk with her, to hold with her a tête-à-tête. Nor was this result achieved with difficulty. Though she was natural and unaffected, the simple dignity about her was sufficient to forbid any such request, or even any such thought in the men who had the pleasure, or, as the reader may think, the grief, of her acquaintance. In short, she was not merely propriety personified; she was propriety magnified and intensified. This particular heroine, who could not consistently have read the book in which her own conduct is described, finally disappears as the wife of an equally remarkable earl. Her story, as it is told, however, strikingly exemplifies the carelessness in working up details which is one of Cooper's marked defects. The novel received its name, as has already been implied, because it aimed to set forth the desirability of precaution in the choice of husband or wife. What it actually taught, however, was its undesirability. The misunderstandings, the crosses, the distresses, to which the lovers were subjected in the tale all sprang from excess of care, and not from lack of it; from exercising precaution where precaution did nothing but harm.

· The work excited but little attention in this country. In the following year it was printed in England by Colburn, and was there noticed without the slightest suspicion of its American authorship. In some quarters it received fairly favorable mention. It could not be hid, however, that the novel, as regarded the general public, had been a failure. Still, it was not so much a failure that the author's friends did not think well of it and see promise in it. They urged him to renewed exertions. He had tried the experiment of depicting scenes he had never witnessed, and a life he had never led. He had, in their opinion, succeeded fairly well in describing what he knew nothing about; they were anxious that he should try his hand at the representation of manners and men of which and whom he knew something. Especially was it made a matter of reproach that he, in heart and soul an American of the Americans, should have gone to a foreign land to fill the imagination of his countrymen with pictures of a social state alien both in feeling and fact to their own. This was an appeal of a kind that was certain to touch Cooper sensibly ; for with him love of country was not a sentiment, it was a passion. As a sort of atonement, therefore, for his first work, he determined to inflict, as he phrased it, a second one upon the world. Against this there should be no objection on the score of patriotism. He naturally turned for his subject to the Revolution, with the details of which he was familiar by his acquaintance with the men who had shared prominently in its conduct, and had felt all the keenness of a personal triumph in its success. The very county, moreover, in which he had made his home was full of recollections. Westchester had been the neutral ground between the English forces stationed in New York and the American army encamped in the highlands of the Hudson. Upon it more, perhaps, than upon any other portion of the soil of the revolted colonies had fallen the curse of war in its heaviest form. Back and forth over a large part of it had perpetually ebbed and flowed the tide of battle. Not a road was there which had not been swept again and again by columns of infantry or squadrons of horse. Every thicket had been the hiding-place of refugees or spies ; every wood or meadow had been the scene of a skirmish ; and every house that had survived the struggle had its tale to tell of thrilling scenes that had taken place within its walls. These circumstances determined Cooper's choice of the place and period. Years before, while at the residence of John Jay, his host had given him, one summer afternoon, the account of a spy that had been in his service during the war. The coolness, shrewdness, fearlessness, but above all the unselfish patriotism, of the man had profoundly impressed the Revolutionary leader who had employed him. The story made an equally deep impression upon Cooper at the time. He now resolved to take it as the foundation of the tale he had been persuaded to write. The result was that on the 22d of December, 1821, the novel of "The Spy" was quietly advertised in the New York papers as on that day published.

The reader, however, would receive a very wrong idea of the feelings with which the author began and ended this work of fiction, should he stop short with the account that has just been given. The circumstances attending its composition and publication are, as a matter of fact, almost as remarkable as the story itself. They certainly present a most suggestive picture of the literary state of America at that time. Cooper, for his part, had not the slightest anticipation of the effect that it was going to have upon his future. In writing it he was carrying out the wishes of his friends full as much as his own. Nor, apparently, did they urge the course upon him because they conceived him capable of accomplishing anything very great or even very good. They felt that he could produce something that was not discreditable, and that was all that could reasonably be expected of an American. There was no other novelist in the field. Charles Brockden Brown had been dead several years. Irving and Paulding were writing only short sketches. John Neal, indeed, in addition to the poems, tragedies, reviews, newspaper articles, indexes, and histories he was turning out by wholesale, had likewise perpetrated a novel; but it was never known

enough to justify the mention of it as having been forgotten. Here, consequently, was a vacant place that
ought to be filled. Cooper was never the man who
would be eager to take a place because there was no
one else to occupy it; and the way he went at the task
he had undertaken gives indirectly a clear insight into
an American author's feelings sixty years ago. He entered upon the work not merely without the expectation
of success, but almost without the hope of it. The
novel was written very hastily; the sheets passed into
the hands of the type-setter with scarcely a correction;
and so little heart had he in the task that the first volume was printed several months before he felt any inducement to write a line of the second. The propriety
of abandoning it entirely, under the apprehension of
its proving a serious loss, was debated. "Should
chance," he said, in a later introduction to the book,
"throw a copy of this prefatory notice into the hands
of an American twenty years hence, he will smile to
think that a countryman hesitated to complete a work
so far advanced, merely because the disposition of the
country to read a book that treated of its own familiar
interests was distrusted." In this respect the difficulty
of his position was made more prominent by its contrast
with that of the great novelist who was then occupying
the attention of the English-speaking world. Scott, in
writing "Waverley," could take for granted that there
lay behind him an intense feeling of nationality, which
would show itself not in noisy boastfulness, but in genuine appreciation; that with the matter of his work his
countrymen would sympathize, whatever might be their
opinion as to its execution. No such supposition could
be made by Cooper; no such belief inspired him to ex-

ertion. He might hope to create interest; he could not venture to assume its existence. One other incident connected with the composition of this work marks even more plainly the almost despairing attitude of his mind. While the second volume was slowly printing, he received an intimation from his publisher that the work might grow to a length that would endanger the profits. The author hereupon adopted a course which is itself a proof of how much stranger is fact than fiction. To placate the publisher and set his mind at rest, the last chapter was written, printed, and paged, not merely before the intervening chapters had been composed, but before they had been fully conceived. It was fair to expect failure for a work which no bookseller had been found willing to undertake at his own risk, and which the author himself set about in a manner so perfunctory. The indifference and carelessness displayed, he said afterward, were disrespectful to the public and unjust to himself; yet they give, as nothing else could, a vivid picture of the literary situation in America at that time.

The reluctance and half-heartedness with which Cooper began and completed this work stand, indeed, in sharpest contrast to the existing state of feeling, when it is only the prayers of friends and the tears of relatives that can prevent most of us from publishing some novel we have already written. But almost as it were by accident he had struck into the vein best fitted for the display of his natural powers. In it he succeeded with little effort, where other men with the greatest effort might have failed. The delicate distinctions that underlie character where social pressure has given to all the same outside, it was not his to depict. Still less could he unfold the subtle workings of motives that often elude the observation of the very persons whom they most influence. Such a power is essential to the success of him who seeks to delineate men as seen in conventional society; and largely for the lack of it his first novel had been a failure. It was only at rare intervals, also, that he showed that precision of style and pointed method of statement which, independent of the subject, interest the reader in men and things that are not in themselves interesting. It was the story of adventure, using adventure in its broadest sense, that he was fitted to tell: and fortunately for him Walter Scott, then in the very height of his popularity, had made it supremely fashionable. In this it is only needful to draw character in bold outlines; to represent men not under the influence of motives that hold sway in artificial and complex society, but as breathed upon by those common airs of reflection and swept hither and thither by those common gales of passion that operate upon us all as members of the race. It is not the personality of the actors to which the attention is supremely drawn, though even in that there is ample field for the exhibition of striking characterization. It is the events that carry us along; it is the catastrophe to which they are hurrying that excites the feelings and absorbs the thoughts. There can be no greater absurdity than to speak of this kind of story, as is sometimes done, as being inferior in itself to those devoted exclusively to the delineation of manners or character, or even of the subtler motives which act upon the heart and life. As well might one say that the "Iliad" is a poem of inferior type to the "Excursion." Again, it is only those who think it must be easy to write what it is easy to read

3

who will fall into the mistake of fancying that a novel of adventure which has vitality enough to live does not owe its existence to the arduous, though it may be largely unconscious, exercise of high creative power. No better correction for this error can be found than in looking over the names of the countless imitators of Scott, some of them distinguished in other fields, who have made so signal a failure that even the very fact that they attempted to imitate him at all has been wholly forgotten.

"The Spy" appeared almost at the very close of 1821. It was not long before its success was assured. Early in 1822 the newspapers were able to assert that it had met with a sale unprecedented in the annals of American literature. What that phrase meant is partly indicated by the fact that it had then been found necessary to publish a second edition. In March a third edition was put to the press; and in the same month the story was dramatized and acted with the greatest success. Still in the abject dependence upon foreign estimate which was the preëminent characteristic of a large portion of the educated class of that day, many felt constrained to wait for the judgment that would come back from Europe before they could venture to express an opinion which they had the presumption to call their own. Contemporary newspapers more than once mention the relief that was afforded to many when Cooper was spoken of in several of the English journals as "a distinguished American novelist." This, it has been implied, was then a condition of the public mind that no writer could dare wholly to disregard. When the project of abandoning this novel, already half printed, was under discussion, the principal reason that finally decided the author to persevere was the fact that his previous work had received a respectful notice in a few English periodicals. It was thought, in consequence, that in his new venture he would be secure from loss. Still, it is due to his countrymen to say that it was to them alone he owed his first success. In later years the declaration was often made that he would never have been held in honor at home, had it not been for foreign approbation. The assertion he himself indignantly denied. " This work," he said afterward, in speaking of " The Spy," " most of you received with a generous welcome that might have satisfied any one that the heart of this great community is sound." Certain it is that the success of the novel was assured in America some time before the character of its reception in Europe was known.

The printed volume was offered to the London publisher Murray, and for terms he was referred to Irving, who was then in England. Murray gave the novel for examination to Gifford, the editor of the " Quarterly." By his advice it was declined, — a result that might easily have been foretold from the hostility of the man to this country. He had made his review an organ of the most persistent depreciation and abuse of America and everything American. A new writer from this side of the ocean was little likely to meet with any favor in his sight, especially when his subject was one that from its very nature could not be flattering to British prejudices. Murray having refused, another publisher was found in Miller, who had also been the first to bring out Irving's " Sketch Book." Early in 1822 the work appeared in England. There its success was full as great as it had been in America. This novel, in fact, made Cooper's reputation both at home and abroad. It is important to bear this in mind, because it is a common notion that it was his delineations of Indian life that brought him his European fame. They established it, but they did not originate it. "The Spy" was a tale of a war, which in character was not essentially different from any other war. So far as the story painted the incidents of a struggle in which the English had been unsuccessful, it could have no right to expect favor from the English public unless there was merit in the execution of the work independent of the subject. The interest with which it was read by a people who could not fail to find portions of it disagreeable, who were moreover accustomed to look with contempt upon everything of American origin, was the best proof that a novelist had arisen whose reputation would stretch beyond the narrow limits of nationality. This was even more strikingly seen, when it came to be translated. If the English opinion was favorable, the French might fairly be called enthusiastic. A version was made into that tongue in the summer of 1822, by the translator of the Waverley Novels. In the absolute ignorance that existed as to its authorship, the work was ascribed by several of the Parisian papers to Fanny Wright, who subsequently achieved a fame of her own as a champion of woman's privileges and denouncer of woman's wrongs. In spite of its anonymous character and of some extraordinary blunders in translation, it was warmly received in France. From that country its reputation in no long space of time spread in every direction; translations followed one after another into all the cultivated tongues of modern Europe; and in all it met the same degree of favor. Nor has lapse of time shaken seriously

its popularity. The career of success, which began sixty
years ago, has suffered vicissitudes, but never suspen-
sion ; and to this hour, whatever fault may be found
with the work as a whole, the name of Harvey Birch is
still one of the best known in fiction. No tale produced during the present century has probably had so
extensive a circulation ; and the leading character in it
has found admirers everywhere and at times imitators.
Of this latter statement a striking illustration is given
in the memoirs of Gisquet, a prefect of the French
police under Louis Philippe. In his chapter on the
secret agents employed by him during his administration, he tells the story of one who by the information he
imparted rendered important services in preventing the
outbreak of civil war. He thus describes the motives
which led the man to pursue the course he did. " Struck
with the reading," he writes, "of one of Cooper's novels
called ' The Spy,' he aspired to the sort of ambition
which distinguished the hero of that work, and was desirous of playing in France the part which Cooper has
assigned to Harvey Birch during the American war of
independence. . . . Harvey Birch — for he adopted this
name in all his reports — never belied his professions of
fidelity. He rendered services which would have merited a competent fortune ; but when the term of them
ended, he contented himself with asking for a humble
employment, barely enough to supply his daily necessi-
ties." The belief in the reality of the hero has, indeed,
been part of the singular fortune of the book. In his
account of Nicaragua, published in 1852, Mr. E. G.
Squier furnished incidentally interesting testimony to
the truth of this statement as well as to the wide circulation of the tale itself. At La Union, the port of San

Miguel, he stayed at the house of the commandant of the place. His apartments he found well stocked with books, and among them was this particular novel. "The 'Espy,'" he went on to say, "of the lamented Cooper, I may mention, seems to be better known in Spanish America than any other work in the English language. I found it everywhere; and when I subsequently visited the Indian pueblo of Conchagua, the first alcalde produced it from an obscure corner of the cabildo, as a very great treasure. He regarded it as veritable history, and thought 'Señor Birch' a most extraordinary personage and a model guerillero."

CHAPTER III.

1822–1826.

COOPER would have been more or less than mortal if the unexpected success achieved by "The Spy" had not incited him to renewed effort. It definitely determined his career, though at the time he did not know it. As yet he was not sure in his own mind whether the favor his book had met was the result of a lucky hit or was due to the display of actual power. There can be no question as to the honesty of his assertion when he published his third novel, that it depended upon certain contingencies whether it would not be the last. But from this time on he wrote incessantly. From 1820 to 1830, including both years, he brought out eleven works. In many respects this was the happiest period of his literary life as well as the most successful. During it he produced many of his greatest creations. One decided failure he made; but with this exception if each new story did not seem to exhibit any new power, it at least gave no sign of weakness, or misdirection of energy. This period is in fact so supremely the creative one of Cooper's life as regards the conception of character and scene that nearly all he did demands careful examination.

He first set about a task that lay near his heart. This was to describe the scenes, the manners and customs of his native land, especially of the frontier life in which he had been trained. In 1823, accordingly, appeared " The Pioneers," itself the pioneer of the five famous stories, which now go collectively under the name of the " Leather-Stocking Tales." It was a vivid and faithful picture of the sights he had seen and the men he had met in the home of his childhood, where as a boy he had witnessed the struggles which attend the conquest of man over nature. In it appear in comparatively rude outlines the personages whose names and exploits his pen was afterwards to make famous throughout the civilized world. They are in this work of a far less lofty type than in those which followed. " The Pioneers," in truth, though not a poor story, is much the poorest of the series of which it forms a part. The almost loving interest he took in the matter about which he was writing tempted the author to indulge his recollections at the expense of his judgment. His first novel, he said in the prefatory address to the publisher which appeared in this one, had been written to show that he could write a grave tale, and it was so grave that no one would read it ; the second was written to overcome if possible the neglect of the public ; but the third was written exclusively to please himself. The story as a story suffered in consequence from the very fascination which the subject had for his mind. So subordinate was it made, especially in the first half, to the description of the scenes, that the details at times become wearisome and the interest often flags.

The expectation with which the appearance of this work was awaited is a striking proof of the impression that the previous novel had made. It was to have been brought out as early as the autumn of 1822. But during the summer of that year the yellow fever ravaged

New York and largely broke up for a time all kinds of business, including printing. Causes beyond control still further delayed the publication, and it was not until the first of February, 1823, that the book appeared. The public curiosity, however, had been fully excited. Extracts from it — according to a custom then prevalent in England — had been furnished in advance to some of the newspapers, and though these were not the most striking passages, they served to direct attention and awaken expectation. At the close of January, announcement of the precise date of publication was made. Success was certain from the start; but the degree of it outran all anticipation. The evening papers of the first of February were able to state that up to twelve o'clock that day there had been sold three thousand five hundred copies. Even at this period, with a population more than five times as numerous, such a half day's sale, under similar circumstances, would be remarkable. It is little wonder, therefore, that the newspapers of that period felt that only largeness of type and profusion of exclamation points could suitably record such a success.

"The Pioneers" was the first work to display a peculiarity of the author's character, which came afterwards into marked prominence. Cooper in a sense belonged to the school of Scott; and he was so far from denying it that in one place he speaks of himself as being nothing more than a chip from the former's block. But his life would have been far happier and his success much greater had he followed in one respect the example of him he called his master. Scott ordinarily did not read criticisms upon his own writings; and when he did, he was careful not to let his equanimity be seriously disturbed even by the severest attacks. Much of this was no doubt due to prudence; but a good deal of it to contempt. For of all the rubbish that time shoots into the wallet of oblivion, contemporary criticism runs about the least chance of being rescued from the forget-fulness into which it has been thrust. This is a result entirely independent of its goodness or badness. If the criticism is both destructive and just, the very death of the subject against which it is directed causes it to per-ish in the ruin it has brought about. If it is unjust, it is certain to be speedily forgotten, unless he who suffers from it takes the pains to perpetuate its memory, or some later investigator drags it from its obscurity for the sake of pointing out its absurdity. The creative literature of the past is the utmost the present can be expected to read. Its critical literature, however cele-brated in its day, is looked upon with contempt, or at best with a patronizing approval, by the following age, which is always confident that it at least has reached the supreme standard of correct taste, and asks no aid in making up its judgments from those who have gone before. But the philosophy which shows this to be true never lessened one iota the pain which the man of sensitive nature suffers. The extent to which Cooper was affected by hostile criticism is something remark-able, even in the irritable race of authors. He man-ifested under it the irascibility of a man not simply thin-skinned, but of one whose skin was raw. Meekness was never a distinguishing characteristic of his nature; and attack invariably stung him into defiance or coun-ter-attack. Unfriendly insinuations contained in ob-scure journals could goad him into remarks upon them, or into a reply to them, which at this date is the only means of preserving the original charge. It was in his prefaces that he was apt to express his resentment most warmly, for he well knew that this was the one part of a book which the reviewer is absolutely certain to read. In these he frequently took occasion to point out to the generation of critical vipers the various offenses of which they were guilty, the stupidities that seemed to belong to their very nature, and that utter lack of literary skill which prevented them from giving a look of sense to the most plausible nonsense they concocted. By Cooper, indeed, the preface was looked upon not as a place to conciliate the reader, but to hurl scorn at the reviewer. In his hands it became a trumpet from which he blew from time to time critic-defying strains, which more than made up in vigor for all they lacked in prudence. This characteristic was early manifested. In the short preface to the second edition of "The Spy," he could not refrain from referring to the friends who had given him good advice, and who had favored him with numberless valuable hints, by the help of which the work might be made excellent. But it is the letter to the publisher, with which "The Pioneers" originally opened, that was the first of his regular warlike manifestoes. Though not very long, two thirds of it was devoted to the men who had publicly found fault with his previous works. He pointed out their discrepancies in taste and the metaphysical obscurity of their opinions. At the conclusion he wrote a sentence which some of them never forgot. He told his publisher that to him alone he should look for the only true account of the reception of his book. "The critics," said he in continuation, "may write as obscurely as they please, and look much wiser than they are; the papers may puff and abuse as their changeful humors dictate ; but if you meet me with a smiling face I shall at once know that all is essentially well."

Little notice, however, was taken at the time of Cooper's preference of the public opinion which showed itself in buying his books, to that which made it its chief aim to teach him how they ought to be written. The country was too pleased with him and too proud of him to pay any special attention to these momentary ebullitions of dissatisfaction. On his part so great had now become his literary activity, that before "The Pioneers" was published he had set to work upon a new novel, of a kind of which he can justly be described as the creator, and in which he was to be followed by a host of imitators.

At a dinner party in New York in 1822, at which Cooper was present, the authorship of the Waverley Novels, still a matter of some uncertainty, came up for discussion. In December of the preceding year "The Pirate" had been published. The incidents in this story were brought forward as a proof of the thorough familiarity with sea-life of him, whoever he was, that had written it. Such familiarity Scott had never had the opportunity to gain in the only way it could be gained. It followed, therefore, that the tale was not of his composition. Cooper, who had never doubted the authorship of these novels, did not at all share in this view. The very reasons that made others feel uncertain led him to be confident. To one like him whose early life had been spent on top-gallant yards and in becketing royals, it was perfectly clear that "The Pirate" was the work of a landsman and not of a sailor. Not that he denied the accuracy of the descriptions so far as they went. The

point that he made was that with the same materials
far greater effects could and would have been produced,
had the author possessed that intimate familiarity with
ocean-life which can be his alone whose home for years
has been upon the waves. He could not convince his
opponents by argument. He consequently determined
to convince them by writing a sea-story.

We who are familiar with the countless hosts of
novels of this nature that have swarmed and are still
swarming from the press, cannot realize the apparent
peril which at that time existed in this undertaking.
No work of the kind, such as he now projected, had
ever yet been published. Sailors, indeed, had been introduced into fiction, notably by Smollett, but in no case
had there been exhibited the handling and movements
of vessels, and the details of naval operations. During
the last half-century we have been so surfeited with
the sea-story in every form, that most of us have forgotten the fact of its late origin, and that it is to Cooper
that it owes its creation. That he created it was not
due to any encouragement from others. He had plenty
of judicious friends to warn him from the undertaking.
Sailors, he was told, might understand and appreciate
it, but no one else would. Minute detail, moreover,
was necessary to render it intelligible to seamen, and to
landsmen it would be both unintelligible and uninteresting on account of the technicalities which must inevita-
bly be found in minute detail. A reputation already
well established would be sunk in the treacherous element he was purposing to describe. Cooper persisted in
his purpose, but he could not fail to be disturbed by the
unfavorable auguries that met him on every side. These
naturally had the more weight, as they came from men

who were attached to him personally, and who were honestly solicitous for his fame. He was at one time almost inclined to give up the project. But a critical English friend to whom he submitted a portion of the manuscript was delighted with it. In this man's judgment and taste Cooper felt so great confidence that he was induced to persevere. Moreover, to try the effect upon the more peculiar public of seamen, he read an extract to one of his old shipmates, who was also a relative. This was the account of the war-vessel working off shore in a gale. The selection was certainly a happy one. The literature of the sea presents no more thrilling chapter than that which, describing the passage of the great frigate through the narrow channel, gives every detail with such vividness and power that the most unimaginative cannot merely see ship, shore, and foaming water, but almost hear the roaring of the wind, the creaking of the cordage, and the dashing of the waves against the breakers. As he read on the listener's interest kept growing until he was no longer able to remain quiet. Rising from his seat he paced up and down the room furiously until the chapter was finished. Then half ashamed of the excitement into which he had been betrayed, he avenged himself just as if he were a professional reviewer by indulging in a bit of special criticism : " It's all very well," he burst out, " but you have let your jib stand too long, my fine fellow." For once Cooper heeded advice. " I blew it out of the bolt-rope," said he, " in pure spite ; " and blown out of the bolt-rope the jib appears in the tale.

He now felt reasonably confident of success, and any doubt that might have lingered in his mind was at once swept away by the favorable reception the work met when it came out. Its publication was for a while delayed. Early in the summer of 1823 the first volume had been finished and a portion of the second, but any further progress was checked for the time by an affliction that then befell the author. On the 5th of August his youngest child, Fenimore, then little less than two years old, died at the family residence in Beach Street, New York, and this calamity was followed by illness of his own. "The Pilot," in consequence, though bearing the date of 1823, was not actually furnished to the trade until the 7th of January, 1824. Its success, both in this country and in Europe, was instantaneous. Far-sighted men saw at once that a new realm had been added to the domain of fiction. "The Pilot" is indeed not only the first of Cooper's sea-stories in point of time, but if we regard exclusively the excellence of detached scenes, it may perhaps be justly styled the best of them all. At any rate its place in the highest rank of this species of fiction cannot be disputed, and in spite of the multitude of similar works that have followed in its wake and which have had their seasons of temporary popularity, its hold upon the public has never been lost.

Cooper was without question exceptionally fortunate in the materials with which he had to deal. He was never under the necessity of getting up with infinite toil what the modern novelist terms his local coloring. This existed for him ready made. He had only to call to mind the men he had himself met, the hazards he had run, the life he had lived, to be furnished with all the incidents and scenes and characters that were capable of being wrought into romance. His descriptions both of forest and of sea have all that vividness and reality which cannot well be given save by him who has threaded at will every maze of the one and tossed for week after week upon the billows of the other. Moreover, in this particular case, while he satisfied his patriotic feeling in the choice of the time, he displayed great judgment in the selection of the hero. The pilot, though never named, we know to be the extraordinary and daring adventurer, John Paul Jones, and the period is of course the American Revolution. In his literary art, likewise, Cooper has never been equaled by his imitators. Provided he could create the desired effect, he dared to let the reader remain in ignorance of the details he introduced. Enough of technicality was brought in to satisfy the professional seaman, but not so much as to distract the attention of the landsman from the main movement of the story. Contented with this the author did not seek to explain to the latter what he could not well understand without having served personally before the mast. From this rule he never varied, save in the few cases where the interest of the tale could be better served by imparting information than by withholding it. He had a full artistic appreciation of the impressiveness of the unknown. For, in stories of this kind, the vagueness of the reader's knowledge adds to the effect upon his mind, because, while he sees that mighty agencies are at work in perilous situations, his very ignorance of their exact nature deepens the feeling of awe they are of themselves calculated to produce. The wise reticence of Cooper in this respect can be seen by contrasting it with the prodigality of information, contained in more than one modern sea-novel, in which the whole action of the story is arrested to explain a technical operation with the result that the ordinary reader finds the explanation more unintelligible than the technical operation itself.

Still, in spite of the excellence of the tales which had followed it, " The Spy " continued with the majority of readers to be the most popular of his works. This fact, coupled with his intense love of country, led him to turn once more for a subject to his native land and to the period in the description of which he had won his first fame. He formed, in fact, a plan of writing a series of works of fiction, the scenes of which should be laid in the various colonies that had shared in the Revolutionary struggle. In pursuance of this scheme, his next work was projected. In February, 1825, appeared " Lionel Lincoln, or the Leaguer of Boston." The first edition had a preliminary title-page, which contained the inscription, " Legends of the Thirteen Republics," followed by this quotation from Hamlet —

> " I will fight with him upon this theme
> Until my eyelids will no longer wag."

When the plan he had conceived was given up, this addition naturally disappeared with it. Nothing that industry could do was spared by Cooper to make this work a success. On this account as well as for its reception by the public it stands in marked contrast to " The Spy." In the preparation of it he studied historical authorities, he read state papers, he pored over official documents of all kinds and degrees of dreariness. To have his slightest assertions in accordance with fact, he examined almanacs, and searched for all the contemporary reports as to the condition of the weather. He visited Boston in order to go over in person the ground he was to make the scene of his story. As a result of all this labor he has furnished us an admirable description of the engagement at Concord Bridge, of the running fight of Lexington, and of the battle of Bunker's Hill. Of the last, it is, according to the sufficient authority of Bancroft, the best account ever given. At this point praise must stop. New England was always to Cooper an ungenial clime, both as regards his creative activity and his critical appreciation. The moment he touched its soil, his strength seemed to abandon him. Whatever excellencies this particular work displayed, they were not the excellencies of a novel. Accuracy of detail, even in historical romance, is only a minor virtue. The modern reader is, indeed, often inclined to doubt whether it is a virtue at all now that modern research is constantly showing that so much we have been wont to look upon as fact is nothing more than fable. So superior is the imagination of man turning out to his memory that one is tempted to fancy that instead of going to history for our fiction we shall yet have to turn about and go to fiction for our history.

"Lionel Lincoln" is certainly one of Cooper's most signal failures. In writing it he had attempted to do what it did not lie in the peculiar nature of his powers to accomplish. It is the story of crime long hidden from the knowledge of men, but dogging with unceasing activity the memories of those concerned in it. But the secret chambers of the soul into which the guilty man never looks willingly, Cooper could neither enter himself nor lay bare to others. Remorse that gnaws incessantly at every activity of the spirit, the consciousness of sin that haunts the heart and hangs like a burden upon the life, can never well be depicted save by him whose words suggest more than they reveal. Cooper was not a writer of this kind. He belonged to that class of literary artists who convey their precise meaning by exactness and fullness of detail. The vagueness and indefiniteness with which this story abounds is not, therefore, that impressive obscurity which springs from the mysterious; it is, on the contrary, the obscurity of the unintelligible and absurd. In all of Cooper's novels, it is a fault that the characters are often represented as acting without sufficient motive. In the story of adventure this can be pardoned, or at least overlooked; for freak plays an important part in determining the movements of many of us. It is not so, however, in tales containing a plot similar to that of " Lionel Lincoln." The mind revolts at finding the actors in the drama represented as having committed monstrous crimes, without any reason that is worth mentioning. This radical defect in the plan is not counterbalanced by any felicity in the execution. Many of the incidents are more than improbable, they are impossible. The style, likewise, is labored, and the conversations combine the two undesirable peculiarities of being both stilted and dull. The characters, female or male, are in no case successfully drawn. The inferior ones, introduced to amuse, serve only to depress the reader. The hero in the course of the tale does several absurd things; but he finally surpasses himself by hurrying away from the woman he loves, without her knowledge, immediately after he has been joined to her in marriage. The representation of the half-witted Job — a character upon which the author clearly labored hard — neither arouses interest nor touches the heart. It is, indeed, impossible to feel much sympathy with one particular imbecile, no matter how patriotic, in a story where most of the actors are represented as acting like idiots.

Nevertheless, his reputation and the real excellence

of the battle scenes, saved this work from seeming at
the time so much of a failure as it actually was.   Certainly whatever loss of credit he may have sustained as
the result of writing "Lionel Lincoln," was much more
than made up by the success of the tale that followed.
In 1824 he had gone on an excursion to Saratoga, Lake
George, and Lake Champlain, with a small party of
English gentlemen.   One of these was Mr. Stanley, the
future Lord Derby.   As they reached Glens Falls and
were examining the caverns made by the river at that
spot, Mr. Stanley told Cooper that here ought to be laid
the scene of a romance.   In reply, the novelist assured
him that a book should be written in which these caverns should have a place.   The promise was fulfilled.
On the 4th of February, 1826, "The Last of the Mohicans " made its appearance.   It was composed the previous year in a little cottage then situated in a quiet, open
country, on which now stands the suburban village of
Astoria.   A severe illness attacked Cooper during its
progress ; but whatever effect it had upon his physical
frame, it certainly did not impair in the slightest his intellectual force.   The success of the work was both instantaneous and prodigious.   Owing, perhaps, to the
novelty of the scenes and characters, it was even greater
in Europe than in America.   But there was no lack of
appreciation in his own land.   In the estimation of his
countrymen, the novel at once took its place at the head
of his productions.   An incidental fact will not only
make clear its success, but the state of the book trade at
that time.   The demand for the work soon became so
great and so persistent, that in April it was decided to
stereotype it.

It deserved fully the success it gained.   Of all the

novels written by Cooper, "The Last of the Mohicans" is the one in which the interest not only never halts, but never sinks. It is, indeed, an open question, whether a higher art would not have given more breathing-places in this exciting tale, in which the mind is hurried without pause from sensation to sensation. But this is a fault, if it be a fault, which the reader will always forgive, whatever the critic may say. The latter, indeed, can see much to blame if he look at the work purely as an artistic creation. He can find improbability of action, insufficiency of motive, and feebleness of outline in many of the leading characters. But these are minor drawbacks. They sink into absolute insignificance when compared with the wealth of power displayed. As they are unable to retard the unflagging interest with which the story is read, so they do not essentially modify the estimation of it after it has been read.

In this work two great achievements were accomplished by Cooper. The first was the idealization of the white hunter whom he had described in "The Pioneers." No one can read the two novels in succession without seeing at once how much Leather-Stocking has gained in dignity. In thought and feeling and habits he is essentially the same; but there was given to his character a poetic elevation which raised it at once to the front rank of the creations of the imagination, and will make it imperishable with English literature. As he appears in "The Pioneers" he is merely an old man who has made his home in the hills in advance of the tide of settlement. He is the solitary hunter who views with dislike clearings and improvements, who cannot breathe freely in streets, who hates the sight of masses of men, who looks with especial loathing upon the civilization whose first work is to fell the trees he has learned to love, whose first exercise of power is to draw the network of the law around the freedom and irresponsibility of forest life. Though full of a simple and somewhat sententious morality, he is querulous, irritable, ignorant. But in "The Last of the Mohicans," while the man continues the same, the aspect he presents is wholly different. All that is weak in his character is in the background; all that is best and strongest comes to the front. He is in the prime of life. Ignorant he still remains of the ways of the world as found in the settlements; but there is no trace of discontent or fretfulness. He has full room for the exercise of his native virtues, and in the character of the acute and daring scout he finds no superior. To him forest and sky are an open book. Knowledge is conveyed to his ears in every sound that breaks the stillness of the summer woods; and to his eyes scarred rock and riven pine and the deserted nest of the eagle have made the paths of the wilderness as plain as the broadest highway. Nor are his moral qualities inferior to his purely professional. His coolness never deserts him, his resources never fail him, and along with the versatility that is never at a loss in the presence of the unexpected is the resolution that never flinches at the approach of the perilous.

This delineation has always met with unqualified praise. But the idealization of the Indian character as seen in Chingachcook and Uncas has been the subject of much controversy. This is not the place to express an opinion upon the truth of the representation. It is enough to say here that the view Cooper took was not hastily formed, nor was it the result of accidental prejudices. He studied all the sources of information accessible at that time which threw light upon the Indian character. He visited the deputations from the various tribes that passed through the state of New York on their way to the national capital. In some instances he followed them to Washington. It is obvious that to a man of his poetic temperament they may have appeared in a different light from what they did to the ordinary government agent. Certainly he never found reason to modify his views, though he was familiar with the criticism made upon them. Toward the close of his life he took occasion to reaffirm them. It is also to be added that if he gave especial prominence to certain virtues, real or imaginary, of the Indian race, he was equally careful not to pass over their vices. Most of the warriors he introduces are depicted as crafty, bloodthirsty, and merciless. But whether his representation be true or false, it has from that time to this profoundly affected opinion. Throughout the whole civilized world the conception of the Indian character, as Cooper drew it in "The Last of the Mohicans" and still further elaborated it in the later "Leather-Stocking Tales," has taken permanent hold of the imaginations of men. Individuals may cast it off; but in the case of the great mass it stands undisturbed by doubt or unshaken by denial. This much can be said in its favor irrespective of the question of its accuracy. If Cooper has given to Indian conversation more poetry than it is thought to possess, or to Indian character more virtue, the addition has been a gain to literature, whatever it may have been to truth.

CHAPTER IV.

1826–1830.

WITH the publication of "The Last of the Mohicans," Cooper's popularity was at its height. His countrymen were proud of him, proud that he had chosen his native land as the scene of his stories, proud that he had in consequence extended among all cultivated peoples its fame as well as his own. His works were more than read. They were in most cases dramatized and acted as soon as published. Artists vied in making incidents depicted in them the subjects of their paintings. Poems, founded upon them or connected in some way with them, made their appearance in the newspapers. If in many cases these things were in themselves of no value, they at least served to show the widespread popular interest which his writings had aroused. Moreover, his reputation was far from being limited to his own land. No other American, before or since, has enjoyed so wide a contemporary popularity. Irving may have been on the whole a greater favorite in England; but if so, it was largely due to the fact that the subjects upon which he was employed were of special interest to English readers, and his manner of treating them was flattering to English prejudices. But the Continental fame of Cooper was unrivaled, and indeed could fairly be said to hold its own with that of Walter Scott. Long before he went to Europe himself, his works appeared simultaneously in America, England, and France. They were speedily translated into German and Italian, and in most instances soon found their way into the other cultivated tongues of Europe. Everywhere his ability had been recognized by those whose approbation, if it could not confer immortality, was certain to bring with it temporary applause. The admiration expressed for him was far less marked in England than upon the Continent; but even there it could often be termed cordial. It came, too, from those who, whatever estimation we may give to their praise, did not praise lightly. From Miss Edgeworth he received personally a tribute to his success in delineating the characters in which her own reputation had been largely won. On reading "The Spy," she sent him a message, that she liked Betty Flanigan particularly, and that no Irish pen could have drawn her better. Scott had been much struck by the scenes and personages depicted in "The Pilot," the novel he first read, and predicted at once the success of the sea-story and of its creator. Many there were, even in England, who looked upon Cooper as being equal to the great master of historical romance. "Have you read the American novels?" wrote in November, 1824, Mary Russell Mitford to a friend. "In my mind they are as good as anything Sir Walter ever wrote. He has opened fresh ground, too (if one may say so of the sea). No one but Smollett has ever attempted to delineate the naval character; and then his are so coarse and hard. Now this has the same truth and power with a deep, grand feeling. . . . Imagine the author's boldness in taking Paul Jones for a hero, and his power in making one care for him! I envy the Americans their Mr. Cooper. . . . There is a certain Long Tom who appears to me the finest thing since Parson Adams." Subsequently, in July, 1826, she spoke thus of "The Last of the Mohicans," in a letter to Haydon: "I like it," she wrote, "better than any of Scott's, except the three first and 'The Heart of Mid-Lothian.'" The praise, indeed, given both then and at a later period, may often seem extravagant. In a passage written in 1835, Barry Cornwall, not merely content with putting Cooper at the head of all American authors, added that he may "dare competition with almost any writer whatever."

It need hardly be said that opinions such as these were not to be found generally in the English literary periodicals. Cooper's name was not even mentioned in the great reviews until his fame had been secured without their aid. The success which he won in Great Britain was not due in the slightest to the professional critics. These men fancied they had exhausted the power of panegyric when they went so far as to term him the American Scott. This fact was triumphantly paraded at a later period by a writer in Blackwood, presumably Wilson, as one of the convincing proofs of the untruthfulness of the charge made by Barry Cornwall, that authors from this country were treated with systematic unfairness in English reviews. "Were we ever unjust to Cooper?" he asked. "Why, people call him the American Scott." This sort of patting on the back was thought a proud illustration of the generosity of the British character, and as putting the recipient of it under obligations of everlasting gratitude.

There is no doubt, indeed, that the reputation of Cooper suffered all his life by the constant comparison

that was made between him and the great Scotch writer.
It was to a certain extent inevitable; but it was none
the less unfortunate. He could never be judged by
what he did; it was always by the fanciful test of how
some one else would have done it. This was even more
true of his own country than of England. Scott's
popularity was greater here than it was anywhere else.
There was a feeling akin almost to moral reprobation
expressed against any one who should presume to fancy
that the best work of any native author could equal
the poorest that Scott put forth. The Continental
opinion which at that time often reckoned the American novelist as equal, if not superior to his British contemporary, seemed to men here like a profanation. It
was, indeed, so said in direct terms.

Comparison with Scott, therefore, always put the one
compared at a great disadvantage. This, however, is a
method of judging that is necessary to some and easy to
all. Genuine appreciation demands study and thought.
For these comparison is a cheap substitute. To call
Cooper the American Scott in compliment in the days
of his popularity, and in derision in the days of his unpopularity, was a method of criticism which enabled
men to praise or undervalue without taking the trouble
to think. Stories were invented and set in circulation
of how he himself rejoiced in being so designated.
Great, accordingly, was the indignation felt and expressed by these gentry at the presumption of the
American author, when at a later period he asserted
that so far from taking pride in the title, it merely
gave him just as much gratification as any nickname
could give a gentleman.

It would be, moreover, far from truth to say that

in this most prosperous portion of his career his popularity was unmixed in his own country. Even then his success had aroused a good deal of envy. In 1823 he was attacked, in common with many prominent citizens of New York, in a satire called "Gotham and the Gothamites." This was the work of a man of the name of Judah, who, in 1822, had published a dramatic poem styled "Odofried the Outcast." The title was ominous of the fate which the production met. The author naturally felt that the age was unappreciative. To relieve his mind he wrote eleven or twelve hundred lines of fresh drivel, in which he assailed everything and everybody. The satire was of that dreadful kind which requires notes and commentaries to point out who is hit and what is meant; and the annotation, as is usual in such cases, took up much more space than the text. This work — for which the author was sent to jail, though a lunatic asylum would have been a far fitter place — is only of interest here because it bears direct and positive evidence to the fact that at this time Cooper was the most widely read of American authors.

But jealousy of his fame could be found among men of much higher pretensions than this wretched poetaster. "The North American Review" had at that time been ponderously revolving through space for several years. It was then a periodical respectable, classical, and dull, all three in an eminent degree. Towards Cooper it struggled in a feeble way to be just, but for all that it was the exponent of a distinctly unfriendly feeling. Among individuals a conspicuous representative of this hostility was the poet Percival. He could not endure the reputation which the novelist had acquired. Percival was a man of a good deal of ability, of a great deal of knowledge, and of an inexhaustible capacity of spinning out verse, never rising much above, nor falling much below mediocrity, which, if mere quantity were the only element to be considered, would have justified him in contracting to produce enough to constitute of itself a national literature. As he invariably proved himself entirely destitute of common sense in his ordinary conduct, he was led to fancy that he was not merely a man of ability, but a man of genius; and during the whole of his life he perpetually posed as that most intolerable of literary nuisances, a man of unappreciated genius. In spite of the fact that he had been hospitably entertained and befriended by Cooper, he could not be satisfied, because their common publisher looked upon the latter as the "greatest literary genius in America." The reception given by the public to the "long, dirty, straggling tales" of the novelist disgusted him. "I ask nothing," he wrote in April, 1823, "of a people who will lavish their patronage on such a vulgar book as "The Pioneers." They and I are well quit. They neglect me, and I despise them." In a later letter he returned to this work. "It might do," he said, "to amuse the select society of a barber's shop or a porter-house. But to have the author step forward on such stilts and claim to be the lion of our national literature, and fall to roaring himself and set all his jackals howling (S. C. & Co.) to put better folks out of countenance — why 'tis pitiful, 'tis wondrous pitiful at least for the country that not only suffers it but encourages it." Percival, indeed, his biographer tells us, was subsequently urged to contribute to "The North American Review" a critical article on "The Prairie," in which simple justice was to be done to Cooper — which

phrase had, of course, its usual meaning, that injustice
was to be done him. The poet's customary indecision
prevailed, however; the country was spared this exhibition of spiteful incapacity, and the novelist was left to
stumble along in uncertainty as to his precise position
among men of letters.

Not but there were plenty of men anxious to show
it. Especially was this true of that class which looked
upon it as the supreme effort of critical judgment to
exaggerate the value of everything written in Europe
and depreciate everything of native origin. There was
a prevailing belief among those who mistook their own
individual impotence for the incapacity of a whole people, that nothing good could come out of America.
Many showed their faith by their conduct. In 1834,
Cooper himself said that he knew of several instances
in which persons had not read anything he had written
for the avowed reason that nothing worth reading could
be written by one of their countrymen. To all of these
it was a subject of some perplexity and of more annoyance that his works should be, if anything, more popular in Europe than they were in his native land. To
account for this fact various sage reasons were early
suggested and are still occasionally heard. One of these
has always been particularly common. This was that it
was the novelty of the scenes and characters depicted
that attracted attention and not the ability shown in
depicting them. At any rate, they wished it understood
that if he satisfied the European, he did not satisfy the
native world : for if creative power had been denied
us, we could at least show that as a compensation we
had been supplied with a double portion of refined taste.
Speaking in behalf of the American people, these critics

expressed anxiety that neither at home nor abroad should Cooper be regarded as obtaining the unqualified admiration or attaining the lofty ideal of "all of us." Against any such impression they entered their humble protest. All that lay in their power should be done to counteract it. This is no one-sided statement of opinions then expressed. These very sentiments in almost these very words can be found in reviews of that period.

Cooper at the time of writing his first novel was dwelling at Angevine. When the success of the second made it probable that he would continue for a while his career as an author, and possibly devote his life to it, the necessity arose of changing his residence. His country home was about five and twenty miles from the city, but twenty-five miles in those days of limited mail facilities and limited means of communication was a distance not to be tolerated. Accordingly, in 1822 he moved into New York. Either there or in its suburbs he dwelt until his departure for Europe. Here his youngest child, Paul, was born in 1824, and here, as has already been mentioned, his infant son Fenimore died. His talents and his reputation gave him at once a leading position in society. Nor were his associates inferior men. He founded a club which included on its rolls the residents of New York then best known in literature and law, science and art. The names of many will be even more familiar to our ears than they were to those of their contemporaries. All forms of intellectual activity were represented. To this club belonged, among others, Chancellor Kent the jurist; Verplanck, the editor of Shakespeare; Jarvis the painter; Durand the engraver; DeKay the naturalist; Wiley the publisher; Morse the inventor of the electric telegraph; Halleck and Bryant, the poets. It was sometimes called after the name of its founder; but it more commonly bore the title of the "Bread and Cheese Lunch." It met weekly, and Cooper, whenever he was in the city, was invariably present. More than that, he was the life and soul of it. Though kept up for a while after his departure from the country, it was only a languishing existence it maintained, and even this speedily ended in death.

His pecuniary situation had been largely improved by his literary success. The pressure upon his means had in fact been one of the main reasons, if not the main reason, that had led him to contemplate pursuing a literary life. The property left by his father had gradually dwindled in value, partly through lack of careful uninterrupted management. His elder brothers, on whom the administration of the estate had successively devolved, had died. The result was, that he found himself without the means which in his childhood he might justly have looked forward to possessing. So far from being a man of wealth he was in the earlier part of his literary career a poor man. From any difficulties, however, into which he may have fallen he was more than retrieved by the success of what he wrote. Precisely what was the sale of his books, or how much he received for their sale, it would be hard and perhaps impossible now to tell. He was careless himself about preserving any records of such facts. But, besides this natural indifference, he seemed to resent any public reference to the price paid him for his writings as an unauthorized intrusion into his personal affairs. Allusions even to the amount of his receipts he apparently regarded as springing not so much from a feeling of pride in his success, as from a desire to represent him as being under great obligations to his countrymen. In some instances he was certainly correct in so regarding it. On one occasion after his return from Europe, he denied the truth of an assertion made in a newspaper, as to the amount he derived from the sale of each of his novels. "It remains for the public to decide," said he, "whether it will tolerate or not this meddling with private interests by any one who can get the command of a little ink and a few types." In the prefatory address to the publisher which appeared in the first edition of "The Pioneers," he made the statement, that the success of "The Spy," should always remain a secret between themselves. This reticence and dislike of publicity continued throughout the whole of his career. It extended to everything connected with his writings. Our knowledge on these points is, therefore, both scanty and uncertain. The size of the editions has never been given to the public. The sale of "The Pioneers" on the morning of its publication has already been noticed; and there are contemporary newspaper statements to the effect that the first edition of "The Red Rover" consisted of five thousand copies, and that this was exhausted in a few days. But it is only from incidental references of this kind, which can rarely be relied upon absolutely, that we at this late day are able to gain any specific information whatever.

He was unquestionably helped in the end, however, by what in the beginning threatened to be a serious if not insuperable obstacle. He was unable to get any one concerned in the book trade to assume the risk of bringing out "The Spy." That had to be taken by the author himself. In the case of this novel, we know positively that Cooper was not only the owner of the

copyright, but of all the edition; that he gave directions
as to the terms on which the work was to be furnished
to the booksellers, while the publishers, Wiley & Halsted, had no direct interest in it, and received their
reward by a commission. It is evident that under this
arrangement his profits on the sale were far larger than
would usually be the case. Whether he followed the
same method in any of his later productions, there
seems to be no means of ascertaining. Wiley, however, until his death, continued to be his publisher.
"The Last of the Mohicans" went into the hands of
Carey & Lea of Philadelphia; and this firm, under
various changes of name, continued to bring out the
American edition of his novels until the year 1844. It
was from the sales in this country that most of the income from his books was derived. England, indeed,
brought him a large sum, at least up to the passage of
the copyright law of 1838; but he gained little pecuniary benefit from the wide circulation of his works on
the European continent, whatever may have been the
renown. In regard to France, he said in 1834 after
his return, that he had paid in taxes to the government
of that country, during his different residences in it, con-
siderably more money than was obtained from the sales
of the sheets of fourteen books. In Germany, where
his writings had an immense circulation, his receipts
were still less.

But whatever may have been the precise amount
acquired by the sale of his works, it was sufficient to
pay off heavy debts incurred by others, but which he
was compelled to assume, to put him in an independent
position and justify him in determining to fulfill a long-
cherished desire of spending some time in Europe. Ac-

cordingly on the 1st of June, 1826, he sailed with his
family — consisting, with the servants, of ten persons —
from the port of New York. On the 5th of November,
1833, he landed there on his return. His original intention was to be gone for but five years. To the fixing
of this particular time he was apparently influenced by
a remark of Jefferson, that no American should remain
away for a longer period from the country, because if
he did, so rapid were the changes, its facts would have
got wholly beyond his knowledge. His absence actually
extended to a little less than seven years and a half.
Most of this time was spent in France. From Henry
Clay, then Secretary of State, he had received the appointment of consul at Lyons. He had asked for it, because he did not wish to have the appearance of expa-
triating himself; for as the service was then conducted,
such a post involved no duties and brought in no re-
turns. His commission bears date the 10th of May,
1826. Even this nominal position he gave up after
holding it between two and three years. No resignation of his is on file in the State Department; but a
successor was appointed on the 15th of January, 1829.
He threw up the place because he had come to entertain the conviction that gross abuses existed in the system of foreign appointments, and it became him to set
an example of the principles he professed.

It may be well at this point to furnish an outline
sketch of his various residences in Europe. The voyage
from America lasted about a month; and after staying
a few days in England he passed over to France, on
the soil of which he first set foot on the 18th of July,
1826. Either in Paris or its immediate neighborhood
he remained until February, 1828, when he crossed

over to England. Leaving London early in June, he
went back to France by the way of Holland and Belgium. In July, 1828, he left Paris for Switzerland,
and took up his residence near Berne. After spending
some weeks in making excursions from that point, he
crossed the Alps in October by the Simplon Pass. The
following winter and spring he spent in Florence and
its vicinity. In the summer of 1829 he sailed down
the Italian coast to Naples, and after staying a few
weeks in that city, made a home for himself and his
family at Sorrento for nearly three months. The winter
of 1829–30 he spent in Rome. In the spring of 1830
he went to Venice. From that place he journeyed to
Munich by the Tyrol, and finally settled down in
Dresden. From his temporary home in Saxony, however, the July revolution speedily drew him to Paris,
and that city he made mainly his residence from that
time until his return to America in 1833. There he
was, and there he stood his ground during the terrible
cholera ravages of 1832. Occasional expeditions he
made, and of one in particular, up the Rhine and in
Switzerland, he has published a full account.

It was eminently characteristic of Cooper, that though
he brought with him letters of introduction, he found
himself unwilling to deliver a single one of them. Yet,
certainly, if any American could be pardoned the use
of a custom that has been so much abused, he was the
man. But after he had resided quietly in France for
a few weeks, he happened to attend a diplomatic dinner
given by the United States minister to Canning, then
on a visit to Paris. This was the occasion of making
his presence known to those who had long before made
the acquaintance of his writings. He was at once sought

out and welcomed by the most distinguished men of the most brilliant capital in the world. The polish, the grace, the elegance, and the wit of French social life made upon him an impression which he not only never forgot, but which he was afterwards in the habit of contrasting with the social life of England and America, to the manifest disadvantage of both, and with the certain result of provoking the hostility of each. He himself says very little of the reception he met; but we know from other sources how cordial and even deferential it was. He was not a man, indeed, to enjoy being lionized, to be set up, as he expressed it, at a dinner-table as a piece of luxury, like strawberries in February or peaches in April. But he was in a capital where attention is always paid to ability, though rarely with noisy demonstration. He received his full share of it. Without mentioning numerous other evidences, the conspicuous position he held is evident from the way Scott speaks of him in his diary. He mentions meeting him one evening at the Princess Galitzin's in November, 1826. " Cooper was there," said he, " so the Scotch and American lions took the field together."

But of all the countries in which he resided he grew to be fondest of Italy. This was partly due to the fact that there he could indulge to the full extent two passions that had come to be a part of his nature — the love of fine skies, and of beautiful scenery. His feelings in regard to this country and to France he expressed on one occasion with a courtliness that was wholly free from the insincerity of the courtier's art. In November, 1830, shortly after his return to Paris from Germany, he was presented to the royal family. The Queen of Louis Philippe, who was the daughter of Ferdinand I.,

of the Two Sicilies, asked him of all the lands visited
by him which he most preferred. "That in which your
majesty was born," was the reply, "for its nature, and
that in which your majesty reigns for its society."
There was not in this the slightest compliment, if by
compliment anything is meant inconsistent with the
severest truth. "Switzerland," he said afterward, "is
the country to astonish and sometimes to delight; but
Italy is the land to love." During the nearly two
years he remained there, its scenery, its climate, its
recollections, and also its people, were constantly gaining a hold upon his heart. No country did he ever
leave with so much regret; and when he came to take
his final departure, his feelings were such as are experienced by him who is on the point of bidding farewell
to a much-loved home. When he passed into the
valley of the Adige on his journey to the Tyrol, in
1830, he reversed the usual practice of the traveler
who has his eyes fixed only on what is to come. He
turned around to cast a last lingering glance at the land
he was about to leave behind. Italy was the only
country, his wife told him, that she had ever known
him to quit looking over the shoulder. His regard for
the people was, perhaps, intensified by the reaction
against the estimation in which he had been wont to
hold them. "The vulgar-minded English," — he said in
one of those deliciously irritating and double-acting
sentences he was afterward in the habit of frequently
uttering — "talk of the damned Italians, and the vulgar-
minded American, quite in rule, imitates his great
model." Certainly his prejudices against the inhabitants of that country were soon swept away. He contrasted them favorably with all their neighbors. They

were more gracious than the English, more sincere than the French, and infinitely more refined than the Germans. In grace of mind, and in love, and even knowledge of the arts, a large portion of the common Italians were, in his opinion, as much superior to the Anglo-Saxons as civilization is to barbarism. He came in time to have a sort of fondness even for the professional mendicants. He furnishes us a curious picture of the beggars who assembled about his residence daily in Sorrento, to whom he invariably gave a grano apiece. The company, starting out from one or two, had been steadily reinforced by recruits from far and near, till it ran up to the neighborhood of a hundred men, who regularly presented themselves for their pittance. There is no more graphic description in his writings than his account of the scene which took place when a new-comer among the beggars had the indiscretion, on receiving his grano, to wish the giver only a hundred years of life ; the indignation of the king of the gang at this exhibition of black ingratitude ; the tumult with which the blunder was corrected, and the shouts and outcries with which the pitiful hundred was changed into a thousand years, and long ones at that.

During this time his literary activity was unceasing. Before the close of 1830 he had completed four novels : " The Prairie," " The Red Rover," " The Wept of Wishton-Wish," and " The Water Witch," — all of which were devoted to the delineation of scenes and characters belonging to his native land. Before he started for Europe he had begun a new Indian story. This was finished during his early residence in Paris. He had felt it to be a hazardous venture to bring into " The Last of the Mohicans " the personages who had been previously drawn in "The Pioneers." But so great had been his success, and so strongly had the characters taken hold of him, that he determined to renew the experiment for a third time. Leather-Stocking, accordingly, was introduced as living in extreme old age on the Western prairies, and the book ends with his death. The idea of transferring the home of the worn-out hunter to these vast solitudes was suggested, it is fair to infer from Cooper's own words, by the actual career of Daniel Boone, the Kentucky pioneer. The simple story of this man's life was sufficiently remarkable; but in the exaggerated accounts of it that were then current, he was represented as having emigrated, in his ninety-second year, to an estate three hundred miles west of the Mississippi, because he found a population of ten to the square mile inconveniently crowded.

On the 17th of May, 1827, "The Prairie" was published. It did not meet with the extraordinary success of "The Last of the Mohicans," nor has it ever been as great a favorite with the general public. It was written in a far more quiet and subdued vein. It never keeps up that prolonged strain upon the feelings which characterizes the work that preceded it, and which while a defect in the eyes of some is to most readers its special charm. There are, indeed, in many of Cooper's stories, situations more thrilling and scenes more stirring than can be found in "The Prairie," though in it there is no lack of these. But of all his tales it is much the most poetical. Man sinks into insignificance in the presence of these mighty solitudes; for throughout the whole book the immensity of nature hangs over the spirit like a pall. Nor were the characters of the principal personages out of harmony with the atmosphere that envelopes the scenes described. In the lonely hunter, now nearing his grave, there is a pathetic grandeur, which is a natural development, and not an artificial addition. Though he has hurried as far away as possible from the din of the settlements, he is no longer querulous and irritable as in his old age in the Otsego hills. He has learned to recognize the inevitable. While he does not cease to regret, he has ceased to denounce. He knows that the majestic solitude of nature will not long remain undisturbed, nor its more majestic silence unbroken; for in every wind that blows from the East he hears the sound of axes and the crash of falling trees that herald the march of civilization across the continent. He sorrows at the ruin impending on all that is dearest to his heart; but he awaits it in dignified submission. In fine contrast to him stands the man who has likewise sought the solitude of the wilderness, not because he loves the beauty and the majesty of primeval nature, but because he hates the restraints that human society has thrown about the indulgence of human passions. Criticism has rarely done justice to the skill and power with which Cooper has drawn the squatter of the prairies, who holds that land should be as free as air ; who has traveled hundreds of miles beyond the Mississippi to reach a place where title-deeds are not registered and sheriffs make no levies ; who neither fears God nor regards man ; to whom the rule of the rifle is the supremest law; and yet who, with all his detestation of the safeguards which society has erected for its security, has a moral code and a rough wild justice of his own.

"The Prairie" was followed by "The Red Rover," which came out on the 9th of January, 1828. During the years that followed the publication of "The Pilot," the reputation of that work had been steadily increasing. Time had more than confirmed the first favorable impression. Not only had any lingering prejudice against the sea-story as a story been entirely swept away, but tales of this kind were beginning to be the fashion. Imitators were springing up everywhere. It was natural, therefore, for Cooper to turn his attention once more to a kind of fiction to the composition of which he himself had originally opened the way. After leaving the navy he had become one of the owners of a whaling vessel, and in it had made one or two voyages to Newport. In the harbor of that place he fixed the introduction of his new story of the sea. He had taken up his residence during the summer of 1827 in the little hamlet of St. Ouen on the Seine, not far from Paris. There, in the space of three or four months, "The Red Rover" was written. From the date of its appearance to the present time it has always been justly one of the most popular of his productions, and perhaps, considered as a whole, stands at the head of his sea-tales.

On the 6th of November, 1829, succeeded an Indian story of King Philip's war, under the name of "The Wept of Wish-ton-Wish." The fanciful title puzzled, and did not altogether please, the public. As a matter of fact it was used only in this country. In England the novel was called "The Borderers;" in France "The Puritans of America, or the Valley of Wish-ton-Wish." This work was begun during his residence in Switzerland in 1828, and was completed at Florence. It has never been popular, particularly in America. The tale is a tragic one throughout, and the prevailing air of sombreness is rarely lightened by any success in the management of minor incidents. The introduction too was marked by one of Cooper's besetting faults, intolerable prolixity. But the main cause of his failure lay in his inability to delineate the Puritan character. It was not knowledge that was wanting, it was sympathy; or perhaps it is better to say that it was his lack of sympathy which prevented his having any genuine knowledge. He tried in all honesty to depict the men who had founded New England, the men of hard heads and iron hearts, in whom piety and pugnacity were, as in himself, so intimately blended that the transition from the one to the other is a vanishing line whose discovery defies the closest scrutiny. Paradoxical as the assertion may seem, he was too much like the Puritans to do them justice. His character was essentially the same as their own; but the influences under which he had been trained were altogether different. Upon their manners, their ideas, and even their appearance he had early learned to look with aversion; and he had not the power to project his mind out of the circle of notions and prejudices in which he had been brought up. The very name of the Reverend Meek Wolf which he bestowed in this story upon his clergyman, revealed of itself the existence of feelings which put him at once out of that pale of sympathetic thought, which enables the novelist or historian to look with the insight of the spirit upon men and motives which his intellect acting by itself would prompt him to distrust and dislike.

To this tale succeeded "The Water Witch." This was begun at Sorrento and finished at Rome, a city which he subsequently used often to speak of as the precise moral antipodes of the capital of the New World, in the harbor of which he had laid much of the scene of this story. It was not till he reached Dresden, however, that he was enabled to have it put in print. On the 11th of December, 1830, it made its appearance in this country. With it ended for a time his fictions that dealt with American life and manners. He now turned to new fields and wrote with different aims.

During all these years his popularity had continued unabated, though his last two novels could hardly be said to have met with the favor which had been accorded to most of those which had preceded them. It is certainly a convincing proof of the wide reputation he had gained before he went to Europe, that five editions of "The Prairie," the first work he wrote after his arrival, were arranged to be published at the same time. Two were to come out in Paris, one in French and one in English; one in London; one in Berlin; and one in Philadelphia. But even this success was soon surpassed. It is hard to credit the accounts that are given on unimpeachable testimony. One statement, however, is too important to be overlooked, coming from the source it does. In the controversy going on in this country in 1833, in regard to the part Cooper had taken in the finance discussion, which will be mentioned in its proper place, Morse, the inventor of the electric telegraph, published a letter in defense of his absent friend. In it he bore witness in the following words to the popularity of the novelist in the Old World: "I have visited, in Europe, many countries," said he, "and what I have asserted of the fame of Mr. Cooper I assert from personal knowledge. In every city of Europe that I visited the works of Cooper were conspicuously placed in the windows of every bookshop. They are published as soon as he produces them in thirty-four different places in Europe. They have been seen by American travelers in the languages of Turkey and Persia, in Constantinople, in Egypt, at Jerusalem, at Ispahan."

CHAPTER V.

1830.

THE month of December, 1830, which saw the publication of " The Water Witch," closed the first and far the most fortunate decade of Cooper's literary life. In the decade which followed began that career of controversy which lasted, with little intermission, until his death. By it his reputation and his fortunes were profoundly affected. It worked a complete revolution both in the sentiments with which he regarded others, and in the sentiments with which others regarded him. The most intense lover of his country, he became the most unpopular man of letters to whom it has ever given birth. For years a storm of abuse fell upon him, which for violence, for virulence, and even for malignity, surpassed anything in the history of American literature, if not in the history of literature itself. Nor did the effect of this disappear with his life. The misrepresentations and calumnies, which were then set in motion, have not ceased to operate even at this day. Full as marked, still, was the influence which the controversies, in which he was engaged, had upon his literary reputation. A direct result of them at the time was not only to impair the estimation in which his previous writings had been held, but to cause the later productions of his pen to be treated with systematic injustice. Both in England and America the effect of this hostile criticism has not yet died away.

On the other hand, it was no one-sided contest that took place. If Cooper was attacked, he, in turn, did his part in attacking. No man has ever criticised his own country more unsparingly, and in some instances more unjustly, than did he, who, in foreign lands, had been its stoutest and most pronounced defender. Nor, in the controversies that followed his return from Europe, did one side conduct itself with perfect righteousness, and the other with deliberate villainy. Had the parties but seen fit to act in this manner, the duties of a biographer would have been sensibly lightened. A fair and dispassionate account of the circumstances that led to the unpopularity which clouded, though it could hardly be said to darken, Cooper's later life, demands a full and careful examination of many facts which, in some instances, seem to have no relation to the subject. Especially is a knowledge of the European estimate of America during the period that the novelist resided abroad a matter of first importance. But even of as great importance is a knowledge of certain traits of his character and of certain sentiments which he strongly felt, and of certain beliefs which he earnestly held. To bring out these points clearly, it is necessary for a while to arrest the progress of the narrative.

It is to be remarked at the outset that the first impression which Cooper made upon strangers was rarely in his favor. To this we have the concurrent testimony of those who knew him slightly, and of those who knew him well. It was due to a variety of causes. He had infinite pride, and there was in his manner a self-assertion that often bordered, or seemed to border, upon arrogance. His earnestness, moreover, was often mistaken for brusqueness and violence ; for he was, in some measure, of that class of men who appear to be excited when they are only interested. The result was that at first he was apt to repel rather than attract. Without referring to other evidence, we need here only to quote the guarded statement of one of his warmest friends in describing the beginning of their acquaintance. "I remember," says Bryant, "being somewhat startled, coming, as I did, from the seclusion of a country life, with a certain emphatic frankness in his manner which, however, I came at last to like and to admire." But besides this he had other characteristics which, to the majority of men, could not be agreeable. Thoroughly grounded in his own convictions, positive and uncompromising in the expression of them, he had no patience with those — and the number is far from being a small one — who embrace their views loosely, hold them half-heartedly, or defend them ignorantly. The opinions of such he was not content, like most men of ability, with quietly and unobtrusively despising. The contempt he felt he did not pay sufficient deference to human nature to hide. It was inevitable that the self-love of many should be offended by the arbitrariness and imperiousness with which he overrode their opinions, and still more by the unequivocal disdain manifested for them. It must be conceded, also, that to those for whom he felt indifference or dislike, he had in no slight degree that capacity of making himself disagreeable which reaches, and then only in rare instances, the ripened perfection of offensiveness in him who has breathed from earliest youth the social air of England. These were traits that were sure to make him enemies in private life. In public life, moreover, the ardor of his temperament was such as to hurry him into controversy;

and the number of those hostile to him on personal grounds, was always liable to receive accessions from men who had never seen him face to face. No gage of battle could be thrown down which he did not stand ready to take up. Opposition only inflamed him; it never daunted him. He had not the slightest particle of that prudence which teaches a man to keep out of contests in which he can gain no advantage, or in which success will be only a little less disastrous than defeat. It hardly needs to be said that a politic line of conduct is usually the very last which a person of such a temperament follows. But when to all these characteristics is added a peculiar sensitiveness to criticism, it is evident that if proper opportunities are offered, personal unpopularity will be certain to result from the ample materials existing for its development.

Against this view of his character, it is fair to add here that he had many qualities which would tend to bring about an entirely opposite result. He was more than ordinarily generous; and gave with a liberality that went at times beyond what most men would look upon as prudence. He was prompt to relieve merit that stood in need of help. Many cases of this kind there are unpublished and unknown out of a very small circle; for Cooper was not one to let his left hand know what his right hand was doing. One fact, however, has been so often mentioned, that it is violating no sanctity of private life to repeat it here. He was the first to discover the excellence of Greenough and to make that sculptor known to his countrymen. "Fenimore Cooper saved me from despair," wrote the latter in 1833, "after my second return to Italy. He employed me as I wished to be employed; and has up to this moment

6

been a father to me in kindness." To this generosity, it
is to be added that his sense of personal honor was of
the loftiest kind. It was sometimes, indeed, carried to
an extreme almost Quixotic; so that men morally fat-
witted could not even comprehend his principles of
action, and men who contented themselves with conventional morality resented his assertion of them as a reflection upon themselves. His loyalty to those who
had become dear to him was, moreover, just as conspicuous as his loyalty to what he deemed right. It with-
stood every chance of change, every accident of time
and circumstance, and only gave way on absolute proof
of unworthiness. Intimate acquaintance was sure to
bring to Cooper respect, admiration, and finally affection. Few men have stood better than he that final test
of excellence which rests upon the fact that those who
knew him best loved him most. Yet even these were
often forced to admit, that it was necessary to know him
well to appreciate how generous, how true, and how
lofty-minded he was.

Besides these traits of character, it is important to understand some of Cooper's political and social opinions.
He was an aristocrat in feeling, and a democrat by conviction. To some this seems a combination so unnatural that they find it hard to comprehend it. That a
man whose tastes and sympathies and station connect
him with the highest class, and to whom contact with
the uneducated and unrefined brings with it a sense of
personal discomfort and often of disgust, should avow
his belief in the political rights of those socially inferior,
should be unwilling to deny them privileges which
he claims for himself, is something so appalling to many
that their minds strive vainly to grasp it. But this feel-

ing was so thoroughly wrought into Cooper's nature
that he almost disliked those of his countrymen whom
he found not to share in it. "I confess," he wrote at
the time when he was generally denounced as an aristocrat, "that I now feel mortified and grieved when I
meet with an American gentleman who professes anything but liberal opinions as respects the rights of his
fellow-creatures." He went on to explain that by liberal opinions he meant "the generous, manly determination to let all enjoy equal political rights, and to bring
those to whom authority is necessarily confided under
the control of the community they serve." He despised
the cant that the people were their own worst enemies.
So far from it, he believed in widening the foundations
of society by making representation as real as possible,
and thereby giving to every interest in the state its fair
measure of power ; for no government, in his eyes,
could ever be just or pure in which the governors have
interests distinct from those of the governed. These
opinions he put sometimes in an extreme form. "I
have never yet been in a country," he said, "in which
what are called the lower orders have not clearer and
sounder views than their betters, of the great principles
which ought to predominate in the control of human affairs." At the same time his belief in democracy was
not in the least one of unmixed admiration. He was
far from looking upon it as a perfect form of government. It was only the one that, taking all things into
consideration, was attended with fewer evils and greater
advantages than any other. It had faults and dangers
peculiar to itself. His liberal opinions, he took frequent
care to say, had nothing in common with the devices of
demagogues who teach the doctrine, that the voice of

the people is the voice of God; that the aggregation of fallible parts, acting, too, with diminished responsibilities, forms an infallible whole.

Along with this clear understanding of the advantages and disadvantages of democracy there was mingled, however, a weakness of feeling on the subject of position, which occasionally degenerated into an almost ridiculous pettiness. This was especially true of his later life. His utterances were sometimes so apparently contradictory, however, that it is hard to tell whether justice has been done to his real meaning on account of the difficulty of ascertaining what his real meaning was. But he spoke often of " the gentry of America," as if there were or could be here a class of gentlemen outside and independent of those engaged in professions or occupations. He seemed at times to attach that supreme importance to descent which we are usually accustomed to see exhibited in this country only by those who have little or nothing else to boast of. His contempt of trade and of those employed in it had frequently about its expression a spice of affectation. Moreover, he subjected himself to much misrepresentation and ill-will by the manner in which he lectured his countrymen on the distinctions that must prevail in society. There are certain things which are everywhere recognized and quietly accepted : they only become offensive when proclaimed. A man may unhesitatingly acquiesce in his inferiority, socially, to one who is politically only his equal; but he will very naturally resent a reference, by the latter, to the fact of his social inferiority. A good deal of Cooper's later writings was deformed by solemn commonplaces on the inevitable necessity of the existence of class distinctions. This drew upon him the condemnation of many who

did not look upon the expression of such views as an offense against truth, but as an offense against good manners. To correct the folly of fools was itself folly ; and
wise men, no matter what their station in life, did not
thank him for the instruction, the very giving of which
implied an insult to their intelligence. His remarks on
the subject were never heeded, if indeed they were ever
read, by those for whom they were specially designed.
But to his enemies they furnished ample opportunities
for misrepresentation and abuse.

But any account of Cooper would be of slight value
that failed to take notice of his love of country. No
other man of letters has there been in America, or perhaps in any other land, to whom this has been a passion so absorbing. It entered into the very deepest
feelings of his heart. Even in the storm of calumny,
which fell upon him in his later years, if the flame of
his patriotism seemed at times to die away, any little
circumstance was sure to revive it at once. No pro-
claimer of " manifest destiny " ever had more faith than
he in the imperial greatness and grandeur to which the
republic was to attain. All that in vulgar minds took
the shape of braggart boasting, was in his idealized and
glorified by his lofty conception of the majestic part
which his country was to play in deciding the destinies
of mankind. In spite of short-comings he deplored, of
perils that he feared, firm in his heart was the conviction that here was to be the home of the great new race
that was to rule the world. Other lands might look to
the future with hope or doubt ; his own was as sure of
it as if it lay already in its grasp. This was a confidence that survived all changes, and despised all forebodings. The question of slavery certainly disturbed

him, but it did not shake his trust. The prophecies of
the dissolution of the Union, current in Europe, he
laughed to scorn. Even in the days of nullification his
faith never wavered one jot. To no one, more justly
than to him, could perpetual thanks have been voted,
because he never despaired of the republic.

Cooper's lofty views of his country he soon found
were essentially different from those entertained abroad.
The knowledge of America even now possessed in Europe is not burdensomely great. But in 1830 its ignorance was prodigious; and the nearest approach to interest was usually the result of something of that same
vague fear which haunted the citizens of the Roman
Empire at the possible perils to civilization that might
lie hid in the boundless depths of the German forests.
On the Continent the ignorance was greater than it was
in England, and Cooper had plenty of opportunities
of witnessing the exhibition of it. In the case of the
common people he was amused by it. That the whites
who had emigrated to America had not yet become entirely black; that it was reasonable to expect that time,
while it could not restore their original hue to these
deteriorated Europeans tanned to ebony, might in the
revolution of the suns elevate them to a fair degree of
civilization; these, and similar sage opinions, did not
disturb him when uttered by the philosophers of the
lower classes. Yet their ignorance, great as it was, he
found not to surpass materially that of men who ought
to have known better, so long as they pretended to
know at all. That the colonies had been settled by
convicts, was a common impression among the best educated. While residing in Paris Cooper had the gratification of having his country quoted in the French

Chamber of Deputies as an example of the possibility of forming respectable communities by the transportation of criminals. Even men who sympathized with republican institutions, he informs us, did not think of denying the fact; they denied merely the inference. The brilliant publicist, Paul Courier, had asserted it would be as unjust to reproach the modern Romans with being descendants of ravishers and robbers, as it would be to reproach the Americans with being descendants of convicts. All could not be expected, however, to be so liberal as this constitutional reformer. The gross vices which in foreign opinion distinguished the inhabitants of the United States, were held to be the natural consequences of their settlement by felons. Cooper subsequently took care to furnish the sons of the Puritans with all needful information as to the light in which their fathers were viewed in Europe. At the time, however, it was far different. Keenly sensitive to his country's honor, and knowing the morals of his countrymen to be far higher than those of the men of any other land, derogatory statements of this kind were galling in the extreme.

But it was the English opinion that Cooper resented most bitterly. This was partly because he believed from the community of origin and speech it ought to be better informed, and partly because he looked upon it as responsible for many of the absurd and erroneous impressions that prevailed in the rest of Europe. His feelings were rendered still keener by the direct contact with English prejudice which he had personally during his residence abroad. The attitude of the Continent towards America was that of supreme ignorance and indifference. But there was at the time something besides that in the attitude of England, so far certainly as it was represented by its periodical literature. In the most favorable cases it was supercilious and patronizing, an attitude which never permits the nation criticising to understand the nation criticised. There was never any effort to penetrate into the real nature of the social and political movements that were taking place on this side of the water. Men were contented with the examination of mere external phenomena, which, whether good or bad in themselves, belonged to a period of growth and were certain to pass away. Not the slightest sympathy existed with the feelings and aspirations of a people closely allied in blood and speech, and the lack of desire involved the lack of ability to enter into the spirit of their institutions. There was no idea that there could be other types of character than those found on British soil, or any room or reason for the play of other social and political forces than were at work in British communities.

At the time, however, that Cooper took up his residence in Europe there was more than supercilious indifference in the character of English criticism. There was steady misrepresentation and abuse, due in a few cases to design, in more to ignorance, in most to that disposition on the part of all men to believe readily what they wish ardently. It made little difference whether the writer were Whig or Tory. If anything the open dislike of the latter was preferable to the patronizing regard of the former. In 1804 the poet Moore visited America. He wrote home a number of poetical epistles, in which he told his friends that he had found us old in our youth and blasted in our prime. The demon gold was running loose; everything and everybody was corrupt; truth, conscience, and virtue were regularly made matters of barter and sale. A succession of English travelers repeated from year to year the same dismal story, and their statements were caught up and paraded and dwelt upon in the English periodical press. In "The Quarterly Review," in particular, our condition was constantly held up as an awful example of the results of democratic institutions and universal suffrage. Certain facts and predictions had been repeated so often that they came to be accepted and believed by all. We spoke a dialect of the English tongue; our manners were bad, if we could be said to have any at all; loyalty we could know nothing about, because we had no king; religion we were entirely devoid of, because there was no established church; the federation was steadily tending towards monarchy; the wealthy were longing to be nobles; and the Union could not last above a quarter of a century. Worse than all, intrigue and bribery were sapping the national life; or to use a still favorite phrase of the newspapers, though the repetition of a hundred years has now made it somewhat stale, corruption was preying upon the vitals of the republic.

There is not the slightest exaggeration in these statements. Their truth any one familiar with the periodical literature of that period will least of all doubt. There was a perfect agreement between those who visited us and described us and those who drew their description from their imaginations. Nothing distinguished the English traveler or the English reviewer so much as his piety, and his profound conviction that religion could not exist where it was not carefully watched over by an established church. Besides this inevitable moral

destitution, we were irreclaimably given over to vulgarity. Manners there could not be in a land abandoned
to an unbridled democracy. In the most praiseworthy
instances even, men lacked that repose, that fine tact,
which were found universally in the higher orders in
the mother country. The defect was ineradicable, according to most; for it had its baleful origin in popular
institutions themselves. In justice it must be added
that there were some who, in consequence of the
American passion for traveling, entertained a mild hope
that in time this rudeness would wear away, and this
total ignorance of good breeding would be enlightened
by the polish and refinement that would be picked up
from the quantity to be found scattered about foreign
courts. The published correspondence of that period
is delicious in its frankness. The Englishman, writing
to his American friend, never descends from his lofty
position of censor both of great and petty morals. The
inferiority of manners in this country is a point insisted
upon by the former with an assiduity and assurance
that are sufficient of themselves to make clear how high
was the breeding to which he himself had attained. It
makes little difference who write the letters. They all
express the same sentiments. They all offer advice as
to the best method America can take to retrieve the
good opinion of Europe which it has lost. They are careful to say that they entertain the kindest of feelings to
the United States; that they neglect no occasion of doing justice to the good and wise that had found there a
home. Unfortunately these are few in number; and
with a lofty sense of justice they never fail to express
disapprobation in strong terms of the vast amount to be
condemned in a land which had fallen under the sway

of a reckless democracy and a godless church. One English gentleman in the British military service, after being some time in this country, writes, after his return, to an American friend, and thus cheerfully records his impressions. "The frightful effects produced by an unrestrained democracy," he says, "the demoralizing effects produced by universal suffrage never appeared to me so odious as they do now by contrast with the good breeding, the order and mutual support which all give to each other in this country, from the highest to the lowest." This letter belongs to the year 1839, and it only continues a line of remark common for the half-century previous. Everything that came from America, if praised at all, was praised with a qualification. Not a compliment could be uttered of an individual without an implied disparagement of the land that gave him birth. The record of every man who was well received in English society will bear out this assertion. Scott wrote to Southey in 1819, that Ticknor was "a wondrous fellow for romantic lore and antiquarian research, *considering his country.*" Even words of genuine affection were often accompanied with an impertinence which has a delightfulness of its own from the utter unconsciousness on the part of the writer or speaker of having said anything out of the way. They were compliments of the kind which intimated that the person addressed was a sort of redeeming feature in a wild waste of desert. "You have taught us," writes in 1840 Mrs. Basil Montagu to Charles Sumner, "to think much more highly of your country — from whom we have hitherto seen no such men."

There is nothing to be gained in raking over at this day the ashes of dead controversies and revilings.

Americans no longer read the writings of the kind described, and Englishmen have largely forgotten that they were ever written. The new commentators on our habits and customs have taken up a new line of remark, and the new prophets of woe foresee an entirely new class of calamities. But it has been necessary to revive here the memory of the old charges and forebodings, in order to show the state of feeling that would be developed by them in a man of a peculiarly sensitive and proud nature, such as was the subject of this biography. Rubbish as they may seem now, they were to the men of that time a grievous sore. Whatever may have been Cooper's feelings previously, it was not until after he had resided for a while in Europe that any hostility towards England is seen in his works. But there it soon began to manifest itself, though at first rather in the way of defense than attack. As time went on it increased rather than diminished. It largely affected his own fortunes by the personal hostility it provoked in return. To some extent, without doubt, his oft-repeated declaration was true, that in the dependence then existing here upon foreign opinion, every American author held his reputation at the mercy of the British reviewer. It would be unjust to say that it seemed at one period almost as if Cooper had sworn towards England undying hate. But it is certainly a fact that he gave utterance to his inmost feelings when he described it as a country that cast a chill over his affections, a country that all men respected but that few men loved. Yet he had been brought up in the school of the Federalist party, in which admiration for the literature, policy, and morals of the motherland was taught as a duty; in which every door was thrown open to visitors from England as an act of hospitality due to kinsmen separated merely by the accident of position. He himself tells us how, an ardent boy of seventeen, he leaped for the first time upon the soil of Great Britain, feeling for it a love almost as devoted as that which he bore the land of his birth, and looking upon every native of it in the light of a brother. It did not take him long to find out that the fancied tie of kinship was not recognized, that it was even despised; and that if he made friends, it must be in spite of his country, and not because of it. His connection with the navy had also led him to be keenly sensitive to the injustice and indignities connected with the impressment of seamen. In his first voyage in a merchant ship he had seen two native Americans taken from the vessel and forced into the British service. His own captain even had on one occasion been seized, though speedily liberated. There had also been an attempt to press a Swede belonging to the crew, on the ground that his country and England were in alliance, and the latter had therefore a right to his help. These were not the acts to inspire devotion towards the people who committed or who authorized them. The keen resentment Cooper felt for the wrongs then perpetrated upon the American marine he afterward expressed in his novels of "Wing-and-Wing" and "Miles Walling-ford." He never forgot those early experiences. When he came to reside in Europe he was as little disposed to forgive the depreciation of his country which he imputed, whether justly or unjustly, to English influence. Distrust became dislike, and dislike deepened into hostility.

There is little doubt that with a man of Cooper's nature the revulsion from his original feelings would tend to swing him to the opposite extreme ; that, as a consequence of that, he would often fancy insult where none was intended, and impute to design conduct that was the result of chance or even of personal timidity. But making full allowance for this inevitable source of error, there was plenty of reason furnished for offense to a man whose personal pride was equal to that of the whole British aristocracy, and whose pride in his country exceeded even his personal pride. The ignorant criticism which amused most Americans was apt to make him indignant. No compliment, in particular, could be paid with safety to him individually at the expense of his country. This was a practice, however, which the Englishmen of that day seemed to regard as the consummate crown of adulation. Depreciation of America of any sort he resented at once. If conversation touched upon matters discreditable to the United States — which was far from being an uncommon topic — it was very much his practice, instead of listening to it patiently, to bring up matters discreditable to Great Britain. There was unquestionably ample material on both sides with which each could blacken the other. But while this tended to make the conversation less monotonous, it likewise tended to make the converser less popular. Cooper lost early by his bearing in English society much of the favor which he had won from his writings. To this we have positive evidence. It is specifically mentioned in the sketch of his life, which along with his portrait appeared in 1831 in Colburn's "New Monthly Magazine." The article went on, after mentioning this fact, to pay a tribute to his somewhat aggressive patriotism. "Yet he seems," it said, "to claim little consideration on the score of intellectual greatness; he is evidently prouder of his birth than of his genius; and looks, speaks, and walks as if he exulted more in being recognized as an American citizen than as the author of 'The Pilot' and 'The Prairie.' "

To a man whose heart was thus full of the future glories of the republic, the indifference and neglect with which it was regarded could not but be galling. Still this was nothing to the positive contempt which often manifested itself in social slights that could be felt but could not well be resented. This was especially noticeable in the case of the legations, the conduct of which was largely under the control of the home government. The English policy was here in marked contrast to that of Russia, which, even at that early day, cultivated almost ostentatiously friendship with America. Between the legations of these two countries there was always the best of understandings. The direct contrary often prevailed between the ministers of Great Britain and of the United States. The influence of the former was frequently thought to be exerted to the social injury of the latter. Whether true or false, this was generally believed. Cooper certainly credited it and looked forward to the time when the whole attitude of England would be altered. We were then less than twelve millions in population; but the day would come when we should be fifty millions. The existing state of things would then be changed. You and I may not live to see it, he wrote substantially to his friends, but our sons and grandsons will. They may not like us any better, but they will take care to hide their feelings. Strong resentment sometimes drove him into taking up positions he would not in his cooler moments have maintained. "As one citizen of the republic," he wrote, "however insignificant, I have no notion of being blackguarded and

vituperated half a century and then cajoled into forget-
fulness at the suggestion of fear and expediency, as circumstances render our good-will of importance." Not
one of these slights and insults would he have the fifty
millions forget. He did not bear in mind that fifty
millions could not afford to remember. It was like
asking the man of middle life to revenge upon the
sons the indignities which the boy had received from
the fathers.

Cooper's residence in England was only for a few
months during the first half of the year 1828. With
his feelings towards that country and with the feeling
entertained in it toward his own, nothing could have
made his stay highly pleasant. But it is one of the
numerous minor falsehoods that came to be connected
with his life, that it was unpleasant. On the contrary,
his company was sought by many of the most distinguished men, though in accordance with his usual
custom he carried no letters of introduction. At a
later period he said that in no country had he been
personally so well treated as in England; he was as
strongly convinced as his worst enemy, that as an author
he had been extolled there beyond his merits; nor had
he failed to receive quite as much substantial remunera-
tion as he could properly lay claim to. But the social
atmosphere there prevailing was not the atmosphere he
loved. The poet Moore relates in his diary a story told
him by Sydney Smith of the "touchiness" of "the
Republican" — so the American novelist is styled —
as evinced by the indignation of the latter at the conduct of Lord Nugent. This nobleman, it appears, in-
vited Cooper to take a walk with him to a certain
street. Arriving there he unceremoniously entered the

house of a friend and left his companion to make his way back alone. Cooper's resentment of the treatment may have been unwisely shown; for though often termed an aristocrat, he never exhibited in the slightest degree that reticence which is or is supposed to be the peculiar characteristic of aristocracy. But few would now be found to deny that his indignation was both natural and just, and that the act of Lord Nugent was the act of a boor and not of a gentleman. It was certainly unreasonable to expect that a society which could rejoice in this method of rebuking republican pretension could itself be agreeable to a republican. Cooper could not but be offended by the prejudices he found existing against his country and the dislike usually felt and sometimes expressed for it. The only man he met whom he thought well informed about America was Sir James Mackintosh. The ignorance of some of his friends was so great that even to him it caused amusement rather than anger. Many readers will have heard of the practice of "gouging," with which, according to the veracious English traveler of early days, the native American gave the charm of diversity and diversion to a life whose serious thoughts were wholly absorbed in the acquisition of pelf. Some will remember the definition given of it in Grose's "Dictionary of the Vulgar Tongue:" "to squeeze out a man's eye with the thumb; a cruel practice used by the Bostonians in America." A curious illustration of the belief in this myth occurred to Cooper. One of his friends in England was an amiable and pleasant man of letters, named William Sotheby, little heard of in these days; and even in his own days he had to endure the double degradation of being called a small poet by the small poets themselves.

7

He was at this time an old gentleman of over seventy, and was preparing to make a creditable close to his career by performing the task, which seems to assume the shape of a duty to every literary Englishman of leisure, of translating the Iliad and the Odyssey. Not unnaturally he was more familiar with the way the wrath of Achilles manifested itself than with the shape taken by the wrath of the men of his race beyond the sea. On one occasion he condoled with Cooper because of the quarrelsomeness and fighting prevalent in America, making during this expression of his sympathy an obvious allusion to gouging. It was useless to attempt setting him right. His interest in ancient fiction had not been so absorbing as to close his mind to the acquisition of modern fact; and to Cooper's denial of what he had implied he listened with a polite but incredulous smile.

CHAPTER VI.

1828–1833.

MISREPRESENTATION and abuse of his native land it was not in Cooper's nature to bear in silence. His resentment for the imputations cast upon his country began to show itself soon after he had taken up his residence abroad. In " The Red Rover," which appeared in 1827, there are satirical references to the benevolence and piety of the moral missionaries which England had sent among us, and to the correctness and wisdom of current foreign opinion. In the next novel, "The Wept of Wish-ton-Wish," his feelings are still more fully expressed. In this work he puts into the mouth of one of the characters, a physician, an elaborate disquisition upon the degeneracy of man in America. In the course of it the leech informs his opponent that the science and wisdom and philosophy of Europe had been exceedingly active in the investigation of this matter of colonial inferiority, that they had proved to their own perfect satisfaction, which was the same thing as disposing of the question without appeal, that man and beast, plant and tree, hill and dale, lake, pond, sun, air, fire, and water were all wanting in some of the perfectness of the old regions. It was plain we could never hope to reach the exalted excellence they enjoy ; and while he respected the patriotism that held the contrary view, he could not, out of deference to it, afford to doubt what had been demonstrated by science and collected by learning.

It was not in this indirect way, however, that he could content himself with defending his country. No sooner had he lived in Europe long enough to become acquainted with the erroneous impressions there prevalent, in regard to America, than he set out to prepare a work which should expose their falsity. In it he determined to lay the precise facts before a public which was indisposed to believe anything to the credit, and disposed to believe everything to the discredit of democratic institutions. On the face of it, this was a futile undertaking, no matter how praiseworthy its motive. Nations, no more than individuals, are convinced by what other nations say of themselves ; it is only by what they do. In this particular case the difficulty was rendered more insurmountable by the fact that these erroneous impressions prevailed among those who did not care enough about the matter to investigate it seriously, and who would be certain in most cases to refrain from investigating it at all, had they a suspicion that their preconceived beliefs would be overthrown or even shaken, as a result of their examination. The question naturally arises, whether such men could be convinced by facts and arguments, and if so, whether they were worth the trouble of convincing. Why grudge the adherents of a dying cause the dismal enjoyment they receive from contemplating the ruin that is always being wrought, or is always to be wrought, by Democracy to Democracy ? Experience led Cooper subsequently to see the uselessness of the experiment he, in this instance, tried. When asked at a later period why some efforts were not made to correct the false notions prev-

alent in Europe in regard to America, he answered with
perfect truth then, that no favorable account would be
acceptable; that it would not be enough to confess our
real faults, but we should be required to confess the precise faults that, according to the opinions of that quarter
of the world, we were morally, logically, and politically
bound to possess. By the wide circulation of his fictions he, in truth, did more to remove wrong impressions, dissipate prejudices, and open the eyes of Europe
to a knowledge of American life and manners, than
could have been accomplished by the longest and most
ponderous array of indisputable facts.

Facts, however, he at this time purposed to furnish.
Accordingly, on the 13th of August, 1828, appeared a
work entitled, "Notions of the Americans, Picked up
by a Traveling Bachelor." Whatever its actual success,
it was a relative failure. Cooper himself tells us that it
occasioned him a heavy pecuniary loss. Manner and
matter, both foredoomed it to the fate which it met.
The plan of it was an unfortunate one as well as a
purely artificial one. The views and observations and
statements of fact are put into the mouth of a European traveling bachelor, a member of a club of cosmop-
olites, who, in consequence of meeting an American,
named Cadwallader, is persuaded to visit and see for
himself the new world. Arriving there he writes letters
to his friends, giving an account of his impressions.
The fiction of foreign authorship was the first mistake.
It could not mislead any one, nor was it intended to
mislead any one. But a grave didactic treatise which
was designed to convey a truthful impression, lost something and gained nothing by being connected with any
artifice, even though not meant to impose upon the

reader. Nor was the work interesting to one not specially interested in the subject. To the American it gave the strongest assurances of loyalty to republican institutions on the part of her most widely-known man of letters ; but it added little or nothing to the information of which he was already in possession. On the other hand, the laudatory style in which this country was invariably spoken of was certain to be offensive to those whom it was the design of the work to enlighten. The weight of matter, moreover, was not rendered any more endurable by lightness of treatment. At the present day the work is chiefly interesting for the keen observations that are found in it, and for its remarks upon the future of the country rather than upon its then existing state. Cooper's predictions were concerned with the minutest, as well as the greatest subjects. They ranged all the way from the indefinite assurance, that New York must eventually become the gastronomic capital of the globe, to the precise statement, as to the exact number of the population there would be in the United States fifty years from the time in which he was writing. This last prophecy, it is to be said, has turned out singularly true. He fixed the number at fifty millions. That this was no chance guess, but a carefully worked out computation, is evident from the fact that he repeats it several times in this work and occasionally in later ones. He, moreover, assigned definitely forty-three millions to the whites and seven millions to the blacks.

It is not for an American to find fault with the laudatory tone of a work which reflects the ardent love of country felt by the writer. Yet in many respects it is a singular production. In manner it is calm, grave,

almost philosophical; there is not the slightest effort at
fine writing; the tone can never be said to be even fer-
vid. Yet it must be confessed that not in the most exalted of Fourth of July orations does the national eagle
scream with a shriller note, or wing his way with a
more unflagging flight. Any one who formed his notions of this country exclusively from this book, would
be sure to fancy that here at last paradise was reopening
to the children of a fallen race. After this remark, it
may seem ridiculous, and yet it is perfectly just to say,
that Cooper, so far from giving way to exaggeration in
his assertions, kept himself well within the bounds of the
truth. In the exercise of that duty which presses heavily upon every reviewer, to seem, if not to be wiser than
his author, many of the English periodicals, even those
most favorable to America, undertook to doubt his
statements of fact, to sneer at his prophecies of the future as ludicrous exaggerations, and to term them striking and whimsical instances of Yankee braggadocio, and
of the love of building castles in the air. Cooper could
not well overstate the material prosperity and progress
of the country, nor the inability of men trained under
different conditions either to believe it or to comprehend
it. Reality soon outran some of his most daring anticipations. His most extravagant statements were speedily more than confirmed by the operation of agencies
whose mighty results he could not foresee, because,
when he wrote, the agencies themselves did not exist.
He had carefully guarded himself in one instance, by
saying that he did not expect that the Northwest
would be settled within an early period. The precaution was unnecessary. He had been brought up in a
town, founded in the wilderness, at a distance of less

than one hundred and fifty miles from the commercial capital of the republic. He lived long enough to see the frontiers of civilization pushed one thousand miles west of the line it had held in his boyhood's home.

Any wrong impression, therefore, which the work conveyed was not due to the spirit of braggadocio pervading it, as asserted and commented upon by the English reviewers. No false statement was made intentionally; there were very few that were made mistakenly. But though Cooper purposed to tell nothing but truth about his country, he did not feel himself under obligation to tell all the truth. The attention was almost exclusively directed to that side of the national character which lent itself most readily to favorable treatment. What was unfavorable was either omitted altogether, or was very lightly passed over. One letter alone, and that not a long one, was devoted to slavery. It is plain that he was annoyed by it; to some extent, in spite of his confidence, disquieted by it, though the dangers he feared were not the dangers that actually came. Even at that early day there was enough to trouble the lover of his country in the criticism it encountered, for the glaring contrast between its professions of liberty and its practice; but far more in the dimly-seen shape of that gigantic struggle which, though itself vague and undefined, was already beginning to cast its lowering shadow over the future of the republic. So in a similar manner the literature, architecture, and art of America were passed over in a few pages, while letter after letter was given up to a description of its progress in wealth and comfort. Yet no one knew better than Cooper, — at a later period he took care his countrymen should not forget it, — that of all standards by which to test national glory, the material standard is in itself the lowest and most vulgar ; and that the difference in real greatness between two places can never be measured by the comparative amount of sugar, or salt, or flour sold in each. Yet he remembered then, what later he seemed to forget, that the necessity of conquering the continent, of making it inhabitable for man, was at the time and must continue long to remain a very positive hindrance to the development of literary and artistic ability, because by the immense rewards it offered it attracted to the development of material resources the intellect and vigor of the entire land.

Cooper tells us, as has been said, that he lost money on this work. But there was something more than pecuniary failure that attended it. There were in it statements which met with disfavor at home. More important than these, however, were remarks that aroused personal hostility abroad. He made several references, in particular, to the people of England, and they were not of a kind to conciliate regard for himself and his work. In one place he spoke of the society of that country as being more repulsive, artificial, and cumbered, and, in short, more absurd and frequently less graceful than that of any other European nation. Theoretically, the English care nothing for foreign opinion. They have said it so often among themselves that most of them look upon it as a point which has been settled by the consent of mankind. But like many other beliefs it has become an article of faith without having become an article of practice. To this extent it is true that they care nothing for the remarks of obscure men of which they never hear. On the other hand, no nation is more sensitive to contemporary foreign opinion, coming from writers of distinction. There will be plenty of instances furnished in this one biography to prove fully this assertion. Cooper's attack was never forgotten or forgiven. From this time there was a distinctly hostile feeling manifested toward him in many of the English periodicals. Even before his next work appeared, London correspondents of American newspapers announced that it was going to be severely criticised, inasmuch as the novelist had made himself unpopular in England by the comments made and the views put forth in the "Notions of the Americans." If this were not true, it was at least believed to be true. Certainly the fact of hostility steadily increasing from this period, on the part of the British press, cannot be denied, whatever we may think of the causes that brought it about. Nor did it stop short with depreciation of his works. Literary criticism, even if based merely upon personal dislike, can always resort with safety to the cheap defense that it is honest. But there were reviewers who went farther, who framed for Cooper imaginary feelings and then proceeded to assail him for having them. He was accused, especially, of pluming himself highly upon the title of the "American Scott." Hazlitt, for instance, seeing him strutting, as he terms it, in the streets of Paris, was enabled to detect by the way the novelist walked the way he felt upon this special matter, and afterward to state the conclusion at which he had arrived as a positive fact. Similar specimens of fine critical insight into Cooper's motives and sentiments can be found scattered up and down the pages of English journals.

At the time he was bringing out "The Water Witch" in Germany, the revolution in France took place that resulted in the expulsion of the Bourbons and the calling of Louis Philippe to the throne. Paris became at once the Mecca to which the lovers of liberty throughout Europe resorted. Thither Cooper hastened from his home in Dresden. He reached the city in August, 1830. There he watched with the profoundest interest the political movements that were going on about him. The reactionary tendencies that early began to manifest themselves in the rule of the Citizen King, brought to him the same disappointment and the same disgust that it did to all the ardent republicans of the Old World. There is much in what he says to remind the reader of the feelings expressed by Heine, who had likewise hurried to Paris after the July revolution, and who was venting his indignation and contempt in the columns of the Augsburg "Allgemeine Zeitung." Occasional passages bear even a close similarity. Cooper on one occasion describes Louis Philippe walking about among his subjects wearing a white hat, carrying a red umbrella, and evidently laboring to act in an easy and affable manner. " In short," he said in a phrase that might have been written by the great German, "he was condescending with all his might."

Close upon the revolution in France followed the revolt of Poland. The insurrection lasted about ten months, and during its progress the feelings of Cooper were profoundly stirred in behalf of that people. With this his personal friendship with the Polish poet, Mickiewicz, had probably a great deal to do; for at Rome a close intimacy had sprung up between him and that author. At a meeting, held in Paris on the 4th of July, 1831, at which Cooper presided, a sum of money was contributed to aid the revolters in their struggle. He

presided also at other meetings to advance the same
cause, and acted as chairman of a committee to raise
funds to assist the Polish soldiers who were fighting for
independence, and when this failed, to relieve the exiles
in their distress. Two addresses to the American people
signed by him in his official capacity — one written in
July, 1831, and the other in June, 1832 — appeared in
the American papers of those years ; and the fervor that
characterizes them both leaves little doubt as to their
authorship.

Into the great struggle going on in Europe, either
openly or silently between aristocracy and democracy,
he now, indeed, threw himself with his whole heart. In
certain respects this was a disadvantage. Whenever
Cooper's feelings on political subjects were aroused, his
literary work betrayed the obtrusion of interests more
dominating than those which belong to it legitimately.
This was manifested in the three tales which followed.
In them the scene of action was not only transferred to
European soil, but a direct attempt was avowedly made
to apply American principles to European facts. These
novels were " The Bravo," which appeared November
29, 1831 ; " The Heidenmauer," which appeared September 25, 1832 ; and " The Headsman," which appeared October 18, 1833. The purpose of all these
was the direct exaltation of republican institutions, and
likewise the exposure of those which paraded in the
garb of liberty without possessing its reality. The
scenes of two were accordingly laid in the aristocratic
cities of Venice and of Berne. The first of the three is
generally spoken of as the best, especially by those who
have read none of them at all. Little difference will be
found, as a matter of fact, between " The Bravo " and

" The Headsman " as regards literary merit. "The Heidenmauer " is, however, distinctly inferior, and is in truth one of the most tedious novels that Cooper ever wrote. All were, however, animated by the same spirit. They all assailed oligarchical, and lauded democratic institutions. They were full of denunciations of the accommodating stupidity of patricians who were never able to see anything beneficial to the interests of the state in what was injurious to the interests of their own order. In particular, the doctrine was held up to derision, that while to the ignorant and the low there was ample power given to suffer, there was no power given to understand ; and that consequently it was their duty always to obey and never to criticise.

In writing this series Cooper was undertaking what was on the face of it a hazardous experiment. The peril was not, as thoughtless criticism has had it, in transferring his scenes and characters to a foreign soil. Human nature suffers no material change in passing from America to Europe. The danger lay in the fact that these were novels written with a purpose. The story was not told for its own sake, but for the sake of enforcing certain political opinions. It required, therefore, unusual skill in its construction and in the management of its details. For whatever may be the exact truth contained in the doctrine of art for art's sake, this is certainly clear, that in a work of fiction designed to advance successfully any cause, or support any theory, the didactic element must be made entirely subordinate to the purely creative element. Otherwise we impart to the novel the tediousness of a homily without its accepted authority. Art must be wooed as a mistress ; she can never be commanded as a slave. He, there-

fore, who seeks to press fiction into a work so foreign
to its nature as the inculcation of political opinions,
must, if he hopes to succeed, make the story suggest the
lesson without conveying it obtrusively. Above all is
there need of delicate touch and skillful handling, if the
aim be to affect those who are prejudiced against the
views expressed, or whose interests are involved in the
fate of those attacked. But Cooper's was never a delicate touch. What he thought he never insinuated ; what
he believed himself he never allowed to make its way indirectly into the minds of others. He always uttered it
boldly, and sometimes offensively. Effective this as-
suredly is in compositions of a certain class ; but it is
entirely out of place in a work of fiction. In the case
of these particular novels the purpose is avowed openly
and repeatedly. Cooper, indeed, takes care never to let
it escape the reader's attention. He may almost be said
to stand by his shoulder to jog him if he once happens
to forget that the story has a moral. American institutions, especially, were constantly held up as models in
which the best results were seen, and which it was the
policy of all other countries to imitate. The course
taken was a mark of patriotism ; but it was not the way
to gain converts. It is, in truth, the misfortune of the
novelist, burdened with a moral purpose, that the reader
usually feels the burden and is not affected by the
moral. It was not by methods like these that Scott
threw about chivalry and aristocracy that glamour which
outlasts the most minute acquaintance with the reality,
and influences the imagination in spite of the protest of
the judgment.

But another result that followed from writing novels
with a purpose, had a more direct influence upon his

reputation. It made it impossible that his work should any longer be criticised fairly. This was immediately seen in the case of " The Bravo." This novel had far more success in Europe than in America. But the success was not of a legitimate kind. Parties were at once arrayed for it or against it, not because it was a good or bad production from a literary point of view, but according as men sympathized with or were hostile to the political principles it advocated. It was not the merit of the work that came under consideration, but the merit of the cause. This at once destroyed almost entirely the value of any criticism which the story received.

A little while before " The Bravo " appeared, Cooper was unwillingly led to take part in a controversy which, according to his own view, was the remote cause of the hostility he afterwards encountered in his own land. It was at the time that the movement began on the part of Louis Philippe to separate himself from the liberals, of whom Lafayette was the chief representative. A discussion had arisen, in the French Chamber of Deputies, on the desirability of a reduction in the expenses of government. It gave rise to a controversy which extended much beyond the body in which it originated. Lafayette had advocated greater economy. In the course of the debate mentioned, he had referred to the United States as being a country which was cheaply governed, and at the same time well governed. The periodical press at once took up the question. M. Saulnier, one of the editors of the " Revue Britannique," came out with an article, the direct object of which was to prove that a government of three powers, such as was the limited monarchy recently established, was not so expensive

as that of a republic. In particular, he claimed that the
tax levied per head on the citizens of France was less
than that similarly levied on the citizens of the United
States. This was a direct attack upon Lafayette, who
had for forty years been maintaining that the government of this country was the cheapest known. The attention of Cooper was called to this article, and he was
asked to reply. He declined. A little later it was
made clear to him that the object with which it was
written was to injure Lafayette. The matter then assumed another aspect. To that statesman Cooper was
bound by ties of intimate personal friendship and by
a common love of this country. At a public dinner,
which had been given to Lafayette on the 8th of December, 1830, by the Americans in Paris, Cooper had
presided, and in a speech of marked fervor and ability,
he had dwelt upon the debt due from the United States
to the gallant Frenchman, who had ventured fortune
and life to aid a nation struggling against great odds to
be free. It was not in his nature to have his deeds
give the lie to his words. The fact above mentioned
at once overcame his reluctance to engage in the controversy. Accordingly in December, 1831, appeared a
"Letter to General Lafayette," preceded by a letter
from Lafayette to himself, dated the 22d of November.
This was a pamphlet of fifty pages, in which he went
into the subject of the cost of the United States government. It produced an immediate reply from M. Saulnier, who went over the ground again, and with a fine
air of candor affected to revise his previous statements.
As a result he made the cost of the American government a little larger than he had done before. To this
Cooper replied in a series of letters published in the

" National." The controversy would have ended sooner than it did, had it not been for the appearance of a fresh actor on the scene. This was a certain Mr. Leavitt Harris. He nominally belonged to New Jersey, but a large share of his life had been spent in Russia, and his political notions had apparently become acclimated to that region. He wrote an article on the subject in the shape of a letter to M. François Delassert, the vice-president of the Chamber of Deputies. In it he took ground opposite to that taken by Cooper, controverted his facts, and denied his inferences. So great weight was attached to it by the French government party that it was published as a supplementary number of the " Revue Britannique." Mr. Harris had once been left as *chargé d' affaires* at St. Petersburg during the absence of John Adams at the peace negotiations at Ghent. His letter was accordingly dwelt upon as the production of an American who had been intrusted by his government with high diplomatic position. We who know out of what stuff our foreign agents are sometimes made, would not be likely to attach much weight to the mere fact. But to a foreign nation the opinion of an official seemed naturally more trustworthy than that of a private citizen.

To the letter of Mr. Harris, Cooper replied on the 3d of May, 1832. This closed the discussion, at least so far as he was concerned.[1] But the controversy was followed by circumstances of a mortifying character. After the return to America of the United States minister,

[1] I express no opinion on the merits of this controversy, for I have seen very slight summaries only of the articles that appeared in the *Revue Britannique*. But it is proper to say that it was the opinion of the French liberals, that Cooper utterly demolished his antagonists in the controversy.

8

William C. Rives, Mr. Harris was nominated by the President, and confirmed by the Senate early in March, 1833, as *chargé d'affaires ;* and this office he held until the arrival of Edward Livingston, who was appointed minister on the 3d of May of the same year. Previously to this discreditable act, the Department of State had committed one of imbecility. It had issued a circular to the different local authorities of the Union with avowed reference to the finance controversy. Its purport was a request for them to furnish information in regard to the amount of public expenditures over which they had control. Against this course Cooper protested at once in. a long and vigorous letter to the American people, written on the 10th of December, 1832, from Vevay, Switzerland, and first printed in the Philadelphia "National Gazette." He took the ground that in such a discussion local burdens ought not to be included. It was, in fact, by confusing various kinds of taxation, and taxation for various objects, that the French government party had been able to make any showing for their own side. The letter was widely circulated, and seems to have served its purpose in suppressing the information that had been asked.

Unfortunately it was not the administration alone that displayed a lack of proper sentiment in this controversy. It is far from being a creditable thing in the history of the country that Cooper was subjected to constant attack, and even abuse, in the American newspapers, for his conduct in this finance discussion. He had been particularly careful to confine his remarks to the cost of government in the United States. He had not touched at all upon the cost of government in France. Yet he was charged with having overstepped the reserve imposed upon foreigners, and of having attacked the administration of a friendly country. The accusation was constantly made against him that he went about "flouting his Americanism throughout Europe," and in this particular case that he had overrated the importance of the controversy, and also the importance of the part he had taken in it. He had, in fact, aroused the hostility of that section of Americans, insignificant in number and ability, but sometimes having social position, who prefer the conveniences of despotism to the inconveniences of liberty. To such men Cooper's intense nationality was a standing reproach. His reputation, moreover, made their own littleness especially conspicuous. Depreciation of him, and of his rank as a man of letters, was a necessity of their case. As they did not express openly their real feelings, they carried on at advantage a war against a man who never had the prudence to hide what he thought. Yet among the better class of Americans abroad, Cooper's attachment to his native land received the recognition it merited. "Cooper's new book, 'The Bravo,'" wrote Horatio Greenough, from Paris, to Rembrandt Peale, in November, 1831, "is taking wonderfully here. If you could transfuse a little of that man's love of country and national pride into the leading members of our high society, I think it would leaven them all."

But the attacks in the American newspapers made a painful impression upon a mind that was morbidly sensitive to criticism even from the most insignificant of men. For an act of generous patriotism for which he deserved the thanks of all his countrymen he had received vilification from many of them. These things embittered him. They made him distrustful of the spirit that prevailed in his own land. He began to fancy that the country had gone back instead of forward in national feeling during the years of his absence. He had determined to return, because he was unwilling to have his children brought up on foreign soil and under foreign influences. But for himself he resolved to abandon literature. As soon as he had finished the manuscript he had in hand, he would give up all further thought of writing. "The quill and I are divorced," he wrote to Greenough in June, 1833, "and you cannot conceive the degree of freedom, I could almost say of happiness, I feel at having got my neck out of the halter." Longings for his old sea-life often came over him. "You must not be surprised," he wrote, half-jestingly, to the same friend, "if you hear of my sailing a sloop between Cape Cod and New York." But he had no definite plans marked out. The only thing about which his mind was made up was not to write any more.

CHAPTER VII.

1833–1838.

ON the fifth of November, 1833, Cooper landed at New York. For a few winters that followed he made that city his place of residence. The summers he spent in Cooperstown. To this village he paid a visit in June, 1834, after having been away from it entirely for about sixteen years. The recollections of his early life had always endeared it to his memory, and in it he now determined to take up his permanent abode. Accordingly he acquired possession of his father's old place, which for a long period had remained unoccupied. The house had received from the inhabitants the name of Templeton Hall, with a direct reference to "The Pioneers." Everything about it was rapidly hastening to ruin. Cooper at once began repairs upon it, and after these had been fully completed he made it his only residence. It was in this little village, upon the shore of the lake which his pen has made famous, that he spent the remainder of his life. There he wrote nearly all the works which he produced after his return to his native land. Its seclusion and quiet gave him ample opportunities for undisturbed literary exertion ; the beauty of the surroundings ministered constantly to his passion for scenery ; and of the world outside he saw sufficient to satisfy his wishes in the frequent journeys which business compelled him to make to the great cities.

Yet, though his latter days were spent in the country, the life he led henceforward deserves anything but the name of a pastoral. With the return from Europe begins the epic period of Cooper's career. The next ten years, in particular, were years of battle and storm. He had been criticised harshly and unjustly; he came back prepared and disposed to criticise. His feelings found expression at once. The America to which he had returned seemed to him much worse than that from which he had gone. In his opinion nearly everything had deteriorated. Manners, morals, the whole spirit of the nation, struck him as being on a lower level. Yet the change was not really in the people; it was in himself. The country had been moving on in the line of its natural bustling development; he, on the contrary, had been going back in sentiment. In one particular there was a certain justification for the dislike expressed by him for the novel things he saw. The business of the entire land was in a feverish condition. The Erie Canal, completed the year before his departure for Europe, had opened an unbroken water way from the Atlantic sea-board to the farthest shores of the great lakes. To this stimulus to population and trade was added the expected stimulus of the railroad system, then in its infancy. Both together were disclosing, though more to the imagination than to the eye, the wealth that lay hid in the unsettled regions of the West. They were active agents, therefore, in creating one of those periods of speculative prosperity which are sure to recur when any new and unforeseen avenue to sudden fortune is laid open. The immense field for endeavor revealed by the prospective establishment of flourishing communities reacted unfavorably

upon the intellectual movement which had begun in a
feeble way to show itself twenty years before. The
attraction of mighty enterprises which held out to the
hope promises of the highest temporal triumphs, was a
competition that mere literary and scholastic pursuits,
with their doubtful success and precarious rewards,
could not well maintain. The country certainly went
back for a time in higher things in consequence of that
rapid material progress which drew to its further development the youthful energy and ability of the entire
land. To make money and to make it rapidly seemed
to be the one object of life.

Such a fever of speculative prosperity wholly absorbing the thoughts and activities of men in the acquisition
of wealth, would have been viewed by Cooper at any
time with indifference, even if it did not inspire disgust.
But a greater change than he knew had come over him.
It is clear that he had now grown largely out of sympathy with the energy and enterprise which were doing so
much to build up the prosperity and power of his country. His nature had come into a profound sympathy
with the quiet, the culture, and the polish of the lands
he had left behind. His spirit could no longer be incited by the romance that lay hid in the fiery energies
of trade. In the tumultuousness of the life about him,
he could see little but a restless and vulgar exertion for
the creation of wealth. The perpetual bustle and
change were not to his taste. He spoke of it afterwards, in one of his works, with a certain grim humor
peculiarly his own. America he said, was a country
for alibis. The whole nation was in motion; and everybody was everywhere, and nobody was anywhere.

Feelings of this kind had begun to come over him

long before his return from abroad. He had been affected by his surroundings to an extent of which he was only vaguely conscious. While in Europe he admitted that he found growing in his nature a strong distaste for the common appliances of common life. He had not been long in Florence before these sentiments found utterance. "I begin to feel," he wrote, "I could be well content to vegetate here for one half of my life, to say nothing of the remainder." He drew sharp distinctions between commercial towns and capitals. Even in Italy, Leghorn with its growing trade, its bales of merchandise, its atmosphere filled with the breath of the salt sea mixed with the smell of pitch and tar, seemed mean and vulgar after the refinement and world-old beauty of Florence. He acknowledged that the languor and repose of towns which glory simply in their collections and recollections, were far more suited to his feelings than the activity and tumult of towns whose glory lies in their commercial enterprises. This preference is not uncommon among cultivated men. But it is too much to ask of a nation that it shall exist for the sake of gratifying the æsthetic emotions of travelers. The process of achieving greatness can never be so agreeable to the looker-on as the sight of greatness achieved; but it is unhappily often the case that many things, which the visitor regards as a charm, the native feels to be a reproach.

Besides the change of view in himself, there were some actual changes in the country that were not temporary in their nature. The constitution of society had altered at home during his residence abroad, or was rapidly altering. The influence of the old colonial aristocracy was fast dying out. New men were pushing to the wall the descendants of the families that had flourished before the Revolution, and had sought after it to keep up distinctions and exclusiveness which the very success of the struggle in which they had been concerned doomed to an early decay. This was especially noticeable in New York. In such a city social rank must tend, in the long run, to wait upon wealth. The result may be delayed, it cannot be averted. Wealth, too, in most cases, will find its way to the hands of those carrying on great commercial undertakings. That this class would eventually become a controlling one in society, if not the controlling one, was inevitable. It was not likely that men, who were bent on the conquest of the continent, who revolved even in their dreams all forms of the adventurous and the perilous, whose enterprise stopped short only with the impossible, would be content long to submit to a fictitious superiority on the part of those whose thoughts were so taken up with the consideration of what their fathers had been or had done that they forgot to be or to do anything themselves. Yet the latter composed no small share of the class with which Cooper's early associations had lain. He naturally sympathized with them rather than with those who were displacing them. Trade began to seem to him vulgar, and it was doubtless true that many engaged in it, who had become rapidly rich, were vulgar enough. But he made no distinction. He longed for the restoration of a state of things that had gone forever by. He was disposed to feel dissatisfaction with much that was taking place, not because it came into conflict with his judgment, but because it jarred upon his tastes and prejudices.

A residence in Europe for a few years had, indeed,

done for him what the coming-on of old age does for most. He had become the eulogist of times past. The views which he expressed in private and in public, during the decade that followed his return to America, were not of the kind to make him popular with his countrymen. The manners of the people were, according to him, decidedly worse than they were twenty or thirty years before. The elegant deportment of women had been largely supplanted by the rattle of hoydens and the giggling of the nursery. The class of superior men of the quiet old school were fast disappearing before the " wine-discussing, trade-talking, dollar-dollar set " of the day. Under the blight of this bustling, fussy, money-getting race of social Vandals, simplicity of manners had died out, or was dying out. The architecture of the houses, like the character of the society, was more ambitious than of old, but in far worse taste ; in a taste, in fact, which had been corrupted by uninstructed pretension. The towns were larger, but they were tawdrier than ever. The spirit of traffic was gradually enveloping everything in its sordid grasp. There had taken place a vast expansion of mediocrity, well enough in itself, but so overwhelming as nearly to overshadow everything that once stood out as excellent.

In most of these remarks I am giving Cooper's sentiments, as far as possible, in his own words. They stung the national vanity to the quick. The bitter resentment they evoked at the time could hardly be understood now; and a great deal of wrath was then kindled at what would meet with assent, at the present day, on account of its justice, or excite amusement on account of its exaggeration. Thurlow Weed, in 1841, expressed a general sentiment about Cooper, with much affluence of capital

letter and solemnity of exclamatory punctuation. " He
has disparaged, American Lakes," wrote that editor,
" ridiculed American Scenery, burlesqued American
Coin, and even satirized the American Flag!" Cooper
could hardly have expected his strictures to be received
with applause, but he was clearly surprised at the outcry
they awoke. Yet he had had plenty of opportunities to
learn that other countries were as sensitive to criticism
as his own. One singular illustration of this feeling
had been exhibited at Rome. He had completed his
novel of "The Water Witch" and wished to print and
publish it in that city. The manuscript was accordingly
sent to the censor. It was kept for days, which grew
to weeks. It was at last returned with refusal, unless
it were subjected to thorough revision. Almost on the
opening page occurred a highly objectionable paragraph. "It would seem," Cooper had written, "that as
nature has given its periods to the stages of animal life,
it has also set limits to all moral and political ascen-
dency. While the city of the Medici is receding from
its crumbling walls, like the human form shrinking into
'the lean and slippered pantaloon,' the Queen of the
Adriatic sleeping on her muddy isles, and Rome itself is
only to be traced by fallen temples and buried columns,
the youthful vigor of America is fast covering the wilds
of the West with the happiest fruits of human industry."
This passage, the censor quietly but severely pointed out,
laid down a principle that was unsound, and supported
it by facts that were false. A rigid pruning could alone
make the work worthy of a license. The consequence
was that Cooper carried the manuscript with him to
Germany, and it was first published in Dresden, in a
land where men were not sensitive to anything that
might be said, at any rate about Italy.

But the personal unpopularity he brought upon himself by his censorious remarks will not wholly account for the unpopularity as a writer, which it was his fortune, in no short time, to acquire. There were other agencies at work besides those which affected the feeling towards him as a man. Throughout the English-speaking world there had been a literary reaction. Men had begun to tire of the novel of adventure. It was not that it had lost its hold upon the public; it had lost the supreme hold which for twenty years it had maintained. The mighty master was dead; to some extent his influence had died before him. The later work he did, had in several instances detracted from, rather than added to the fame he had won by the earlier. Cooper's own ventures in the field of foreign fiction, whatever their absolute merit, could not be compared with those in which he had drawn the life of the ocean, or the streams and forests of his native land. But outside of any effect produced by poorer production, there could be no doubt of the fact of a change in the public taste. The hero of action had gone by. In his place had come the hero of observation and reflection, who did not do great things, but who said good things. The exquisite and the sentimentalist were the fashion, to be speedily followed, according to the law of reaction, by the boor and the satirist. At the time when Cooper returned from Europe, Bulwer was the popular favorite. Both in England and America he was styled the prince of living novelists; and nowhere was enthusiasm, in his behalf, crazier than in this country. The revolution in taste, moreover, worked directly in his favor in more ways than one. Scott and Cooper's heroes, whether intelligent or not, were invariably moral. But of this sort of men readers were tired. No character could please highly the popular palate in which there was not a distinct flavor of iniquity. More ability and less morality was the opinion generally entertained, though probably not often expressed. Hence it was not unnatural that the sentimental dandies and high-toned villains of Bulwer's earlier novels should have been the heroes to captivate all hearts.

The comparatively low estimate into which the novel of adventure had sunk, undoubtedly had a marked effect upon Cooper's reputation. Some of his later work is superior to his earlier from the artistic point of view. Yet it was never received with the same praise, at least in English-speaking countries. More than that, the criticism it received was often excessively depreciatory; nor was this all due to personal unpopularity, though a good deal of it certainly was. He simply wrote in a style which the age had temporarily left behind, and fancied it had outgrown. All that Cooper had to do, all that under any circumstances he could do, was to keep on producing the best that lay in his power; sure to find a certain body of readers in sympathy with him; sure also that some time in the future the revolution of taste would bring him into fashion if he had written anything that really deserved to live.

These facts and considerations must, however, be borne in mind in order to understand the gradual growth of the ill-feeling that sprang up between Cooper and his countrymen. To the change of view in himself and to the change of taste in the public, were soon added special circumstances that tended to bring about or increase alienation. But there did not exist toward him, when he came back from Europe, any hostility on the part of his countrymen. Circumstances had led him to suspect such a feeling; but it was mainly the creation of a nature that was morbidly sensitive to criticism. He was not, to be sure, the popular idol at his return that he had been at his departure. But this decline, outside of the causes already mentioned, was due to ignorance rather than dislike. A new generation had, during his absence, come on the scene of active life. To it the influence of his personal presence was unknown. He had been away so long that many looked upon him with the indifference with which foreigners are regarded by the majority; on the other hand, the fact of his being a native prevented others from feeling that interest in him which a foreigner has to some. Whatever hostility actually existed sprang mainly from causes creditable to himself. If Cooper disliked England for its depreciation of America, he hated with a hatred akin to loathing, the recreant Americans who mistook the relation they bore to their native land, and apologized for its character and existence, instead of apologizing for their own. For these men he made no effort to hide the contempt he felt. This class, far larger then in numbers than now, came mainly from the great cities. Many of them had wealth and social position to make up for their lack of ability; some of them were attached to the legations. They naturally resented the low opinion entertained and expressed of them by their countryman, and had doubtless done him some harm, though far less than he supposed. Besides these, however, there were certainly a pretty large number by whom his aggressive patriotism was felt to be a positive bore. To this feeling there had been a good deal of expression given in the newspaper press. Cooper, who never could learn

· how little effect of itself hostile criticism has upon the reputation of a popular writer, gave to these attacks far more weight than they deserved.

It was, therefore, with exaggerated and unnecessary feelings of distrust that he had returned to his native land. He looked for indifference and aversion. Men seldom fail to find in such cases what they expect. He was present at a reception given, a few days after his return, to Commodore Chauncey. Men whom he knew, but had not seen for years, did not come up to speak with him ; those who did, addressed him as if he had been gone from the city a few weeks. So much was he chilled by this apparent coldness that he left the room before the dinner was half over. He did not appreciate his own reserve of manner. The indifference which he found was, in many cases, due not to any lack of cordiality in others, but to hesitation at the way in which advances would be received by himself. There was a brusqueness in his address, an apparent assumption in his manner, which had nothing consonant to them in his feelings. But it was only those who knew him intimately that could venture, after long separation, to break in upon this seeming unsociableness and hauteur.

On Monday, May 29 1826, just before his departure for Europe, a dinner had been given to Cooper at the City Hotel by the club which he had founded. It partook almost of the nature of an ovation. Chancellor Kent had presided. De Witt Clinton, the governor of the state, General Scott, and many others conspicuous in public life, had honored it with their presence. Charles King, the editor of the "New York American," and subsequently president of Columbia College, had addressed him in a speech full of the heartiest interest in his fut-

ure and of pride in his past. The Chancellor had voiced
the general feeling by toasting him as the "genius
which has rendered our native soil classic ground, and
given to our early history the enchantment of fiction."
No one, in fact, had ever left the country with warmer
wishes or more enthusiastic expressions of admiration
and regard. It was but little more than a week after
his return when another invitation to a public dinner
was offered him by some of the most prominent citizens
of New York. In this they expressly asserted that he
had won their esteem and affection, not merely by his
talents, but by his manly defense, while abroad, of the
institutions of his country. The invitation seemed to
surprise Cooper as well as the language in which it was
couched. He thanked the proposers warmly, but he declined it. The refusal was perhaps unavoidable. If so,
it was unfortunate ; if not, it was a mistake. Had the
dinner taken place, it would have shown him the estimation in which he was really held, and would have modified or destroyed any prejudices entertained towards
him by others, if any such existed.

Up to this period in his public career, Cooper had certainly not done anything to undermine his popularity.
He now entered upon a line of conduct which it is char-
ity to call blundering. He began, or at any rate pursued, a controversy, in which nothing was to be gained
and everything to be risked, if not actually lost. He
not only set himself to defend a course that needed no
defense, he replied to attacks, real or imaginary, which
could only be raised into importance by receiving from
him notice. These attacks were a criticism on "The
Bravo" which had appeared in the "New York American;" a criticism on his later writings which was found

in the columns of the " New York Commercial Advertiser ; " and an editorial article in the " New York Courier and Enquirer." He could not have done a more
foolish thing. He knew perfectly well that no writer
could be written down save by himself. He has quoted
the very remark. But a hundred similar sayings, con-
densing in a line the wisdom of ages, could never have
kept him quiet when an attack was made upon himself.
A popular writer has always immense odds in his favor
in any controversy he may have with inferior men. He
is ordinarily sure of the verdict of posterity, for his is
likely to be the only side that will reach its ears. Even
during his own time there will always be a large body
of admirers who will defend him with more fervor, and
advocate his cause with more effect than he has it in his
own power to do. But it can and will be done only in
the case that he does little or nothing himself. If
Cooper had lost any ground in the estimation of the
public, all he had to do, in order to regain it, was to remain quiet. The one thing that Cooper could not do was
to remain quiet. He determined to set himself right before his countrymen. He speedily had full opportunity
to ascertain the results that are pretty sure to follow ex-
periments of this kind.

In June, 1834, appeared Cooper's " Letter to His
Countrymen." Its publication was no sudden freak, for
the year before he had announced the preparation of it.
The work is a thin octavo of a little more than one hundred pages ; but the damage it wrought him was out of
all proportion to its size. The first half of it was taken
up with a reply to the comments and criticisms made in
the New York journals already mentioned. This was of
itself sufficiently absurd, for it revived what had already

been forgotten, and gave importance to some things that had not been worth reading, let alone remembering. But to this blundering was added a wrongheadedness, of which Cooper's later life was to afford numerous illustrations. The article from the " Courier and Enquirer " is quoted in full in the book. Some of its statements are inaccurate ; but no one can read it now without seeing at once that it was written in a spirit that was the very reverse of hostile. To attack a powerful journal for comments clearly dictated by friendly feeling, betrayed more than a lack of prudence; it betrayed a lack of common sense. Moreover, there were other serious defects in the Letter. He criticised at some length certain forms of expression used by one of his assailants. Cooper's remarks on language are almost invariably marked by the pretension and positiveness that characterize the writers on usage who are ignorant of their ignorance ; but in this case they are in addition frequently puerile. His personal references were not especially objectionable. But the best that can be asserted of them is, that he said with good taste what it would have been better taste not to say at all. He, however, so contrived to state his position that he laid himself open to the charge that he looked upon the unfavorable opinion expressed of " The Bravo " as being instigated by the French government, and that, in consequence, the ill reception here accorded to his book was not due necessarily to any inferiority in the work itself, but to the machinations of foreign political enemies. He did not so mean it. He meant to imply that there was no limit to the volunteer baseness of men who stand ready to gratify power by doing for it what it would gladly have done, but would never ask to have done. But the other was a natural inference, and it was used against him with marked effect.

Worse even than all this, he succeeded in accomplishing in the latter half of his Letter. A most exciting controversy was going on at the time between the President and the Senate of the United States. The bitterness had been aggravated into fury by the removal of the deposits. The Senate had passed a resolution declaring the conduct of the President unconstitutional. Against this resolution Jackson had published a protest. The whole country was in a flame. Into the purely personal controversy in which he was engaged, Cooper lugged in a discussion of the political question that was agitating the nation. He remarked, in the course of it, that if the Union were ever destroyed by errors or faults of an internal origin, it would not be by executive but by legislative usurpation. In order apparently to have neither of the two parties in full sympathy with him, he criticised the appointing power of the President, and his action in filling embassies. It is by the most strained interpretation of the danger to our institutions from imitation of those found in foreign countries, that the political discussion was dragged into this production. The force of folly could hardly go farther.

The inevitable result followed. The work pleased nobody, and irritated nearly everybody. Three influential journals were at once made open and active enemies, and in their wake followed a long train of minor newspapers. More than that was effected. The Letter called down upon him the wrath of a great political party, which in the North embraced a large majority of the educated class ; and its hostility followed him relentlessly to the grave. Unwise as the work was, how-

ever, there was nothing in it to justify the abuse that in
consequence fell upon its author. To his statement of
the danger of legislative usurpation Caleb Cushing
made a dignified, though somewhat rhetorical reply;
but while controverting his opinions, he spoke of
Cooper personally with great respect. But such was
not the treatment he generally received. The language
with which he was assailed was of the most insulting
and grossly abusive kind. In those days it was called
appalling severity. It reads now like very dreary and
very vulgar billingsgate. One example will suffice.
The " New York Mirror " was then supposed to be the
leading literary paper in New York. It was nominally
edited by Morris, Willis, and Fay, though the two last
were at that time in Europe. Morris is still remembered by two or three songs he wrote. Besides being
an editor, he held the position of general of militia;
accordingly he was often styled by his admirers, " he of
the sword and pen," which was just and appropriate to
this extent, that he did as much execution with the one
as with the other. His paper intimated that Cooper
was willing to transform himself into a baboon for the
sake of abusing America, and that his inordinate ambition prompted him to distance all competitors, whether
the race were fame or shame. It is proper to add that
the tone of the " Mirror " in regard to Cooper was rad-
ically changed after the return of Willis from Europe.

In his Letter Cooper announced publicly, what he
had long before said to his friends, that he had made up
his mind to abandon authorship. Such resolutions are
mainly remarkable for the fact that they are never kept.
But the howl of denunciation that immediately arose
would never have suffered him to keep still. From this

time dates the beginning of the long and gallant fight he carried on with the American people. Gallant it certainly was, whatever may be thought of its wisdom ; for it was essentially the fight of one man against a nation. In politics he had joined the Democratic party, but with some of their tenets he was not in the slightest sympathy. He was, for example, a fierce protectionist, and neglected no opportunity to cover with ridicule the doctrine of free trade. But though practically standing alone, his courage never faltered. The storm of obloquy that fell upon him made him in his turn bitter and unjust in many things he said ; but it never once daunted his spirit or shook his resolution. On the contrary, it almost seems as if he were aiming at unpopularity ; at any rate he could not be accused of seeking the favor of the public. Its acts he criticised, its opinions he defied. His literary reputation and the sale of his works were seriously affected by the course of conduct he pursued and the hostility it provoked. But he was of that nature that if the certain result of following the path he had marked out for himself had been the hatred of the world, he would never have once deviated from it the breadth of a hair.

He was not a man to remain on the defensive. He at once began hostilities. His first attempt was unfortunate enough. This was the satirical novel called " The Monikins," which was published on the 9th of July, 1835. Of all the works written by Cooper this is most justly subject to the criticism conveyed in the German idiom, that " it does not let itself be read." To the immense majority of even the author's admirers, it has been from the very beginning a sealed book. It is invariably dangerous to assert a negative. But if a personal reference may be pardoned, I am disposed to say, that of the generation that has come upon the stage of active life since Cooper's death, I am the only person who has read this work through. The knowledge of it possessed by his contemporaries did not, in many cases, approach to the dignity of being even second-hand. The accounts of it that have come under my own notice, seem often to have been gathered from reviews of it which had themselves been written by men who had never read the original. It is no difficult matter to explain the neglect into which it immediately sank. The work was a satire mainly upon certain of the social and political features to be found in England and America, designated respectively as Leaphigh and Leaplow; though one or two things characteristic of France were transferred to the former country. But satire Cooper could not write. The power of vigorous invective he had in a marked degree. But the wit which plays while it wounds, which while saying one thing means another, which deals in far-off suggestion and remote allusion, this was something entirely unsuited to the directness and energy of his intellect. Moreover, some of his most marked literary defects were seen here exaggerated and unrelieved. In many of his novels there is prolixity in the introduction. Still in these it is often compensated by descriptions of natural scenery so life-like and so enthusiastic that even the most *blasé* of novel readers is carried along in a state of what may be called endurable tediousness. But in "The Monikins" the introductory tediousness is unendurable. It is not until we are nearly half-way into the work and have actually entered upon the voyage to the land of the monkeys, that the dullness at all disappears. After the country of Leaphigh is reached the story is far less absurd and more entertaining; though Cooper's descriptions are of the nature of caricature rather than of satire. There are, however, many shrewd and caustic remarks scattered up and down the pages of the latter part of the work, but they will never be known to anybody, for nobody will read the book through.

The work fell perfectly dead from the press. But its failure had not the least effect in deterring Cooper from continuing in the course upon which he had started. During the years 1836, 1837, and 1838, he published ten volumes of travels. In these he repeated, with emphasis, everything that he had uttered privately or had implied in his previous publications. The first of these works was entitled " Sketches of Switzerland." It was divided into two parts. The first, which was published on May 21, 1836, gave an account of his residence and excursions in that country during the summer and autumn of 1828. The second part, which appeared October 8, 1836, was largely taken up with accounts of matters and things in Paris during the winter of 1831–32, a journey up the Rhine, and a second visit to Switzerland. These two parts made four volumes. The remaining six had the general title of " Gleanings in Europe," and two each were devoted to France, England, and Italy. The first of these was published March 4, 1837; the second September 2 of the same year; and the third, May 26, 1838. They were written in the form of letters, and were pretty certainly made up from letters actually written or memoranda taken at the time. But they were likewise largely interpersed with the expression of views and feelings that he had learned to adopt and cherish since his return to his native land.

In the case of England and America, in particular, his

remarks may have been full of light, but they did not exhibit sweetness. Probably no set of travels was ever more elaborately contrived to arouse the wrath of readers in both countries, nor one that more successfully fulfilled its mission. His keen observation let no striking traits escape notice. The individual Englishmen he meets and describes could furnish entertainment only to men that were not themselves Englishmen. There is, for instance, the sea-captain who endeavors to compensate for his lack of energy by giving his passenger an account of the marvelous riches of the nobility and gentry. Even more graphically drawn is the islander he met in the Bernese Oberland, who appeared to regard the peak of the Jungfrau with contempt, as if it did very well for Switzerland; and who, when his attention was called to a singularly beautiful effect upon a mountain top, began to tell how cheap mutton was in Herefordshire. Nor were many of his general remarks flattering. As one descended in the social scale he thought the English the most artificial people on earth. Large numbers of them mistook a labored, feigned, heartless manner for high-breeding. The mass of them acted in society like children who have had their hair combed and faces washed, to be shown up in the drawing-room. They were conventional everywhere. The very men whom he met after his arrival in the streets of Southampton, all looked as if they had been born with hat-brushes and clothes-brushes in their hands. As a race, moreover, they had special defects. They lacked delicacy and taste in conferring obligations or paying compliments. They were utterly indifferent to the feelings of others. There was a national propensity to blackguardism; and the English press, in particular, calumniated its enemies, both political and personal, with the coarsest vituperation.

These were not the sort of remarks to draw favorable notices from British periodicals. Cooper soon had an opportunity to verify, in his own experience, the truth of the last of his observations that have been cited. Harsh, however, as was his language about England, it bore little comparison to the severity with which he expressed himself about America. The attacks on the newspaper press belong not here, but to the account of the war he waged with it. The omission, however, will hardly be noticed in the multitude of other matters he found to criticise. Manners, customs, society, were touched throughout with an unsparing hand. Common crimes, he admitted, were not so general with us as in Europe, though mainly because we were exempt from temptation, but uncommon meannesses did abound in a large circle of our population. Our two besetting sins were canting and hypocrisy. We had far less publicity in our pleasures than other nations; yet we had scarcely any domestic privacy on account of the neighborhood. The whole country was full of a village-like gossip which caused every man to think that he was a judge of character, when he was not even a judge of facts. In most matters we were humble imitators of the English. All their mistakes and misjudgments we adopted except such as impaired our good opinion of ourselves. It was a consequence that all their errors about foreign countries had become our errors also. In a few cases, indeed, we were compelled to be American; but whenever there was a tolerable chance we endeavored to become second-class English. Wherever making money was in view, we had but one soul and that was inventive enough; but when it came to spending it we did not know how to set about it except by routine. No people traveled as much as we; none traveled with so little enjoyment or so few comforts. Taste and knowledge and tone were too little concentrated anywhere, too much diffused everywhere, to make head against the advances of an overwhelming mediocrity. Of society there was but little; for what it suited the caprice of certain people to call such was little more than the noisy, screeching, hoydenish romping of both sexes. The taint of provincialism was diffused over all feelings and beliefs. Of arts and letters the country possessed none or next to none. Moreover, there was no genuine sympathy with either. To all this dismal prospect there was slight hope of improvement, because there was a disposition to resent any intimation that we could be better than we were at present.

It would be a gross error to infer the general character of Cooper's travels from these extracts. They are gathered together from ten volumes, without any of the attendant statements by which they are there in many cases modified. Equally erroneous would it be to suppose that he did not find much to praise as well as to condemn in both England and America. These extracts, however, explain the almost savage vituperation with which Cooper was thenceforth followed in the press of the two countries. The works themselves met with a very slight sale: none of them ever passed into a second edition. Men were not likely to read with alacrity, however much they might with profit, unfavorable opinions entertained of themselves. Cooper himself could not have hoped for much success for his strictures. In fact, he expressly declared the contrary.

The most he should expect, he said, would be the secret assent of the wise and good, the expressed censure of the numerous class of the vapid and ignorant, the surprise of the mercenary and the demagogue, and the secret satisfaction of the few who should come after him who would take an interest in his name.

Notwithstanding the ferocious criticism with which they were assailed at the time and the forgetfulness into which they have now fallen, Cooper's accounts of the countries in which he lived are among the best of their kind. Books of travel are from their very nature of temporary interest. It requires peculiar felicity of manner to make up long for the fresher matter about foreign lands which newer books contain. Striking descriptions and acute observations will still, however, reward the reader of Cooper's sketches. There are often displayed in them a vigor and a political sagacity which of themselves would justify his being styled the most robust of American authors. Pointed assertions are scattered up and down his pages. Could, for instance, one of the dangers of a democracy be more clearly and ill-naturedly put than by his statement, that the whole science of government in what are called free states, is getting to be a strife in mystification, in which the great secret is to persuade the governed that he is in fact the governor? His books, moreover, while they reflect his prejudices, show an honest desire to be just. He undoubtedly preferred the Continent to England. But in his account of that country, while he had the unfairness of dislike, he never had the unfairness of intentional misrepresentation. There is nothing of that exulting yell with which the British traveler of those days fell foul of some specimen of American ill-breeding or

American bumptiousness. Nor did he fail to pay a high tribute to what was best in English society or English character. The gentlemen of that country, in appearance, in attainments, in manliness, and he was inclined to add in principles, he placed at the head of their class in Christendom. His censure of America and the Americans was not at all in the nature of indiscriminate abuse. The fault he found with his countrymen was based mainly upon their mistaken opinion of themselves and of their advantages and disadvantages. You boast, he practically said to them, of the superiority of your scenery, in which you are not to be compared with Europe; but you constantly abuse your climate which is equal to, if not finer, than that of any region in the Old World. You stand up manfully for your manners and tastes, which you ought to correct; but you are incessantly apologizing for your institutions of which you ought to be proud. The defects imputed in Europe to the inhabitants of the United States, such as the want of morals, honesty, order, decency, liberality, and religion, were not at all our defects. These, in fact were, as the world goes, the strong points of American character. On the other hand, those on which we prided ourselves, intelligence, taste, manners, education as applied to all beyond the base of society, were the very points upon which we should do well to be silent. This is certainly not an extreme position. But men are far more affected by the blame bestowed upon their foibles than by the praise given to their virtues; and both in England and America the censures were remembered and the commendations forgotten. Other circumstances also came in now to add to his unpopularity in his own country. A local quarrel in which he accidently became concerned, was followed by consequences which affected his estimation throughout the whole land; but the details of this will require a separate chapter.

CHAPTER VIII.

1837–1838.

THREE miles from Cooperstown, on the western side of Otsego Lake, a low, wooded point of land projects for some distance into the water. It combines two characteristics of an attractive resort: beauty of scenery and easiness of access. On these accounts Cooper's father had refused to sell it when he disposed of his other lands. He had, in fact, specially reserved it for his own use, and for that of his descendants. In 1808, a year before his death, he drew up his will. In it he made a particular devise of this spot. "I give and bequeath," ran the words of the document, "my place, called Myrtle Grove, on the west side of the Lake Otsego, to all my descendants in common until the year 1850; then to be inherited by the youngest thereof bearing my name." Two small buildings had been successively erected by him on the spot. The first he tore down himself, but the second was set on fire after his death, by the carelessness of trespassers using it, and burned to the ground. Shortly after 1821, the only representative of the family living in Cooperstown who was of proper age to be consulted, gave his consent, so far as he was concerned, to the erection of a new building by the community. From that time the Point came to be a place of general resort. To it fishing and picnic parties were in the habit of repairing. An impression sprang up, moreover, that the spot was public property. This impression in the course of years advanced to the dignity of positive assertion. It became in time a universally accepted belief in the minds of the citizens that the place belonged to them. It then only remained to furnish the explanation of how it had happened to come into their possession. This was no difficult achievement. The story was soon generally received that Cooper's father, instead of permitting the public to use the Point, had actually made a gift of it to the public.

When Cooper took up his summer residence in the village, after his return from Europe, he found the notion prevalent that the place in question belonged to the community. As executor of his father's will he took pains to correct the error. He informed his fellow-citizens that the Point was private property, and not public; and that while he had no desire to prevent them from resorting to it, he was determined to insist upon the recognition of the real ownership. He might as well have talked to the winds. The community did not bother itself about examining the question of title. It had been in the habit of using the Point without asking any one's consent, and the Point it purposed to keep on using in the same way.

Matters reached a crisis in 1837. The building erected on the spot had become dilapidated. Workmen were sent out to repair it, without going through the formality of consulting the owners of the property. A tree was also cut down, which, on account of certain associations connected with his father, Cooper valued particularly. This was not the way to win over to the view of the community the executor of the property. He sent a card at once to the editor of the Democratic newspaper of the village, stating that the Point was private property, and cautioning the public against injuring the trees. Nothing, however, was said about trespassing. The card came too late for publication that week and before another number of the paper appeared, rumor of its existence had got about. Its reported character created ill-feeling, and messages and even threats were sent to Cooper on the subject. These had the effect which might have been expected. He withdrew the original card and published in its stead a simple, ordinary notice of warning against trespassing on the Point, with a few additional facts. The notice, which is dated July 22, 1837, reads as follows : —

" The public is warned against trespassing on the Three Mile Point, it being the intention of the subscriber rigidly to enforce the title of the estate, of which he is the representative, to the same. The public has not, nor has it ever had, any right to the same beyond what has been conceded by the liberality of the owners."

The notice was signed by Cooper as the executor of his father's estate. Great was the excitement in the village when it was published. A hand-bill was immediately put into circulation calling a meeting of the citizens, to take into consideration the propriety of defending their rights against the arrogant claims and assumed authority of "one J. Fenimore Cooper." The meeting was accordingly held. There was little difference of sentiment among those present. All were animated, according to the newspaper reports, by the determination to use the Three Mile Point without being indebted to the liberality of Cooper or any one else. Stirring speeches were made. Two or three persons were anxious to delay any action until the question of title had been examined. This proposition was deemed by the immense majority of those present to have a truckling character, and consequently met with no favor. The meeting, accordingly, found immediate relief for its feelings in the usual American way, by passing a series of resolutions. The vigor of these was out of all proportion to the sense. The disposition to defy Cooper shot, in some instances, indeed, beyond its proper mark, and extended even to the rules of grammar. After reciting in a preamble the facts as they understood them, the citizens present went on to express their determination and opinions as follows : —

" Resolved, By the aforesaid citizens that we will wholly disregard the notice given by James F. Cooper, forbidding the public to frequent the Three Mile Point.

" Resolved, That inasmuch as it is well known that the late William Cooper intended the use of the Point in question for the citizens of this village and its vicinity, we deem it no more than a proper respect for the memory and intentions of the father, that the son should recognize the claim of the citizens to the use of the premises, even had he the power to deny it.

" Resolved, That we will hold his threat to enforce title to the premises, as we do his whole conduct in relation to the matter, in perfect contempt.

" Resolved, That the language and conduct of Cooper, in his attempts to procure acknowledgements of ' liberality,' and his attempt to force the citizens into asking his permission to use the premises, has been such as to render himself odious to a greater portion of the citizens of this community.

" Resolved, That we do recommend and request the trustees of the Franklin Library, in this village, to re-

10

move all books, of which Cooper is the author, from said library.

" Resolved also, That we will and do denounce any man as sycophant, who has, or shall, ask permission of James F. Cooper to visit the Point in question.

" Resolved, That the proceedings of this meeting be signed by the chairman and secretary, and published in the village papers."

Whatever else these proceedings show, they make it clear that the people of Cooperstown had not well improved the opportunity afforded by his residence among them, of becoming well acquainted with the character of their distinguished townsman. Still there was knowledge enough about him to make the officers of the meeting unwilling to publish the resolutions as they had been ordered. He was not a man to be trifled with; and no one cared to make himself personally responsible for what had been said. As a matter of fact the secretary of the meeting furnished Cooper with a copy of the resolutions; and it was the latter that first caused them to be printed. But the story of the meeting speedily found its way into the newspapers. In the accounts of the proceedings that were in circulation, it was said that a resolution had been passed that the works of the novelist should be taken from the library and publicly burned. This was caught up by the press and repeated everywhere throughout the country. To this day the baseless tradition lingers in Cooperstown itself, that this act was not only determined upon but actually done. The matter doubtless was discussed among the other sage proposals that were brought forward at this meeting; and it may be true, as was afterwards suspected, that the original resolution on this point was modified before it was allowed to go out to the public.

Under the circumstances only one result was possible. The community were very speedily satisfied that they did not own the Point, and were equally convinced that their prospect of obtaining possession of it by clamor was far from good. Two letters, marked by anything but timidity or amiability, Cooper wrote to the Democratic newspaper of the village. In them he gave fully all the facts in the case. To the assertion paraded in many of the Whig journals of the state, that this meeting showed the spirit of the people in Cooperstown, he made an indignant reply. Such a remark, he said, was a libel on the character of the place. The meeting, he declared, was not composed of a fourth part of the population, or a hundredth part of the respectability of the village. The resolutions he described as being the work of presuming boys, who swagger of time immemorial; of strangers who had lived but a brief time in the county; and of a few disreputable persons who, bent on construing liberty entirely on their own side, interposed against palpable rights and sacred family feelings their gossiping facts, their grasping rapacity, and their ruthless disposition to destroy whatever they could not control. "There is but one legal public," he defiantly concluded his first letter, "and that acts under the obligation of precise oaths, through prescribed forms, and on constitutional principles. Let 'excitement' be flourished as it may, this is the only public to which I shall submit the decision of my rights. So far as my means allow, insult shall be avenged by the law, violence repelled by the strong hand, falsehood put to shame by truth, and sophistry exposed by reason."

It is perfectly clear that on the merits of this controversy Cooper was wholly in the right. The bluster of these resolutions exhausted all the courage of his opponents. The question of ownership was at once settled definitely and forever. No one on the spot ever questioned the point any farther, though the original false-hood was steadily repeated by newspapers at a distance, and apparently never once contradicted after its untruth had been shown. Some may think the result, might have been reached by milder means, but the spirit shown at the meeting renders this more than doubtful. Cooper even had to pay for the insertion of his letters in the village newspaper. Unfortunately the ill-feeling aroused did not stop here. It gave rise to what may be described as a semi-political controversy — that is, a controversy in which one party attacks a man, and the party to which he belongs does not think it expedient or worth while to defend him. The libel suits to which it directly or indirectly led with the Whig newspapers of the state will demand a separate chapter. Before they were well under way, however, the novelist made up his mind to right himself in another manner, and brought out a work of fiction which seemed expressly contrived to meet the thought of the sacred writer who wished his adversary had written a book.

Cooper determined to write a story in which he would set forth the principles involved in the controversy about the Point. There is perhaps no subject that cannot be made interesting by the right treatment. But he was now in a state of mind that would not have permitted him to discuss any matter of this nature in the spirit that belongs to the composition of a work of the imagination. The dispute had embittered his feelings already sore. It had tended to give him a still more distorted view of the country to which he had come back. So completely had his feelings swung around that he now had an eye for little but the worst features of the national character. Passion had largely unbalanced his judgment. Ancient fable has pointed out the danger of falling under the fascinations of the sirens; but even that seems preferable to becoming bewitched by the furies.

Still he could not well make a book out of this one event. It could be used to suit all his purposes, however, by being introduced as an incident of an ordinary tale. In this way his side of the story would travel as far as the false assertions about his conduct in the matter which had been circulated not only over America but over Europe. He also set out to bring together in the work he was contemplating all the things that he looked upon with disapprobation and dislike in the social life of this country. His original intention was to begin a story with the landing here of an American family long resident in Europe. Happily he was induced to give an account of the voyage home, and this in the end necessitated the division of the work into two parts. Accordingly on the 16th of August, 1837, appeared the novel of "Homeward Bound," followed in November of the same year by its sequel, entitled "Home as Found." The leading characters are the same in both tales, but the events are entirely unlike. The scene of the first is laid wholly on the water. In its movement, its variety of incidents, and the spirit and energy with which they are told, it is one of the best of Cooper's sea-novels. Nor is this estimate seriously impaired by the fact that it is in some places marred by controversial discussions on liberty and equality, and by the withering exposure of views that no man maintained whose opinions were worth regarding. But these are only occaional blemishes. They do not materially interfere with the progress of the story, which moves on with little variation of interest to the end. On the other hand, the characters are generally as uninteresting as the events are exciting. The chief ones among them have all reached that supreme refinement which justifies them in feeling and decisively pronouncing that whatever is done by anybody but themselves is coarse. But in this work the personages are so subordinate to the scenes that any failure in representing the former is more than counterbalanced by the success shown in depicting the latter.

The reverse was the fact when the sequel followed. In this the characters and their views became prominent, and the events were of slight importance. "Home as Found" was far poorer than "Homeward Bound" was good. Never was a more unfortunate work written by any author. This is the fact, whether it be looked at from the literary or the popular point of view. For the latter it is enough to say that the opinions about America which have already been given in the account of his European travels were more than reënforced. He said again what he had said before, and he took pains to add a great deal that had been left unsaid. The new matter surpassed in the energy of invective the old, and its attack was more concentrated. There were in the novel, to be sure, the remarks that had now got to be habitual with Cooper upon the provincialism of the whole country; but it was upon New York city that the vials of his wrath were especially poured. The town, according to the view here expressed of it, was nothing more than a huge expansion of commonplace things. It was a confused and tasteless collection of flaring red brick houses, martin-box churches, and colossal taverns. But the assault made upon its external appearance bore no comparison to that upon its internal life. The city in a moral sense resembled, according to Cooper, a huge encampment. It stood at the farthest remove from the intellectual supremacy and high tone of a genuine capital as distinguished from a great trading port. In its gayeties he saw little better than the struggles of an uninstructed taste, if indeed that could properly be styled gay which was only a strife in prodigality and parade. The conversation of the elders was entirely about the currency, the price of lots, and the latest speculations in towns. The younger society was made up of babbling misses, who prattled as waters flow, without consciousness of effort, and of whiskered masters who fancied Broadway the world; and the two together looked upon the flirtations of miniature drawing-rooms as the ideal of human life in its loftiest aspects. Upon the *literati* the attack was even more savage. He described this appellation as being given to the most incorrigible members of the book clubs of New York. These had been laboriously employed in puffing each other into celebrity for many weary years, but still remained just as vapid, as conceited, as ignorant, as imitative, as dependent, and as provincial as ever.

It is not an easy matter to condense the bitterness of two volumes into a few sentences. Enough has been given, however, to show the character of the strictures. Whatever may be thought of their justice, few will be disposed to deny their vigor. But Cooper, unfortunately for himself, was not satisfied with demolishing what seemed poor in his eyes. He undertook the business of reconstruction, and set up an ideal of how things ought to be. His main agents in this work were the members of the Effingham family, whom he had brought over from Europe in " Homeward Bound." In these and the train dependent upon them, we were to find realized that pure and perfect social state which he contemplated in his own mind. To them were added a few survivors from the old families, as he termed them, which after a manner had ridden out the social gale that had made shipwreck of so many of their original companions. Out of these materials Cooper attempted to build his ideal framework of a life in which men thought rationally and lived nobly. It was here he made his mistake, and it was a signal one. His inability to portray the higher types of character was an absolute bar to success. This was largely due to his inability to catch and reproduce the tone of polished conversation. Never was his weakness in this respect more painfully manifested than in " Home as Found." He could appreciate such conversation ; he could bear a part in it; but he could not represent it. His characters taken from low life, whatever critics may say, have usually a marked individuality. But whenever Cooper sought to draw the men and women of cultivated society he achieved at best a doubtful success. In this instance he tried to make them and their words and deeds the vehicle of reproof and satire. His failure was absolute. Modern culture, we all know, consists largely in the most refined method of finding fault. But this his ideal family had not reached. An essentially coarse method of finding fault was the only one to which it had attained. Never, indeed, was a more bumptious, conceited, and disagreeable set of personages created by an author, under the impression that they were the reverse. The simple-minded, thoughtful, and upright Mr. Effingham can speedily be dismissed as merely a mild type of bore. Not so with his daughter Eve, and his cousin John Effingham. The latter plays the part of critic of his country and countrymen. It seems hardly possible that in this narrow-minded, disagreeable, and essentially vulgar character, Cooper could have fancied he was creating anything but a contemptible boor. The contrast between what is said of him, and what is said by him, almost reaches the comic. We read constantly of his caustic satire ; we find little of it in his conversation. His fine face is, according to the author, always expressing contempt and sarcasm ; but the examples of these that are shown in his speeches are usually specimens of that forcible-feeble straining to be severe which marks the man of violent temper and feeble intellect. As represented, he has neither the feeling, the instincts, nor the manners of a gentleman. He so much dislikes untruth that he insinuates to a guest, very broadly as well as very unjustly, that he is lying. In short, he is one of those rude and vulgar men who fancy that they are frank simply because they are brutal. No civilized society would long tolerate the presence, if even the existence, of such an animal as he is here represented to be.

Even he, however, shines by comparison with the heroine. Of her we hear no end of praise. Her delicacy, her plastic simplicity, the simple elegance of her attire, her indescribable air of polish, her surpassing beauty and modesty of mien, are referred to again and again. She is simple, she is feminine, she is dignified. To men her smiles are faint and distant. Across her countenance no unworthy thought has ever left a trace. Once and once only did she fail to keep up to the high level of deportment which she ordinarily maintained. On one occasion " her little foot moved " in spite of the fact that " she had been carefully taught, too, that a lady-like manner required that even this beautiful portion of the female frame should be quiet and unobtrusive." Something, however, must always be pardoned to human nature; and Cooper doubtless felt that it would not do to make his heroine absolutely free from frailty. As a sort of foil to her was introduced her cousin Grace Van Cortlandt. She, to be sure, had not had the advantage of foreign travel; but there was a redeeming feature in her case. She belonged to an old family. She was saved in consequence from being entirely submerged in that sweltering, foaming tide of mediocrity, which called itself New York society. Belonging to an old family did not, however, preserve her from being provincial. She is taken along with the rest to Templeton. On her way thither she is steadily snubbed by the masculine element of the party, and henpecked by the feminine. The reader comes in time to have the sincerest pity for this unfortunate girl, who is made to pay very dearly for the misfortune of being akin to a family whose members had become too superior to be gracious and too polished to be polite.

In the composition of this work Cooper seems to have lost all sense of the ridiculous. The personages whom he wished to make particularly attractive are uniformly disagreeable. A French governess appears in the story, who is simply insufferable. He brings in an American woman, Mrs. Bloomfield, as a representative, according to him, of that class which equals, if it does not surpass, in the brilliancy of its conversation the best to be found in European salons. She is introduced discoursing on the civilization of the country in a way that would speedily empty any of the parlors of her native land. Indeed, throughout the work the characters converse as no rational beings ever conversed under any sort of provocation. But it is in the speeches of the heroine that the language reaches its highest development. She can emphatically be said to talk like a book. She does not guess, she hazards conjectures. She playfully addresses her father as " thoughtless, precipitate parent." When she is asked what she thinks of the country now that an attempt was made to take possession of the Point, she describes her character, as drawn in this novel, as no words of another can. " Miss Effingham," she says, " has been grieved, disappointed, nay, shocked, but she will not despair of the republic." Indeed the only person in the work who has any near kinship to humanity is one of the inferior characters, named Aristobulus Bragg. He is the more attractive because he says bright things unconsciously ; while the heavy characters say heavy things under the impression that they are light.

This book had a profound influence upon Cooper's fortunes. From beginning to end it was a blunder. It cannot receive even the negative praise of being a work in which the best of intentions was marred by the worst of taste. Its spirit was a bad spirit throughout. It was dreadful to think some of the things found in it ; but it was more dreadful to say them. There was a great deal of truth in its pages, but if the views expressed in it had been actually inspired, the attitude and tone the author assumed would have prevented his making a convert. To some extent this had been true of " Homeward Bound." Greenough expostulated with Cooper, after reading that novel. "I think," he wrote from Florence, "you lose hold on the American public by rubbing down their shins with brickbats as you do." The most surprising thing connected with "Home as Found," however, is Cooper's unconsciousness, not of the probability, but of the possibility, that he would be charged with drawing himself in the character of Edward Effingham, and to some extent in that of John Effingham. The sentiments advanced were his sentiments, the acts described were in many cases his acts. The absence in a foreign land, the return to America, the scene laid at Templeton, with a direct reference to "The Pioneers," the account of the controversy about the Three Mile Point, — all these fixed definitely the man and the place. Variations in matters of detail would not disturb the truth of the general resemblance. Still Cooper not only did not intend to represent himself, he was unaware that he had done so. Nearly three years after in the columns of a weekly newspaper he stoutly defended himself against the imputation. It was useless. From this time forward the name of Effingham was often derisively applied to him in the controversies in which he was engaged.

It was not merely the intemperate spirit exhibited, which destroyed the effect of the shrewd and just comments often appearing in "Home as Found." This was full as much impaired by the display of personal weaknesses. Cooper's foible about descent he could not help exposing. No thoughtful man denies the desirability of honorable lineage, or undervalues the possession of it; but not for the reasons for which the novelist regarded it and celebrated it. There was much in this single story to justify Lowell's sarcasm, uttered ten years later, that Cooper had written six volumes to prove that he was as good as a lord. He traces his families up to remote periods in the past. He thereby shows their superiority to the newly-created family of the English baronet who is brought into the tale. It was to correct the erroneous impression, prevalent in Europe, that there was no stability, no permanent respectability in the society of this country, that he enlarged upon the date to which ancestry could be traced. The difficulty was to persuade anybody that the men who took the pains to look up their forefathers had any superiority to those who shared in the general indifference as to who their forefathers were. He went farther than this in some instances, and expressly implied that blood and birth were necessary to gentility. This was provincialism pushed to an extreme. Whatever we may think of its actual value, English aristocracy resembles in this gold and silver, that it has an accepted value independent of the character of its representatives. It is, therefore, current throughout the civilized world; whereas American aristocracy is like local paper money: worth nothing except in its own country, and even there receiving little recognition or circulation outside of the immediate neighborhood in which it is found. Still, the subject of blood and birth is a solemn one to those who believe in it, and they are absolutely incapable of comprehending the feelings of a world of scoffers, or, if they do, impute them to imperfect mental or spiritual development. On this point Cooper had the misfortune to say what some think but dare not express.

The wrath aroused, especially in New York city, by this particular novel, had about it something both fearful and comic. In one respect Cooper had the advantage, and his critics all felt it. His work was certain to be translated into all the principal languages of modern Europe. The picture he drew of New York society would be the one that foreigners would naturally receive as genuine. By them it would be looked upon as the work of a man familiar with what he was describing, the work of a man, moreover, who had been well known in European circles for his intense Americanism. It was vain to protest that it was a caricature. The protest would not be heeded even if it were heard. His enemies might rage; but they were powerless to influence foreign opinion, and they felt themselves so. Rage they certainly did; and if the assault made upon him had been as effective as it was violent, little would have been left of his reputation. Even as late as 1842, during the progress of the libel suits, some one took the pains to produce a novel in two volumes called "'The Effinghams, or Home as I Found It,' by the Author of the 'Victims of Chancery.'" The whole aim of this tale was to satirise Cooper. Mere malignity, however, has little vitality; and in spite of the fact that the work was widely praised by the journals for its "sound American feeling," and for its hits at "the conceited, disappointed, and Europeanized writer of 'Home as Found,'" it passed so speedily to the paper-makers that antiquarian research would now be tasked to find a copy. About the contemporary newspaper notices there was a certain tiger-like ferocity which almost justified much that Cooper said in denunciation of the American press. A specimen, though a somewhat extreme one, of a good deal of the sort of criticism to which the novelist was subjected, can be found in the "New Yorker" for the

1st of December, 1838. This journal was edited by Horace Greeley, but the article in question came probably from the pen of Park Benjamin. It defended Cooper from the charge of vilifying his country in order to make his works salable in England, but it defended him in this way. No motive of that kind was necessary to be supposed. He had an inborn disposition to pour out his bile and vent his spleen. "He is as proud of blackguarding," the article continued, "as a fishwoman of Billingsgate. It is as natural to him as snarling to a tom-cat, or growling to a bull-dog. . . . He is the common mark of scorn and contempt of every well-informed American. The superlative dolt!" In this refined and chastened style did the defenders of American cultivation preserve its reputation from its traducer.

Criticism of the kind just quoted, hurts only the man who utters it and the community which tolerates it. It injured the reputation of the country far more than the work could that it criticised. "Home as Found," as a matter of fact, was prevented from doing any harm, partly by its excessive exaggeration but more by its excessive poorness. As a story it stood in marked contrast to its immediate predecessor. It was as difficult to accompany Cooper on land as it had been to abandon him when on the water. The tediousness of the tale is indeed something appalling to the most hardened novel-reader. The only interest it can possibly have at this day is from the opportunity it affords of studying one phase of the author's character, and of accounting for much of the bitter hostility with which he was assailed.

While he was lecturing his countrymen on manners, his own were spoken of in turn in a way that gave especial delight to the enemies he had made by his criticisms. In 1837 Lockhart's " Life of Sir Walter Scott " was appearing. In the diary of that novelist were some references to the American author. "This man," he said, describing his first interview, "who has shown so much genius, has a good deal of the manners, or want of manners, peculiar to his countrymen." Cooper's personal acquaintance with Scott had begun in 1826, just after the latter had set about his gigantic effort to pay off the load of debt in which he had involved himself. The American novelist had made then an attempt to secure for the man he regarded as his master some adequate return from the vast sale of his works in the United States. In this he had been foiled. In the " Knickerbocker Magazine " for April, 1838, he gave an account of these fruitless negotiations. In a later number of the same year he reviewed Lockhart's biography. This work is well known as one of the most entertaining in our literature. But on its appearance it gave a painful shock to the admirers of the great author by the revelations it made of practices which savored more of the proverbial canniness of the Scotchman than of the lofty spirit of the man of honor. Equally surprising was the unconsciousness of the biographer, that there was anything discreditable in what he disclosed. Cooper criticised Scott's conduct in certain matters with a good deal of severity. In regard to some points he took extreme, and what might fairly be deemed Quixotic ground. Yet the general justice of his article will hardly be denied now by any one who is fully cognizant of the facts. Nor, indeed, was it then. "I have just read," wrote Charles Sumner from London to Hillard, in January, 1839, "an article on Lockhart's 'Scott,' written by Cooper in the " Knickerbocker," which was lent me by Barry Cornwall. I think it capital. I see none of Cooper's faults; and I think a proper castigation is applied to the vulgar minds of Scott and Lockhart. Indeed, the nearer I approach the circle of these men the less disposed do I find myself to like them." Sumner subsequently wrote, that Procter fully concurred in the conclusions advanced in the review. But these were not the prevalent opinions, in this country at least. Great was the outcry against Cooper for writing this article; great the outcry against the " Knickerbocker" for printing it. The latter was severely censured for its willingness to prostitute its columns to the service of the former in his slanderous " attempts to vilify the object of his impotent and contemptible hatred." Americans who were averse to Scott's being honestly paid proved particularly solicitous that he should not be honestly criticised. They showed themselves as little scrupulous in defending him after he was dead as they had been in plundering him while he was living.

Cooper had previously aroused the resentment of many because he had failed to express gratification or delight at being termed " the American Scott." He had then been assured again and again that there was no danger of the title being applied to him in future; that in ten years their names would never be coupled together, and that he himself would be totally forgotten. It could hardly have been deemed a compliment in a land where scarcely a petty district can exist peacefully and creditably, with a hill three thousand feet in height, which is not in time rendered disreputable by being saddled with the pretentious name of " The American Switzerland." Personal malice alone, however, could

11

impute his disclaimer either to malice or to envy. His
own estimate of his relations to the British novelist, he
had given many times; and indirectly at that very time
in his account in the first "Knickerbocker" article, of his
interview with Sir Walter Scott. The latter had been
so obliging, he observed, as to make him a number of
flattering speeches, which he, however, did not repay in
kind. His reserve he thought Scott did not altogether
like. In this he was probably mistaken, but the reason
he gave for his own conduct savored little of feelings of
envy or rivalry. "As Johnson," he wrote, "said of his
interview with George the Third, it was not for me to
bandy compliments with my sovereign." No attention
was paid to these and similar utterances of a man whom
his bitterest enemies never once dared to charge with
saying a word he did not mean.

Few at this day will be disposed to deny the justice
of a good deal of the criticism that Cooper passed upon
his country and his countrymen. Even now, though
many of his strictures are directed against things that
no longer exist, there is still much in his writings that
can be read with profit. The essential justice of what
he said is not impaired by the fact that he was usually
indiscreet and intemperate in the saying of it. Nor
were his motives of a low kind. He loved his country,
and nothing lay dearer to his heart than to have her
what she ought to be. The people were the source of
power; and it was his cardinal principle that power
ought always to be censured rather than flattered. It
needed to be told the truth, however unwelcome; and
in his eyes, that man was no true patriot who was not
willing to encounter unpopularity, if it came in the line
of duty. At the same time, while doing full justice to

the purity of his motives, we cannot shut our eyes to the defects of his method. His abilities, his reputation, his acquaintance with foreign lands, gave him inestimable advantages for influencing his countrymen, and of educating them in matters where they stood sadly in need of it. But the spirit in which he went to work deprived him of the legitimate influence he should have exerted. Excitement, and passion, and indignation led him often to say the wrong thing. More often they caused him to say the right thing in the wrong way. Nor did he escape the special temptation which speedily besets him who starts out to tell his fellow-men unpleasant truths. Duty of this kind soon begins to have a peculiar fascination of its own. The careful reader cannot fail to see that in process of time the more disagreeable was the truth the more delightful it became to Cooper to tell it. Most unreasonable it certainly was to expect that constant fault-finding would be looked upon as a proof of special attachment. The means, moreover, were not always adapted to the end. Men may possibly be lectured to some extent into the acquisition of the virtues, but they never can be bullied into the graces.

Besides all this, in a great deal of Cooper's criticism there were fundamental defects. He constantly confounded the unimportant and the temporary with the important and the permanent. Many of his most violent strictures are devoted to points of little consequence, and the feeling expressed is out of all proportion to the significance of the matter involved. Nothing, for instance, seemed to irritate him more than the preference given by many of his countrymen to the scenery of America over that of Europe. Especially was he indignant with the "besotted stupidity" that could compare the bay of New York with that of Naples. He returned to this topic in book after book. Yet of all the harmless exhibitions of mistaken judgment, that which prefers the scenery of one's own land is what a wise man would be least disposed to find fault with ; certainly what he would think least calculated to inspire, the wrath of a Juvenal. Cosmopolitanism is well enough in its way. But that ability to see things exactly as they are, which enables a man to criticise his mother with the same impartiality with which he does any other woman, can hardly be thought to mark a high development of his loftier feelings, however creditable it may be to the judicial tone of his mind. Undue preference of the scenery of one's own country is an amiable weakness at which the philosopher may smile, but the patriot can afford to rejoice.

There was, moreover, a certain vagueness about much of Cooper's criticism that deprived it of effect. No more striking illustration of this could be found than his constant charge of provincialism made against this country. He repeated it in season and out of season. For several years he hardly published a work which did not contain a number of references to it or assertions of its existence. Provincial enough we certainly were then, if looked at from the point of view of the present time. We in turn may seem so to our descendants. This possibility shows at once the somewhat unreal nature of the accusation. Provincialism, like vulgarity, is a term that defies exact explanation. It is the indefinite and, therefore, unanswerable charge that men constantly bring against those whose standard of living and thinking is different from their own. It depends upon the point of view of the speaker full as much as upon the conduct and opinions of those spoken of. It changes as manners change. Nations not only impute it to one another, but even to themselves at different periods of their history. Made by itself, therefore, it means nothing. Without a specific description of what in particular is meant by provincialism, the charge cannot and ought not to have any weight with those against whom it is directed.

Certain incidental facts mentioned in these observations bring also to light another marked defect of Cooper's course. This was not in his views but in his method of enforcing them. He could not refrain from the constant repetition of the same censures. He had never learned literary self-restraint ; that special criticisms, in order to have their full weight, must not be forced too often upon the attention, and especially at unseasonable times. The mind revolts at having the same exhibition of personal feeling thrust upon it in the most uncalled-for manner and in the most unexpected places. Even when originally disposed to agree with the view expressed, it will, out of a pure spirit of contradiction, take the side opposed to that which is enforced with exasperating frequency. The fullest sympathizer is sure to get tired of this everlasting slaying of the slain. A similar effect is, indeed, likely to be produced upon the victim of the criticism. Instead of being stirred to reflection, repentance, or even indignation, he simply becomes bored. After a man has been told a hundred times that he is provincial, the remark ceases to be exciting. The things, therefore, that Cooper said incidentally are even now the only ones that make any deep impression upon the mind. Like all men, sensitive to the national honor, he felt keenly the refusal of Congress to pass a copyright law. It led him to say twice, but both times very quietly, that in spite of loud profession there was little genuine sympathy in this country with art, or scholarship, or letters. The absence of all heat and excitement gives to the remark a weight that never belongs to his violent utterances and fierce denunciations. We may hope that we have gained since his time; but even at this day we have little to boast of, if the average cultivation of the people, as well as its average morality, finds expression in the laws. The record in these matters of the highest legislative body in the land is still the most discreditable of that of any nation in Christendom. To gratify the greed of a few traders, it has never refused to lay heavy burdens upon scholarship and letters. It has steadily imposed duties on the introduction of everything that could facilitate the acquisition of learning, and further the development of art. It has persistently stabbed literature under the pretence of encouraging intelligence. It has never once been guilty of the weakness of yielding for a moment to the virtuous impulse that would even contemplate the enactment of a copyright law. If it ever does pass one, it will do so, not because foreign authors have rights, but because native publishers have quarrels. Thus consistent in its unwillingness to do an honest thing from an honest motive, it will even then grant to selfishness what has been invariably denied to justice.

There were other than faults of view or faults of statement that mark Cooper's writings at this time. The two novels published during the year 1838 show a radical change in the attitude he assumed to his art. What had been indicated in the stories whose scenes were laid in Europe, was now carried out completely. He may have been unconscious of the difference of his point of view, but none the less did it exist. The novel was no longer something in which he could embody his conceptions of beauty fairer, or truth higher than could actually be found in nature. It no longer served him as a refuge from the din of a clamorous, or the hostility of a censorious world. It became a sort of fortress, from the secure position of which he was enabled to deal out annoyance and defiance to his foes. He had not now so much a story to tell as a sermon to preach; and with him, as with many others, to preach meant to denounce. His spirit for a time became captive to the prejudices and the heated feelings which had been aroused by the sense of the injustice with which he had been treated. Though he at intervals worked himself out of this state of mind, upon much of his later work rested the shadow of the prison-house which he, for a season, had made his abiding-place. The result was that a good deal of what he afterwards wrote was marred by the obtrusion of personal likes and dislikes, and the taint of controversial discussion. These things rarely concerned the story in which they appeared, and they inspired hostility to the writer. Cooper, indeed, never learned to appreciate the fact that a reader has rights which an author is bound to respect. By dragging in irrelevant discussions, moreover, he was taking the surest way to lose the audience he most sought to influence. A little reflection would have taught him that there was little use in a prophet's crying in the wilderness, unless he can succeed in gathering the people together.

While, therefore, there can be no justification for the ferocity with which Cooper was assailed, there was some

palliation. His course from his return to the country
had been wanting in prudence, and at times in common
sense. He had plunged at once as a combatant into one
of the bitterest political controversies that ever agitated
the republic. Hard blows were given and taken. He
could scarcely expect that, in the heat of the strife, regard would in all cases be paid to the proprieties and
even the decencies of private life. There was much in
his later productions, moreover, to alienate many who
were honestly disposed to admire him as a writer. Politics we could get at all times and from everybody. If,
again, we were hopelessly provincial, if we were irreclaimably given over to vulgarity, we could find out all
about it from the latest English traveler, or the review
of his work that had appeared in the latest English
periodicals. But by Cooper the life of the wilderness
and of the sea had been told as by no other writer. Over
the fields and forests and streams of his native land he
had thrown the glamour of romantic association and
lofty deeds. There was something unpleasant in witnessing a man who could do this turning his attention
to the discussion of points of etiquette and manners. Be-
side the waste of power, which is something always disagreeable to contemplate, the subject itself could hardly
be called an attractive one. It was a sandy desert to
travel over at best. But even those who thought it a
thing worth while to do once, could hardly help feeling
surprise at the spirit which could induce a man to go
over it again and again, enlarge upon its discomforts, its
perpetual sameness and barrenness, and point out its
incapacity of being made much better. There were even
worse things than this. It could scarcely fail to inspire
a sentiment almost like disgust to have the creator of

Leather-Stocking argue with heat the question whether it is right for a lady to come into a drawing-room at a party without leaning upon the arm of a gentleman; or discourse solemnly upon the proper way of eating eggs, and announce oracularly that all who were acquainted with polite society would agree in denouncing the wine-glass or egg-glass as a vulgar substitute for the egg-cup. Questions like these are usually left to those who have the taste to delight in them and the mental elevation to grasp the difficulties involved in them. They were the more disagreeable when met with in Cooper, because in addition to the pettiness of the subject, there was an apparent unconsciousness on his part that the limits of his own preferences and conclusions were not necessarily those of the human mind.

Cooper indeed exemplified in his literary career a story he was in the habit of telling of one of his early adventures. While in the navy he was traveling in the wilderness bordering upon the Ontario. The party to which he belonged came upon an inn where they were not expected. The landlord was totally unprepared, and met them with a sorrowful countenance. There was, he assured them, absolutely nothing in his house that was fit to eat. When asked what he had that was not fit to eat, he could only say in reply that he could furnish them with venison, pheasant, wild duck, and some fresh fish. To the astonished question of what better he supposed they could wish, the landlord meekly replied, that he thought they might have wanted some salt pork. The story was truer of Cooper himself than of his innkeeper. Nature he could depict, and the wild life led in it, so that all men stood ready and eager to gaze on the pictures he drew. He chose too often to inflict upon them, instead of it, the most commonplace of moralizing, the stalest disquisitions upon manners and customs, and the driest discussions of politics and theology.

But the moral injury which Cooper received from these controversial discussions and their results was far greater than the intellectual. They swung him off the line of healthful activity. They perverted his judgment. He looked upon the social and political movements that were going on about him with the eye of an irritated and wronged man. Years did not bring to him the philosophic mind, but the spirit of the opinionated partisan and the heated denouncer. He fixed his attention so completely on the tendencies to ill that manifested themselves in the social state, that he often became blind to the counterbalancing tendencies to good. Hence his later judgments were frequently one-sided and partial. He too often took up the rôle of prophesying disasters that never came to pass. Moreover, this habit of looking at one side not only narrowed his mental vision, but turned it in the direction of petty objects. No reader of his later novels can fail to see how often he excites himself over matters of no serious moment; or which, whether serious or slight, are utterly out of place where they are. By many of these exhibitions the indifferent will be amused, but the admirers of the man will feel pained if not outraged.

CHAPTER IX.

By the end of 1837 Cooper had pretty sedulously improved every opportunity of making himself unpopular. His criticisms had been distributed with admirable impartiality. Few persons or places could complain that they had been overlooked. The natural satisfaction that any one would have felt in contemplating the punishment inflicted upon his friend or neighbor, was utterly marred by the consideration of the outrage done to himself. There was scarcely a class of Cooper's fellow-citizens whose susceptibilities had not been touched, or whose wrath had not been kindled by something he had said either in public or in private, and by his saying it repeatedly. The sons of the Puritans he had exasperated by styling them the grand inquisitors of private life, and by asserting that a low sort of tyranny over domestic affairs was the direct result of their religious polity. He had roused the resentment of the survivors of the old Federalist party by declaring that its design during the war of 1812 had been disunion, and that in secret many of them still longed for a restoration of monarchy, and sighed for ribbons, stars, and garters. He had not conciliated the party with which he was nominally allied by his incessant attacks upon the doctrine of free-trade. He had made Boston shudder to its remotest suburbs, by stating again and again in the strongest terms that it was in the Middle States alone that the English language was spoken with purity. The New England capital he had further described as a gossiping country town with a tone of criticism so narrow and vulgar as scarcely to hide the parochial sort of venom which engendered it. He had charged upon New Yorkers that their lives were spent in the constant struggle for inordinate and grasping gain; that to talk of dollars was to them a source of endless enjoyment; and that their society had for its characteristic distinction the fussy pretension and swagger that usually mark the presence of lucky speculators in stocks. He had attributed to the whole trading class a jealous and ferocious watchfulness of the pocket, and a readiness to sacrifice at any time the honor of the country for the sake of personal profit. To the native merchants he had denied the name of real merchants. They were simply factors, mere agents, who were ennobled by commerce, but who did not themselves ennoble it. The foreign traders resident here fared no better. They had never read the Constitution of the country they had made their home, and were incapable of understanding it if they should read it. Always judging of American facts in accordance with the antiquated notions in which they had been brought up, they were largely responsible for the erroneous opinions entertained and blundering prophecies made in Europe in regard to the condition and future of the United States. The educated class, above all, he had denounced for its indomitable selfishness and its hatred of the rights of those socially inferior. It was entirely behind the fortunes of the country and still cherished prejudices against democracy that the very stupidest of European conservatives had begun to lay aside. The newspaper press he had assailed with a pungency and vigor which it in vain sought to rival. He was spattered by it, however, with almost every opprobrious term that belongs to the vocabulary of wrath and abuse. Invention was tasked to furnish discreditable reasons for all that he said and did. That inexhaustible capacity of devising base motives for conduct, which is an especial attribute of mean minds, had now opportunity to put forth its full powers in the way of insinuation and assertion. It did not go unimproved. A common charge brought against him after the publication of the "Letter to His Countrymen" was that it had been written for the sake of gaining office. It was even said that Van Buren had a hand in it. Then and afterward, the Whig newspapers represented Cooper as seeking the position of Secretary of the Navy. Denial availed him nothing. It would certainly have not been at all to his discredit to have desired the place; for he knew a great deal about the navy, and its interests were very dear to his heart. For these very reasons his appointment to it would have been in violation of the traditional policy of the government. It was probably never once contemplated by any administration, as it was certainly never asked by Cooper himself.

The two extracts that have already been given are doubtless sufficient to satisfy any curiosity that may exist in regard to the way in which he was spoken of by the press of America. Yet coarse as was its vituperation, it was surpassed by that of Great Britain. Englishmen may have felt, and have felt justly, that Cooper took an unfair view of their social life and political institutions. National character sweeps through a range so vast that a man will usually be able to find in it what he goes to seek.   Even under the most favorable conditions the tastes of a coterie or the habits of a class are made the standard by which to estimate the tastes and habits of a whole people.   Certain it is that the view of any nation is to be distrusted which is not taken from a station of good-will.   But granting that Cooper was unjust in his observations, there was nothing he said which afforded the least excuse for the coarse personality with which he was followed from the time he published his volumes on England.   The remarks of the ordinary journals can be dismissed without comment. But brutal vituperation was found in abundance in periodicals which claimed to be the representatives of the highest cultivation and refinement.   According to "Blackwood's Magazine," Cooper was a vulgar man, who from having been bred to the sea had been enabled to give some striking descriptions of sea-affairs, and in consequence had unluckily imagined himself a universal genius.   It went on to add, that on the strength of the trifling reputation he had acquired by stories descriptive of American life, he had come to Europe, and had since been partly traveling on the Continent to pick up materials for novels, and partly residing in England, actively employed in the effort to introduce himself into society. In this it admitted he might have been partially successful, for the English were a very yielding people and did not take much trouble to resist attempts of this kind. "Blackwood," however, was outdone in this rowdy style of reviewing by "Fraser's Magazine."   From that periodical we learn that Cooper was "a passable scribbler of passable novels," a "bilious braggart," a "liar," a "full jackass," "a man of consummate and inbred vulgarity," "a bore of the first magnitude in society," who went about fishing for introductions. "But this," it concluded, speaking of his England, "was his last kick, and we shall not disturb his dying moments." Two years later the magazine seemed to think he had some power of kicking left, for it returned to the charge in consequence of his review of Lockhart's "Life of Scott." In this article he was called a "spiteful miscreant," an "insect," a "grub," a "reptile." The "Quarterly Review" was as virulent and violent as the magazines, but the attack was more skillful as well as longer and more elaborate. By garbling extracts it cleverly insinuated a good deal more than it said, and it so contrived to put several things that the reader could hardly fail to draw inferences which the writer must have known to be false. Even these attacks were equaled if not surpassed at a later period by the "London Times." A nominal review in that journal of "Eve Effingham," as "Home as Found" was entitled in England, was really devoted to personal vituperation of the novelist. It ended with the assertion that he was more vulgar than ever, and was the most "affected, offensive, envious, and ill-conditioned" of authors. Altogether Cooper must have been impressed with the effectiveness of the blow which he had struck by the violence with which it was resented. It seems hard to believe that remarks such as have been quoted should have been thought to establish anything but the vulgarity of the men who wrote them. Yet they apparently answered their purpose. The very latest notice of Cooper's life which has appeared in Great Britain, characterizes his work on England as an "outburst of vanity and ill-temper." It certainly contained some ill-judged remarks which have been made the most of by his enemies; but this estimate, like many other assertions in the same sketch, was not got from reading the work itself, but from what British periodicals had said about it.

Such was the kind of criticism that the novelist now mainly received in the two great English-speaking countries. These flowers of invective do not constitute an anthology which an Englishman or American of to-day can read with pleasure, or contemplate with pride. It was the comments made by his countrymen that naturally touched Cooper most nearly. His nature was of a kind to feel keenly, and resent warmly insinuations and charges that impugned the purity of his motives. Nor was his a disposition to rest quiet under attack or to assume merely the defensive. He retorted in letters, in works of fiction, and in books of travel. Finally he resorted to libel suits. Never, indeed, was a fiercer fight carried on by an individual against a power more mighty than Cooper carried on with the press. It had a thousand tongues, he had but one; but it often seemed as if his one had the force of a thousand. The epithets he applied to newspapers were not of the kind with which they were in the habit of celebrating themselves. Their enterprise in obtaining news he described as a mercenary diligence in the collection and diffusion of information, whether true or false. Nor were his comments upon those concerned in carrying them on more favorable. What we should call a reporter he, on one occasion, mildly spoke of as a " miscreant who pandered for the press." In the last novel he wrote, he energetically termed this whole class the funguses of letters who flourished on the dunghill of the common mind ; and that in their view the sole use for which the universe was created was to furnish paragraphs for newspapers. Men in the higher grades of the profession fared little better. Against the political journals, in particular, he brought the charge that under the pretence of serving the public they were mainly used to aid the ambition or gratify the spite of their editors.

Even as early as 1832, Cooper had awakened the indignation of the press by an incidental remark made in the introduction to "The Heidenmauer." He was describing a journey through a part of Belgium in which the Dutch troops had been operating the week before his arrival. They had been reported as having committed unusual excesses. Of these excesses he said he could find no trace. He went on to add a sentence which has apparently only a slight connection with what had gone before. "Each hour, as life advances," he wrote, "am I made to see how capricious and vulgar is the immortality conferred by a newspaper." This remark was warmly resented. It was asserted to be a declaration, not merely of indifference to the opinion of the press, but of a preference on his part of its censure to its praise. Its business, therefore, was to see that his wishes should be carried out.

After the controversy in regard to the Three Mile Point, the attacks of the Whig journals increased in bitterness. The state of mind it caused in Cooper can be seen in a little volume, published by him in April, 1838, entitled "The American Democrat." This work is made up of a singular mixture of abstract discussions on liberty and equality, on the nature of parties, on forms of government, and of remarks on national habits and manners. It is not an interesting book. Yet it is fair to say of it, that it is animated throughout by a lofty patriotism, and it manifests a clear view of the dangers and duties of a democracy, with its comparative advantages and disadvantages. But it likewise exhibited some of the most uncompromising traits of the author's character. In writing it, he was not aiming at popularity; it might not be much out of the way to say that he was aiming at unpopularity. The doctrine with which he sets out is, that in this country power rests with the people, and power ought always to be chidden rather than commended. He was accordingly liberal in criticism. But the value of what he said was largely impaired, if not wholly destroyed by the one-sidedness of view and tendency to over-statement into which his ardor of feeling now habitually hurried him. In nothing is this extravagance more strikingly seen than in the comments in this work upon the press. There was a great deal of truth in what he said; but the justice of some of his views was deprived of any effect by the exaggeration and consequent injustice of others. The substance of his remarks was that there were more newspapers in this country than in Europe, but they were generally of a lower character. The multiplication of them was due to the fact that little capital was required in their creation, and little intelligence employed in their management. Their number was, therefore, not a thing to be boasted of but rather to be sorrowed over, since the quality diminished in an inverse ratio to the quantity. Nor was there anything in the methods employed by the press that justified any exultation in its prosperity. It tyrannized over public men, over letters, over the stage, over even private life. Under the pretence of preserving public morals, it corrupted them to the core. Under the semblance of maintaining liberty, it was gradually establishing a despotism as rude, as grasping, and as vul-

gar as that of any state known. It loudly professed
freedom of opinion, but exhibited no tolerance. It paraded patriotism, but never sacrificed interest. But its
great fundamental failing was the untrustworthiness of
its statements. It existed to pervert truth. Its conductors were mainly political adventurers. They were
unscrupulous, but they were not so utterly ignorant that
they failed to see the necessity of occasionally making
correct assertions. It was, however, this mixture of
fact with fiction that was the chief cause of the evil influence exerted. The result of it all was that the entire nation, in a moral sense, breathed an atmosphere of
falsehood. He concluded his indictment by declaring
that the American press would seem to have been expressly devised by the great agent of mischief, to depress and destroy all that was good, and to elevate and
advance all that was evil.

This style of remark was certainly not designed to
win newspaper favor or support. But he went even farther in his novels of " Homeward Bound " and " Home
as Found." In those two works he drew the portrait
of an American editor in the person of Steadfast Dodge
of the Active Inquirer. All the baser qualities of human nature were united in this ideal representative of
the press. He was a sneak, a spy, a coward, a demagogue, a parasite, a lickspittle, a fawner upon all from
whom he hoped help, a slanderer of all who did not care
to endure his society. Such a picture did not rise even
to the dignity of caricature. Nor is it relieved either
in this work or elsewhere by others drawn favorably.
The reader of Cooper will search his writings in vain
for a portrait which any member of the editorial profession would be glad to recognize as his own.

All this was vigorous enough, but it could hardly be called profitable. Cooper had now cultivated to perfection the art of saying injudicious things as well as the art of saying things injudiciously. His ability in hitting upon the very line of remark that would still further enrage the hostile, and irritate the indifferent and even the friendly, assumed almost the nature of genius. The power of his attacks could not be gainsaid. But while they inspired his opponents with respect, they filled his friends with dismay. He was soon in a singular position. He enjoyed at one and the same time the double distinction of being reviled in England for his aggressive republicanism, and of being denounced in America for aping the airs of the English aristocracy. It hardly seemed a favorable time for beginning hostilities in a new field. Yet it was then that he entered upon his famous legal war with the Whig newspapers of the state of New York.

A detailed account of the libel suits instituted by Cooper would form one of the most striking chapters in the history of the American press ; and for some reasons it is to be regretted that the plan he had of writing a full account of them was never carried out. Here only a slight summary can be given. It is well to say at the outset that many assertions ordinarily made about them are utterly false. For certain of these prevalent misconceptions Greeley is responsible. He spoke of these trials with some fullness in commenting upon libel suits in his " Recollections of a Busy Life." But Greeley's life was too busy for him always to recollect accurately. While he had not the slightest intention to say anything untrue, what he said was in some instances of this character; though more often it was mis-

leading rather than false. But outside of what Greeley
has written, there are several erroneous assertions current. One of the most common of these is the statement that Cooper's success in them was mainly due to
the application of the law maxim, that the greater the
truth the greater the libel. There was never any
ground for even an insinuation of this kind. Cooper,
when his attention was called to it, treated it with contempt. "The pretense," he wrote in 1845, "that our
courts have ever overruled that the truth is not a complete defense in a libel suit in the civil action, can only
gain credit with the supremely ignorant." In criminal
indictments the New York statute of 1805 had expressly declared that the truth might be pleaded in evidence by the defense. The Constitution of 1821 made
this provision part of the fundamental law, and it was
adopted from that into the Constitution of 1846. The
assertion owed its origin wholly to the effort of beaten
parties to explain their defeat on some other ground
than that they had been found guilty of the offense with
which they had been charged.

A more preposterous statement even than this was
that the question involved in these suits was the right
of editors to criticise the productions of authors. In
not one of these trials was the literary judgment passed
by the reviewer mentioned as having the slightest bearing on the case. It ought not to be necessary to say
that it was the attack upon the character of the man
that alone came under the consideration of the courts,
and not that upon the character of the book. The
impudent pretense was, however, set up at the time that
the press had a right to go behind the writer's work,
and assail him himself. " Does an author," said " The

New Yorker" in February, 1837, "subject himself to personal criticism by submitting a work to the public? If he makes his work the channel of disparagement upon masses of men, he does."

The most marked feature of these trials is that Cooper fought his battle single-handed. With a very few exceptions, — notably the "Albany Argus" and the "New York Evening Post," — the press of the party with which he was nominally allied, remained neutral. Some of them were even hostile; for the novelist's criticism of editors had known no distinction of politics. On the other hand, the press of the opposition party was united. From East to West they bore down upon Cooper with a common cry. No event in his life showed more plainly the fearless and uncompromising nature of the man; nor again did anything else he was concerned in mark more clearly his versatility and vigor. In these trials he was assisted by his nephew, Richard Cooper, who was his regular counsel. But outside of him, in the civil suits, he had very rarely any help, and in most of them he argued his own cause. Wherever he appeared in person he seems to have come off uniformly victorious. Nor were his victories won over inferior opponents. The reputation of the lawyer is under ordinary conditions limited necessarily to a small circle. Even in that, considering the amount of intellectual acuteness and power displayed, it is an exceedingly transitory reputation. But the men against whom Cooper was pitted stood in the very front rank of their profession. They were leaders of the bar in the greatest state in the Union. Nor have times so far swept by that their names are not still remembered; and stories are still told of their achievements by those who have taken their places. Cooper, not a lawyer by profession, met these men on their own ground and defeated them. It was not long, indeed, after these suits were instituted, that it was claimed by his friends, and often conceded by his foes, that he was the one man in the country best acquainted with the law of libel. Our surprise at his success is increased by the fact that he was not only unpopular himself, but he was engaged in an unpopular cause. The verdicts he won were usually small in amount, but they were wrung from reluctant juries, and frequently in the face of bitter prejudices that had to be overcome before he could hope for a fair consideration of his own side.

At the outset the editorial fraternity were disposed to take these libel suits jocularly. They were looked upon as a gigantic joke. Nor did this feeling die out when the first trial resulted in Cooper's favor. It was proposed that the newspapers throughout the country should contribute each one dollar to a fund to be called " The Effingham Libel Fund," out of which all damages awarded the novelist were to be paid. Every additional suit was welcomed with a shout. As time went on this insolence gave way to apprehension. In nearly every case the plaintiff was coming off successful. The comments of the press began to assume an expostulatory tone. Cooper was gravely informed that were he to be tried in the High Court of Public Opinion — this imaginary tribunal was usually made imposing by dignifying its initial letters — for his libels upon his country and his countrymen, the damages he would have to pay would not only sweep away the amounts given him by the results in the regular courts, but even the profits that had accrued from the sale of his novels.

These remonstrances were often animated also by a new-born zeal for his literary fame. He was told he was his own greatest enemy. He was doing himself irreparable injury by the course he was taking. He was so acting as to lose the reputation he had early won. This feeling naturally increased in intensity as suits continued to be decided in his favor. The newspapers at last rose to the full appreciation of the situation. The liberty of the press was actually in danger. The trials were said to be conducted in defiance of law as well as justice. The judges belonged to the Democratic party, and they wrested the statutes from their true intent in order to oppress the Whig editor. There came finally to be something exquisitely absurd in the utterances of the journals on the subject of these suits. One would fancy from reading them that the plaintiff was a monster resembling the bloodthirsty ogre of a fairy tale, bullying judges, overawing juries, maliciously bent on crushing the free-born American who should have the temerity to express an unfavorable opinion of his writings. Coriolanus, indeed, never fluttered the dove-cotes in Corioli more effectively than for some years Cooper did the Whig newspaper offices of the state of New York.

The origin of the suits was as follows: An account of the circumstances connected with the Three Mile Point controversy appeared, immediately after they had taken place, in the " Norwich Telegraph," a paper published in the neighboring county of Chenango. The article began with a reference to Cooper. " This gentleman," it said, " not satisfied with having drawn upon his head universal contempt from abroad, has done the same thing at Cooperstown where he resides." In this spirit it went on to give its report of the events told in the preceding chapter. "So stands the matter at present," it closed its account, "Mr. J. F. C. threatening the citizens on the one hand, and being derided and despised by them on the other." In conclusion it called upon the "Otsego Republican," the Whig newspaper of Cooperstown, to furnish all the facts in the case.

The latter journal was edited by a man named Barber. He was not slow to comply with the request, and in one of the numbers of August, 1837, he republished the article of the "Chenango Telegraph" with additional assertions of his own. The latter belonged more to the realm of fiction than of fact. Three Mile Point he declared had been reserved expressly for the use of the inhabitants of Cooperstown by the father of the novelist. When the notice was published depriving them of their rights, a meeting had been called which had been largely attended. The room was crowded with the industry, intelligence, and respectability of the village. Powerful addresses were made and a series of resolutions were passed. These expressed the feelings of all present. "The remarks," the newspaper continued, "were of a lucid character, and the resolutions, full, pungent, and yet respectful."

Two days after this article had appeared, the editor received a letter from Cooper's counsel which was to the effect that he would be prosecuted for libel unless he retracted his statements. On his side the novelist undertook to make perfectly clear to him that his assertions were untrue; but he expected, after the real facts had been set before him and fully examined, that he would take back what he had said. "No atonement," the letter concluded, "will be accepted, that is not first

approved of by the plaintiff in the suit." Barber was not
disposed either to retract or to investigate the accuracy of
the facts he had stated. He published the letter, however, with the usual solemn declaration that seems to be
kept in type in all newspaper offices, that in doing what
he had done he had been actuated solely by the noblest
motives; that he had not published anything libellous;
that if in anything he had been misinformed, he held
himself always ready to make the proper correction.
"In conclusion," he said, "not being sensible of having
injured Mr. Cooper, we consider that we have no atonement to offer." Under these circumstances the suit
went on. It did not come to final trial until May,
1839, at the Montgomery circuit of the Supreme Court.
Joshua A. Spencer was the principal lawyer for the
defense, while Cooper conducted his own case. The jury
returned a verdict of four hundred dollars for the plaintiff. Eventually the editor sought to evade in various
ways the payment of the whole award, and did succeed
in evading the payment of a good part of it. A terrible outcry was, however, raised against Cooper because the sheriff levied upon some money that had been
carefully laid away and locked up by Barber in a trunk.

With this begins the famous series of suits that occupied no small share of the few following years of the
author's life. At the time the first one was decided,
another was pending against the editor of the "Chenango
Telegraph." The leading Whig newspapers naturally
took the side of their associates. For a time they had
a good deal to say about the greatest slanderer of the
whole profession pouncing upon one of the fraternity
least able to defend himself, simply because in a moment
of haste and excitement he had been guilty of what they

were pleased to call a technical libel. It did not seem to occur to them that any one could be so foolhardy as to make them the object of attack. They did not have to wait long to discover that the influence wielded by a journal was no protection. Besides the newspapers already mentioned, Cooper prosecuted the "Oneida Whig," published at Utica. This suit was tried in April, 1842. Though successful in it, the damages awarded were slight, being but seventy dollars. A suit, tried little more than six months before against the "Evening Signal," of New York city, edited by Park Benjamin, had resulted in the recovery of a larger sum. The amount in this case was three hundred and seventy-five dollars. With these exceptions his suits were directed against the "Courier and Enquirer," edited by James Watson Webb; "the Albany Evening Journal," edited by Thurlow Weed; the "Tribune," edited by Horace Greeley, and the "Commercial Advertiser," edited by William Leet Stone. These were the leading Whig journals in the state, and among the most influential in the whole country. It could not be said that Cooper hesitated about flying at high game.

In the controversy with Webb, Cooper had the least success. This was partly due to the fact that it was not a civil action that was brought against the former, but a criminal indictment. Juries might make editors pay for the privilege of expressing their feelings of contempt or hate, but they were not inclined to send them to prison. The indictment in this case was based upon a criticism of "Home as Found." The review, which was of several columns in length, had appeared in the "Courier and Enquirer" of November 22, 1838. There was very little in the way of hostile insinuation and assertion and

personal depreciation that could not be found in this
article and in some which followed. The attack was
moreover a skillful one. It was directed largely against
those points where Cooper had fairly laid himself open
to ridicule. Especially was this the case in the matter
of descent and family. Webb represented the novelist
as the son of a humble hawker of fish through the streets
of Burlington, who had afterward become a respectable though not a first-class wheelwright. By probity,
industry, and enterprise he had finally risen to wealth
and position. The maternal grandmother of the author
had, according to this same story, for more than twenty
years occupied a stall and sold fresh vegetables in the
Philadelphia market, and was remarkable for the superior quality of the articles she kept. Webb praised
the father at the expense of the son. The former had
never been ashamed of his humble origin. On the contrary, he was justly proud of the intelligence and ability which, unaided by any mere external advantages,
had raised him to a station in life so much higher than
he at first held. Of such a career any child had a right
to be proud. These were statements that could not
well be resented, conceding that they were injurious, nor
could they well be corrected, conceding that they were
untrue. Webb, who had recently returned from Europe, asserted, moreover, that he had been present at
a dinner-party in London, where "Home as Found"
came under discussion. On that occasion he had fallen
into a conversation about it with "a nobleman of distinction." The latter informed him that Cooper's attack upon English society had materially injured the
sale of his works in that country, and it was evident
that he was now seeking to regain the ground and the

market he had lost, by praising everything English at the expense of everything American; but as his base motives were now fully understood, no one was led astray. The reported conversation carries internal evidence of its authenticity. It required a very noble lord to impute to a well-known writer motives so very noble; and none but an Englishman could have appreciated so fully the eternal conditions of success in the English market. These remarks of Webb's are, however, merely incidental. His direct personal attack on Cooper rivaled that of the British periodicals in ferocity. "We may and do know him," said he in the only extract for which there is room, "as a base-minded caitiff who has traduced his country for filthy lucre and low-born spleen; but time only can render harmless abroad the envenomed barb of the slanderer who is in fact a traitor to national pride and national character."

For this article Webb was indicted by the grand jury of Otsego County, in February, 1839. In June of the same year a second indictment was found against him for saying that the first was secured by political trickery. The trial, for various reasons, did not come off until November, 1841. Webb made a public retraction of the statements upon which the second indictment was found; and this was accepted on the part of the prosecution. On the trial for the first indictment the jury disagreed. The defendant objected to Cooper's summing up the case, and this objection the court sustained. It was a wise policy: for the trials in the civil suits showed that the novelist was full as effective in addressing a jury orally as he ever was in addressing the public in his most successful stories. One amusing feature of this case was that the two volumes of "Home as Found" were read to the jury from beginning to end by the plaintiff's counsel, Ambrose L. Jordan.

Cooper was not discouraged by the ill result of this trial. The indictment was still pressed. A second trial took place at Cooperstown in June, 1843. Again the jury disagreed. A third trial is reported to have taken place and to have resulted in the acquittal of Webb; but I find no account of it in the newspapers to which I have had access.

The suits brought against the "Albany Evening Journal" were, however, the most striking in this whole contest. They show, too, more clearly than the others, the spirit and methods with which it was waged on both sides. Some features are especially marked. One is the illustration furnished of the onslaughts that were made upon the novelist's character and reputation, not from any real ill-will, but from pure wantonness or at least very slight political hostility. Another is the jaunty superciliousness with which the conductors of the press at first affected to treat the threats of prosecution. More noteworthy than anything else, however, is the view given of the deliberate manner in which Cooper began these suits, and the relentless tenacity with which he followed them up. The "Evening Journal," of which Thurlow Weed was then the head, partly from the political skill of its editor, and partly from its being the organ of the party at the state capital, was, at that time, the most influential Whig journal in New York. Weed published in it, in two different numbers of August, 1837, the articles which had appeared in the "Chenango Telegraph" and the "Otsego Republican" about the Three Mile Point controversy. He accompanied them with some comments of his own in regard to

Cooper. " He was, as is known," said he in his second notice, " pretty generally despised abroad. He is now equally distinguished at home." The editor then went on to speak of the act of meanness, as he termed it, which had excited the contempt of the novelist's neighbors ; and that the more precise account now furnished by the " Otsego Republican" would rather increase than diminish the measure of scorn that had been aroused. Much was Weed's surprise when, on the 18th of April, 1840, he received a letter from Cooper's counsel requiring a retraction of what had been said in 1837, and a further statement that it must be made within a certain time or a suit for libel would be begun. He treated this notice cavalierly. He was amused by it even more than he was astonished. As it had taken three years for Cooper to bring the suit, he concluded that he would take three weeks at any rate to reply to the demand for a retraction. A second letter from Cooper's counsel, dated the 4th of May, met with the same neglect. Accordingly on the 25th of that month he had the pleasure of announcing that he had been sued for libel by "Mr. John Effingham."

The case after being put off once on a very frivolous pretext, came to trial at the Montgomery circuit of the Supreme Court, held at Fonda, in November, 1841. When it was called Weed was not present, nor was counsel for him. Cooper consented to have the case go over for a day. It was then called again. Nothing was seen of the defendant, nothing had been heard from him. The case was accordingly sent to the jury with a speech from the plaintiff's counsel. A verdict of four hundred dollars was returned. Weed arrived at Fonda the evening of that day, and wrote anonymously to the

" New York Tribune " an account of what had taken place. In some of its details it was more entertaining than accurate. The reason he gave for his absence from the trial was that he had been kept at home by severe illness in his family. But the result enabled him to notice in this manner the sum awarded by the jury.

" This meagre verdict under the circumstances is a severe and mortifying rebuke to Cooper, who had everything his own way.

" The value of Mr. Cooper's character, therefore, has been judicially determined.

" It is worth exactly four hundred dollars."

For the publication of this letter a suit was immediately begun against the " Tribune." But though he wrote for that journal an amusing account of the trial, in his own paper Weed gave vent to the anger which the result had excited. The verdicts gained in his various cases by " this man Cooper," he said, had made " deep inroads upon a fame once bright and enviable, but now sadly dim and dilapidated." He then recited in full the misdeeds of the novelist. " For all this," concluded the aggrieved editor, " connected with the attempt to deprive the citizens of a social privilege with which they were invested by his honored father, we said Mr. Cooper was despised. And for this he prosecuted us. And now having again said it he may again prosecute us, if he wants and thinks he can obtain four hundred dollars more."

Weed did not appreciate the fact that he was not dealing with a politician, but with a man indifferent to or rather contemptuous of popular clamor. His challenge was immediately accepted. Early in December,

1841, he was able to announce the fact that he had been sued again. "The sheriff," he said, "has served another writ upon us for an alleged libel upon Cooper. It remains to be seen how much longer courts and juries will sanction this legal persecution of a man, who after libeling his country and calumniating his countrymen, seeks to muzzle a free press." The jocular tone used at first had all vanished. Instead it was replaced by a fierce spirit of wrathfulness and defiance. During the whole of December, 1841, Weed kept constantly republishing extracts from other newspapers reflecting upon and attacking Cooper's character and conduct. These were, he said, "sharp rebukes" of the novelist's "ridiculous and unworthy attempt to disgrace his own country to gain the favor and smiles of the nobility abroad." Some of these newspaper comments furnish very amusing reading now, especially as the impunity of most of the writers was due to their insignificance. "We rejoice," said one of them, "to witness the spirit of independence manifested by the conductors of the press. It proves their incorruptible integrity and their love of principle, their firm hostility to foreign notions, and their detestation of the man who seeks to ape the high and aristocratic manners of English nobility." These valorous declarations came mainly from the country papers of the state of New York, for the "Evening Journal" was the Triton of these minnows. Weed, however, eagerly reproduced everything that came from outside. One article, in particular, from a Chicago paper, was published, in order that Cooper might see "what right-minded and unprejudiced people say and think of him far away in the boundless West."

The appeal was to deaf ears. Neither contracted

13

East nor boundless West affected Cooper's resolution. As fast as the articles were republished, they were carefully examined, and prosecutions begun against the "Evening Journal" for those of them containing libelous matter. By the middle of December five suits had been commenced, and more were under consideration. A little later, if contemporary newspaper reports can be trusted, the number had swelled to seven. The editor began to appreciate the difficulty and danger of the situation. His courage, however, did not falter. In fact he looked upon himself as manfully standing in the gap for freedom of speech. "These suits," he said, "will determine whether an Independent Press is to be protected in the free exercise of honest opinion, or whether it is to be overawed and silenced by the persecutions of an inflated, litigious, soured novelist, who, in his better days by the favor of the Press, made the money with which he now seeks to oppress its conductors, and sap its independence." He did not purpose to flinch from his duty. Accordingly he announced that he should continue publishing these attacks until Cooper ceased prosecuting.

In this determination he was encouraged by the result of two suits tried in April, 1842, in the Otsego County Court. Though he was beaten in both, the verdict was for small amounts. In one case it was fifty-five dollars, in the other eighty-seven dollars. This convinced the press that the tide was turning. Again the country newspapers were filled with libelous paragraphs. Again the novelist was denounced for his heartless abuse of his country, and his soulless and contemptible vanity. Again these strictures were carefully collected from every quarter, no matter how insignificant, and republished in the columns of the "Evening Journal." But these cheerful anticipations were speedily dissipated. Another suit, tried at Fonda in the Supreme Court in May, 1842, resulted in a verdict of three hundred and twenty-five dollars for the plaintiff. The country papers were indignant. One of the editors sagely suggested that "if judge and jury are to carry on this war on the press to gratify individual malignity much further, it would be well for all editors to unite in petitioning the legislature to pass a law that judges should discharge their duties impartially, and juries be composed of honest and intelligent men." This profound suggestion marks pretty plainly the intellectual grade to which most of the writers of these paragraphs had attained. Before it could be acted upon another suit had been decided. In the September term of the Supreme Court held at Cooperstown, a further verdict of two hundred dollars was awarded. In the following month a new suit was begun.

Weed had fought his fight manfully. But the business of publishing libelous paragraphs at these rates, low as they were, was ceasing to be either pleasant or profitable. Besides his own counsel fees, the adverse verdicts carried with them heavy costs. He concluded to let the liberty of the press take care of itself. Accordingly, on the 14th of December, 1842, he published, though with a grumbling comment, a retraction of all his previous statements. It had been previously submitted to the eminent lawyer, Daniel Cady, and by him approved. It withdrew, first, the allegations contained the previous year in a specific article in the paper. "On a review of the matter and a better knowledge of the facts," were the words of the retraction, " I feel it to be my duty to withdraw the injurious imputations it contains on the character of Mr. Cooper. It is my wish that this retraction should be as broad as the charges. The 'Albany Evening Journal' having also contained various other articles reflecting on Mr. Cooper's character, I feel it due to that gentleman to withdraw every charge that injuriously affects his character."

The course of instruction had been protracted and expensive, but the lesson had been learned at last. The independence of the press had been crushed by the domineering despot of Cooperstown. The controversy threatened to break out again in 1845, but it seems never to have got beyond words. There is a comic element introduced into the whole affair by the fact that the editor of the "Journal" was a profound and even bigoted admirer of his adversary's novels. So fond was he of quoting from them, that according to Greeley, jokers at that time gravely affirmed that Weed had never read but three authors, — Shakespeare, Scott, and Cooper. In the very heat of the controversy he was said to have sat up all night reading "The Pathfinder," which had come out a little while before. Greeley also asserts that the paragraphs which appeared in the "Evening Journal" were merely designed as gentle reminders to the novelist of the folly of the course he was pursuing. This might find belief in a society in which telling a man that he was an object of universal contempt would be deemed an expression of friendly interest in his welfare. When he says, in addition, that there was no shred, no spice of malice in these assaults, he takes away the sole ground on which a plea of palliation can be brought. If not due to that they had not even the poor excuse of weak human nature. They were the

wanton acts of a man who attacks another, not from indignation or wrath, but from the mere desire of inflicting
annoyance or pain.

The controversy with the " Commercial Advertiser "
belongs not here but to the account of the "Naval History." It has already been said that the " Tribune "
had been sued for the publication of Thurlow Weed's
letter describing the trial at Fonda in November, 1841.
In December, 1842, this case came off at Ballston.
Greeley assumed the conduct of the defense. He was
unsuccessful. The jury brought in against him a verdict of two hundred dollars and costs. " We went back
to dinner," he wrote, " took the verdict in all meekness,
took a sleigh and struck a bee-line for New York." No
sooner had he reached the city than he published a most
entertaining account of the whole trial. It filled eleven
columns of the " Tribune," and the demand for it became so great that it was found necessary to publish it
in pamphlet form. For some expressions in it Cooper
began another suit. In this instance Greeley gave up
the plan of defending himself and intrusted the conduct
of his side to Seward. The case dragged on for years
'n the New York courts, and, so far as I have been able
to discover, had not been brought to a final trial before
the plaintiff's death.

By the end of 1843, Cooper had pretty well reduced
the press to silence, so far as comments on his character
were concerned. It was insignificance or remoteness
alone that protected the libeler. The leading newspapers of the state, however much they might abuse his
writings, learned to be very cautious of what they said
of him personally. But it was a barren victory he had
won. He had lost far more than he had gained. That

such would be the result, he knew, while he was engaged in the controversy. It affected, at the time, his literary reputation, and, as a result, the sale of his writings ; and since his death it has been a principal agency in keeping alive a distorted and fictitious view of his personal character. A common impression came to be of him something like the description which Greeley's lawyers gave of the estimation in which he was held in Otsego County, in some legal papers bearing the date of July, 1845. This was to the effect that he had acquired and had among his neighbors " the reputation of a proud, captious, censorious, arbitrary, dogmatical, malicious, illiberal, revengeful, and litigious man." This one-sided and hostile view of a strongly-marked character had just enough of truth in it to cause it to be widely received as an accurate and complete picture. In a similar way the notion became current that he sought to ape the manners of the English aristocracy. Whatever Cooper's foibles were, they were none of them imported. He was too proud in feeling and too self-centred in opinion ever to think of aping anything or anybody. But on these points the prejudices and misrepresentations of that day have lasted down to this.

The account given makes it clear that the occasion of bringing the first of these libel suits was accidental. But as time went on the prosecution of them assumed to Cooper the shape of a duty. When once it had taken on that character, no possible degree of unpopularity or odium could have prevented him from persisting in his course. He treated with disdain the common arguments used to persuade him to abandon them. To one of these he referred directly in a novel published in 1844. He was insisting upon the superiority of the past to the present, a sentiment which became a favorite burden of his latter-day utterances. " The public sense of right," he said, " had not become blunted by familiarity with abuses, and the miserable and craven apology was never heard for not enforcing the laws that nobody cared for what the newspapers say." He certainly had some justification for the hardest things he thought and said of the press. The newspapers which circulated the false reports about his father's disposition of the property at Three Mile Point never corrected them after the precise facts had been published. Many of them continued to repeat the original statements after they must have known them to be untrue. Nor did they stop here. As the British press had in his case done all it could to justify the charge Cooper made against it of ferocious blackguardism of personal and political foes, so many of the American editors seemed anxious to realize, so far as it lay in their power, the picture that had been drawn of them in the character of Steadfast Dodge. Papers containing offensive paragraphs about Cooper were carefully sent, not directed to him personally, but to his wife and daughters. The fear of punishment is the only motive by which those who commit acts of this kind can possibly be influenced. On the other hand, it is an idle claim that the character of the press has been elevated by libel suits that Cooper or any one else has ever brought. Such prosecutions may be both justifiable and necessary ; but the agencies that form and build up intelligence and taste and high principle are not of this negative and restraining character.

CHAPTER X.

1839–1843.

On the 10th of May, 1839, appeared Cooper's "History of the United States Navy." The work was one which he had long contemplated writing. As far back as 1825 there were newspaper reports that he had the undertaking in mind. He himself, in his parting speech at the dinner given him in May, 1826, just before his departure for Europe, had publicly announced his determination of devoting himself to this subject during his absence abroad. "Encouraged by your kindness," he said, "I will take this opportunity of recording the deeds and sufferings of a class of men to which this nation owes a debt of lasting gratitude — a class of men among whom, I am always ready to declare, not only the earliest, but many of the happiest days of my youth have been passed." The necessity of providing for his family and of paying off debts incurred by others, but for which he was responsible, had prevented the immediate carrying out of this resolution. But it had always been in his thoughts. The delay in the preparation probably added to the value of the history; but its reception would unquestionably have been far different had it been brought out in the height of his popularity.

It was a work which for many reasons it was a hard task to make accurate, and a still harder one to make interesting. With slight exceptions the history could be little more than a record of detached combats; and a string of episodes, no matter how brilliant, can never have the attraction which belongs to unity and grandeur of movement. These last can alone characterize the operations of great fleets.

Still, for the writing of this history Cooper was peculiarly fitted. He had belonged to the navy in his early life. He had never ceased to feel the deepest interest in its reputation and prosperity. He had contributed to the "Naval Magazine," a periodical published during 1836 and 1837, a series of papers connected with the improvement of its condition. He was, moreover, on terms of intimacy with many of the officers who had won for it distinction; and through them he had access to sources of information that could not be gained from written authorities. He had, besides, the characteristic of loving truth for its own sake, and the disposition to endure any amount of drudgery and encounter any sort of toil in order to secure it. To this was added the special qualifications of the historical eye, which enabled him to seize the important facts in an infinite mass of detail, and the power of describing vividly what he saw clearly. Under such circumstances it was reasonable to expect that his work would satisfy all fair-thinking men. It is, perhaps, correct to say that it did so. But it also gave rise to a controversy which stretched over a longer period and surpassed, in the bitter feelings it aroused, any of the wars in which the navy itself had ever been engaged.

There were special difficulties to be encountered with readers on both sides of the ocean. On the one hand, Englishmen had usually forgotten to remember that during the war of 1812 there was any naval combat of importance fought except between the Shannon and the Chesapeake; and even at this day it would be difficult to find in an English writer any account of the naval operations of that war in which that particular engagement does not play the principal part. If any other was forced upon their attention it had become an article of their creed that an American frigate was little else than a line-of-battle ship disguised. Moreover, the effective force of the American vessel was, according to their theory, made up of deserters from the British service. These two explanations of any failure were often combined. It is in this way Captain Brenton, one of their naval historians, calmly shows how it was that the Constitution happened to capture the Guerrière. "We may justly say," he concludes his account, "it was a large British frigate taking a small one." On her part America was not to be outdone in her estimate of national prowess. It had become matter of firm faith with the inhabitants of the United States that their side had suffered no losses worth mentioning during the war of 1812; that the American vessel had been invariably successful, whenever there was any approach to equality of force; and that in every case it was the superior seamanship, courage, and skill of their officers and men that had decided the result in their favor, and not superiority in weight of metal.

Neither of these beliefs was of a kind likely to influence Cooper. He had got to that point of feeling in which he looked upon the public opinion of both England and America with a good deal of contempt. It was not to pamper the vanity or flatter the prejudices of either that he wrote, but to state the truth. For this he neglected nothing that lay in his power. He studied public documents of every kind, official reports, all the printed and manuscript material to which he could get access. From officers of the navy who had shared in the actions described he gathered much information which they alone were able to communicate. In one sense he was fully satisfied with what he had done. He did not pretend that in a work which involved the examination and sifting of an almost infinite number of details he had not made some errors. It was only that he had made none intentionally, and that he had put forth his most strenuous exertions to have what he wrote entirely free from mistake. Nor is it possible for any unprejudiced mind to read the history now and not feel the truth of the assertion. Its accuracy and honesty have sometimes been flippantly questioned, but usually by men who have not spent as many days in the study of the subject as Cooper did months. During his life-time imputations were made in a few cases upon the correctness of his statements. They met then, however, so speedy and effectual a refutation that it was not thought worth while to repeat the criticisms until he was in his grave. Cooper might be wrong in his conclusions ; but it was rarely safe to quarrel with his facts. There is more, however, in this history than freedom from intentional perversion of the truth. There are throughout the whole of it the calmness, the judicial spirit, the absence of partisanship which may not of themselves add anything to the interest of the narrative, but are worth everything for the impression of truthfulness it makes.

Impartiality is a quality, however, little apt to be commended where our own feelings and interests are concerned. Still, the general fairness of the work was admitted in England, with the qualification, of course that a perfectly trustworthy history could not come from this side of the water. A few malignant attacks were made upon it. One of these, which appeared in the "United Service Journal" for November and December, 1839, is of the nature of a prolonged roar rather than a criticism ; but it is worth noticing for the incidental evidence it furnishes of the intense rancor felt towards Cooper by many in England on account of his strictures upon that country in the two volumes devoted to it in his "Gleanings in Europe." The writer made the then usual profession of faith, that the work referred to had been completely crushed by the "Quarterly ;" moreover, that the novelist had been convicted by it of the blackest ingratitude for traducing the nation which, we learn from this notice, had fostered his talents for romance. No critic of Cooper, either in Europe or in this country, it is to be remarked here, ever seemed willing to concede that the author had any hand in gaining his own reputation. In America the newspapers constantly assured him that it was due entirely to them. Great Britain assumed that it was to her generous appreciation alone that he was known in either hemisphere. The European main-land was not behind the island in this feeling. "Undoubtedly," wrote Balzac, "Cooper's renown is not due to his countrymen nor to the English: he owes it mainly to the ardent appreciation of France." This sentiment of the novelist's obligation to Great Britain was uppermost in the heart of the reviewer in the "United Service Journal." An uneasy impression, however, weighed upon his mind lest Cooper, who had now suffered annihilation several times without injury, might have survived the particular one inflicted by the " Quarterly." He honestly confessed, therefore, that he had waited some months before criticising the " Naval History," so that he might not look at it with a jaundiced or malignant eye in consequence of his recollections of the previous work on England.

It is not worth while to take any further notice of this article, in which wretched criticism was put into still poorer English. But there was one of these reviews to which Cooper felt it incumbent on him to reply. This appeared in the " Edinburgh " for April, 1840. It was studiously fair in tone. It commended the American author's work in many respects. While doing so, however, it attacked him for having made no use of the " Naval History of Great Britain " by William James, a history which it spoke of in a gushing way as approaching " as nearly to perfection in its own line as any historical work perhaps ever did." It also labored heavily to break the force of some of Cooper's statements by charging him with making assertions without evidence or against evidence. James was a veterinary surgeon who had come to this country before the war of 1812 to practice his profession. After the breaking out of hostilities he left it, or rather, as he says, " escaped from it, before being taken prisoner into the interior " — whatever that may mean. In the early part of " the steelyard and arithmetical war," as Cooper phrased it, which has raged with extreme violence ever since the peace of Ghent, James bore a gallant and conspicuous part. He published a pamphlet on the subject, which, in 1817, came out expanded into a volume. In it he showed conclusively that his countrymen had been utterly wrong in supposing that they had met with any naval reverses during the war of 1812. The falsity of this assumption he satisfactorily established by explaining that the Americans were the most inveterate liars upon the face of the earth. By their deceptive and fraudulent accounts they had beguiled the English, a self-distrustful and self-depreciating people, into believing that they had been defeated, where they had really been victorious. Heroes, indeed, can be overcome by sufficient odds ; and James was always prepared with ample explanations to account for failure in special cases. He also convicted the officers of the American navy not merely of lying in their official reports — which was a duty expected of them both by government and people — but of cowardice in action, of misconduct in their operations, and of brutality toward enemies whom the chance of war threw into their power. A work like this not merely filled a gap in historical literature, it supplied a national want. It was accordingly received with such favor that its author went on to produce a history of the British navy from 1793 to the accession of George IV. In this he embodied his previous narrative ; and a grateful people has never ceased to cherish a work which showed it that it had succeeded where previously it had been laboring under the impression that it had failed.

For James and his history Cooper had unbounded contempt. This horse-doctor, as he termed him, he looked upon as being as well fitted to describe a naval engagement as the proverbial horse-marine would be to take part in one. Besides being incapable, he regarded him as eminently dishonest; as vaunting impartiality while elevating discreditable and improbable hearsay into positive assertion, and fortifying his falsehoods by a pretentious parade of figures and official documents.

It is hardly going too far to say that, in Cooper's opinion, the remarks of James on American affairs combined all possible forms of misstatement from undesigned misrepresentation to deliberate falsehood. There may be difference of opinion on this point; on another there can be none. The period covered by the British writer is on the whole the most glorious in the long and brilliant naval history of the greatest maritime power the world has ever known. Never was there a greater contrast between the spirit with which things were done and the spirit with which they were told. In no other history known to man does tediousness assume proportions more appalling, do figures seem more juiceless, do the stories of heroic achievement furnish less inspiration than in this of James. If it be true, as some modern writers say, that history to be of value must be void of interest, it may be conceded that this particular work is entitled to that praise of perfection accorded it by the Edinburgh Reviewer.

The judgment that held up such a history as a model was not likely to impress a man, who was still under the sway of the old-fashioned notion, that there was no absolutely necessary connection between dullness and accuracy. To this particular criticism Cooper replied in the "Democratic Review" for May and June, 1842. In the first article he exposed the ignorance and dishonesty of James. In the second he devoted himself to the assertions of the "Edinburgh." The game was hardly worth the candle. His arguments could not reach the men who alone needed to know them. In international quarrels of any kind there are few who read both sides. The feeling exists that it is not safe to contaminate the purity of one's faith in his country by the doubts that might arise from merely fancying that an opponent has reasons for his course worth considering. So it was in this case. Few people in the United States saw the " Edinburgh Review," none believed what it said. In England fewer knew even of the existence of the " Democratic Review."

The controversy that arose in this country was on an entirely different ground. It was one that could hardly have been foreseen. The personal hostility which Cooper had succeeded in drawing upon himself was never so conspicuously shown as in the treatment which his " Naval History" underwent. At first, indeed, it was received with general favor, though by many it was thought to give too much credit to the English. In a short time, however, attacks were made upon it so virulent, so causeless, and withal so simultaneous, that the mere fact would of itself afford reason for the suspicion that they were concerted. This was practically the case. A certain amount of preliminary detail will make the circumstances clear. The controversy was entirely about the account of a particular action in the war of 1812, and a work containing over fifty chapters was absolutely condemned as partisan and worthless for what was found on a few pages of one chapter.

The battle of Lake Erie was fought and won by Commodore Perry on the 10th of September, 1813. It presented the peculiarity that the Lawrence, the flagship of the victorious squadron, had struck to the enemy in the course of the engagement. There was a feeling prevalent among many at the time that Elliott, the second in rank, had not been cordial in his support of his commander, and had left him to bear for a long while the brunt of the fight without hastening in his vessel, the Niagara, to his help. This was, in particular, the general belief among those on board the Lawrence. Perry did not sanction this view at first. Urged by good-nature, according to the theory of his friends, he praised Elliott's conduct in his official report. He went even farther in a letter of the 19th of September. This was in reply to a note from Elliott stating that rumors were current that the Lawrence had been sacrificed because of the lack of proper exertion on the part of the second in command. "I am indignant," wrote Perry, "that any report should be in circulation prejudicial to your character as respects the action of the 10th instant. It affords me pleasure that I have it in my power to assure you that the conduct of yourself, officers, and crew was such as to merit my warmest approbation. And I consider the circumstance of your volunteering and bringing the smaller vessels up to close action as contributing largely to our victory." Such was the situation at the time. A few years later, however, a bitter quarrel sprang up between Perry and Elliott, which apparently owed a good deal of its rancor to the exertions of good-natured friends of both in communicating to each remarks made, or supposed to be made, by the other. An envenomed correspondence took place in 1818. It led to Elliott's challenging Perry, and Perry preferring charges against Elliott for his conduct at the battle of Lake Erie. In the letter accompanying the charges he gave as his reason for changing his opinion as to the behavior of his second in command, that he had been put into possession of fresh facts. The government took no action in the matter, and in the following year Perry died. In 1834 Elliott became the mark of hostility of the Whig press on account of his putting

14

the figure of Andrew Jackson at the figure-head of the Constitution, the war-ship of which he was in command. The old scandal about his conduct at Erie was revived. Elliott did more than defend himself. A life of him was published in 1835, written by another, but from materials evidently that he himself had furnished. It claimed that the success of the battle of Lake Erie was mainly due to his efforts. It naturally produced a feeling of intense bitterness among Perry's friends and relatives. This was the way matters stood at the time that the " Naval History " was brought out.

Cooper entered upon the account of the battle of Lake Erie with the common prejudice against Elliott. Nor were efforts lacking to keep it alive and strengthen it, when it was reported in naval circles that he had begun to be uncertain about the justice of his original impressions. Captain Matthew Perry, the brother of the Commodore, forwarded him all the sworn documentary evidence that made against Elliott. He neglected to send any that was given in his favor. Cooper was not the man to be satisfied with this way of writing history. As he examined the subject more and more, he was struck by the conflicting character of the testimony, and the doubt that overhung the whole question. He came finally to the conclusion that it was not a matter he could settle, or, perhaps, any one. He accordingly contented himself with giving as accurate an account of the battle of Lake Erie as he could without entering at all into the details of the controversy. He made not the slightest effort to detract from the praise due to Perry, and, indeed, paid the highest tribute to his skill and conduct. Nor did he give to Elliott any prominence whatever.

He had committed, however, the unpardonable sin. He had refused to attack Elliott. He had preferred to accept Perry's original account of the battle, written within five days after it had taken place, to the view he took of it not only five years later, but also after a bitter personal quarrel had sprung up between him and his former second in command. While Cooper had made no special mention of the latter, he had spoken of him respectfully. There was a general feeling that Elliott ought to have been attacked. He was a very unpopular man, and, perhaps, deservedly so; while Perry was both a popular favorite and a popular hero. The refusal of Cooper to join in the general denunciation brought down upon him, not only those who honestly believed him in the wrong, but the whole horde of his own personal enemies who knew little and cared less about this particular subject. In the long list of controversies which the student of literature is under the necessity of examining, none seems so uncalled for and so discreditable to the assailants as this. For it is to be borne in mind that the historian had not made the slightest attempt to injure Perry in the popular estimation, or to elevate the subordinate at the expense of the commander. Yet assertions of this kind were constantly bandied about, though it would not have taken five minutes' reading of the work to have shown their falsity. Cooper was frequently spoken of by the press as the detractor of American fame and the slanderer of American character, because he refused to say, on one-sided evidence, that an officer of the United States navy had been willing to sacrifice his superior in a hotly contested battle and imperil the result for the sake of ministering to his own personal ambition, or of gratifying a feeling of personal dislike and envy, of the existence of which at the time there was no proof.

Space here exists to notice only the elaborate attacks to which Cooper himself felt constrained to reply. The first of these appeared in four numbers of the " New York Commercial Advertiser " during June, 1839. The articles were written by William A. Duer, who had lately been president of Columbia College. They purported to be a review of the " Naval History," but nothing whatever was said about that work beyond the few pages in which the battle of Lake Erie is described. They were, moreover, so personal in their nature and contained imputations so gross on his character, that Cooper began a libel suit against the journal in which they were published. This finally resulted in one of the most extraordinary trials that has ever been recorded in merely literary annals. The attack in the " Commercial Advertiser " was followed by a similar one in the " North American Review." This was written, however, with more decency, though it again devoted itself mainly to the battle of Lake Erie. It was the work of Alexander Slidell Mackenzie, a naval author, who by three books of travel had gained at the time some literary notoriety. But the notoriety never rose to reputation; and the history which preserves his name at all, preserves it in connection with an event it were well for his memory to have eternally forgotten. It is to be added that he was the brother-in-law of Captain Matthew Perry, and that Duer was his uncle. Hardly had his broadside been delivered, when another attack appeared. The victor of Lake Erie had come from Rhode Island, and Rhode Island rushed to the fray, not to defend her son — for he had not been attacked — but to build up his reputation by ruining that of his enemy. Tristam Burges, when the biography of Elliott, already referred to, had appeared, had delivered a lecture on the battle of Lake Erie before the Rhode Island Historical Society. It was not printed at the time; but no sooner was Cooper's work published than, at the request of Perry's friends and relatives, it was brought out with documents appended. The lecture reads very much like a stump speech of the extreme florid type. It is needless to say that in it Elliott got his full deserts for betraying his commander. It made no direct reference to Cooper, but the whole object was to discredit the account of the battle which he had given.

Even this was not all. Mackenzie prepared a life of Perry, which was published early in 1841. In it he attacked Elliott with great bitterness, and was careful to give in an appendix all the sworn testimony on one side, and leave out all the sworn testimony on the other. The biography met with general favor. It was styled a noble work, and the courage manifested by the author in assailing an unpopular man and celebrating a popular hero was, for some reason hard now to be understood, highly commended on all sides. The intense partisanship of the biography can be read on almost every page. But it was warmly welcomed everywhere, for Elliott had few friends even in his own profession. The " North American Review " for July, 1841, in an article written by the present Admiral Charles H. Davis, congratulated the navy on now having a work which gave a true and faithful report of the battle of Lake Erie, and stigmatized Cooper's account as false in spirit, statement, and comment.

This was, indeed, the general charge. For a while

Cooper was under as heavy a bombardment as Perry himself had been in his flag-ship. That his feelings were outraged by the injustice of it there can be no question, but it never daunted his spirit. Yet he took not the slightest step without being sure of his ground. He went over the evidence again and again. He talked with officers of the navy who held views opposed to his own; though he said afterward he rarely found that they knew anything about the matter beyond common report. With the exception of a few newspaper articles, however, he published nothing directly in reply until four years after his history was published. In the mean while he pressed the suit against William L. Stone, the editor of the "Commercial Advertiser." That paper at first took the prosecution in the jocular and insolent way then common with the press. Under an announcement of "Stand Clear," it informed its readers early in August, 1839, that "the interesting Mr. J. Effingham Fenimore Cooper is to bring a libel suit against us. None will approach it in interest, importance, or amusement." The editor was telling more truth than he thought. No action, however, was taken by Cooper for nearly a year to carry out his expressed intention. But he could always be depended upon. His suits, though sometimes long in coming, were sure to come at last. Great was the surprise of the editor when, in May, 1840, a process was served upon him for a libel printed eleven months before. He was indignant that the prosecutor had waited so long. A demurrer was filed and argued in July, 1840, at the Utica term of the Supreme Court. The decision was against the defendant. Things now began to look more serious; for while the importance of the suit was increasing, its amusement was diminishing.

It, however, hung on in the courts for a year and a half longer. The defendant was naturally unwilling to hasten a trial which was almost certain to end in an adverse verdict. Negotiations between the parties in the autumn of 1841 resulted in a novel agreement. Cooper did not care for damages. It was not money he sought; it was to vindicate the truth of his history and his character as an historian. When, therefore, his adversary suggested that an ordinary jury of twelve men could not well pass upon a question involving the value of conflicting evidence, and minute technical detail, he seized upon the occasion to arrange that it should be tried before a body of referees, consisting of three distinguished lawyers. The proposal was accepted. Never was the eternal question between author and reviewer settled in a more singular and a more thorough way. For the referees were to decide, not merely upon legal points, but upon moral ones. They were to decide whether the author had written a truthful account of the battle of Lake Erie, and whether he had written it in a spirit of truth. On the other hand, they were to decide whether the reviewer had written matter libelous enough to justify a verdict from a jury, and whether in the treatment of the subject for which he criticised the history he had been just and impartial. If the decision were in favor of the author the defendant was not to pay more than two hundred and fifty dollars besides the costs. In any case the beaten party was to publish the full text of the decision, at his own expense, in the cities of New York, Albany, and Washington. The referees agreed upon were Samuel Steevens, named by Cooper; Daniel Lord, Jr., named by Stone; and Samuel A. Foot, chosen by mutual consent. The attendance of many witnesses was rendered unnecessary by the stipulation that a vast mass of documentary testimony in possession of Cooper should be taken in evidence.

The referees met in the United States court room in New York city, on the afternoon of Monday, May 16, 1842. A large crowd was in attendance. Public interest had been aroused, not only by the question involved and the novel character of the suit, but by the fact that the historian was to assume the principal conduct of his own side. The trial lasted for five days. After the opening speeches had been made, the taking of oral testimony began. Among the witnesses for the defense were Sands, Mackenzie, and Paulding, all officers of the navy. They were examined in reference to Cooper's account of the battle of Lake Erie and the diagrams by which he represented the positions of the vessels during the engagement. Their views were in all respects opposed to the theory of operations which he had assumed. After the taking of the oral testimony was ended and certain legal questions had been argued, the summing up was begun by William W. Campbell of Otsego, the leading lawyer for the defense. His speech was exceedingly able and effective. Men who were present at the proceedings asserted, when it was finished, that there was no possible way in which its reasoning could be shaken, still less overthrown. At eight o'clock on Thursday evening Cooper began summing up for the prosecution, and continued until ten. On Friday he resumed his argument at four in the afternoon, and six hours had passed before he concluded. His conduct of the case from the beginning had excited surprise and admiration. Friends and foes alike bore witness to the signal ability he had displayed throughout;

but his closing speech made an especially profound impression. Its interest, its ingenuity, and its effectiveness were conceded by the defendant himself. It was for a long time after spoken of as one of the finest forensic displays that had ever been witnessed at the New York bar. Among those present at the trial was Henry T. Tuckerman, who has left us an account of the circumstances and of the bearing of the man. "A more unpopular cause," he wrote, "never fell to the lot of a practiced advocate; for the hero of Lake Erie was and had long been one of the most cherished of American victors. We could not but admire the self-possession, coolness, and vigor with which the author, on this occasion, played the lawyer. Almost alone in his opinion, — the tide of public sentiment against his theory of the battle, and the popular sympathy wholly with the received traditions of that memorable day, — he stood collected, dignified, uncompromising; examined witnesses, quoted authorities, argued nautical and naval precedents with a force and a facility which would have done credit to an experienced barrister. On the one hand, his speech was a remarkable exhibition of self-esteem, and on the other, a most interesting professional argument; for when he described the battle, and illustrated his views by diagrams, it was like a chapter in one of his own sea-stories, so minute, graphic, and spirited was the picture he drew. The dogmatism was more than compensated for by the picturesqueness of the scene; his self-complacency was exceeded by his wonderful ability. He quoted Cooper's 'Naval History' as if it were 'Blackstone;' he indulged in reminiscences; he made digressions and told anecdotes; he spoke of the manœuvres of the vessels, of the shifting of the wind, of the

course of the fight, like one whose life had been passed
on the quarter-deck. No greater evidence of self-re-
liance, of indifference to the opinion of the world, and
to that of his countrymen in particular, of the rarest descriptive talent, of pertinacity, loyalty to personal conviction, and a manly, firm, yet not unkindly spirit, could
be imagined than the position thus assumed, and the
manner in which he met the exigency. As we gazed
and listened, we understood clearly why, as a man,
Cooper had been viewed from such extremes of prejudice and partiality ; we recognized at once the generosity
and courage, and the willfulness and pride of his character : but the effect was to inspire a respect for the man,
such as authors whose errors are moral weaknesses
never excite."

On the 16th of June the referees rendered their decision on the eight points submitted to them for adjudi-
cation. In regard to five of these they were all in full
agreement ; but in three instances one of the referees
dissented from certain portions of the report made by
the other two.

The first point was whether, according to the evidence and the rules of the law the plaintiff would be
entitled to the verdict of a jury in an ordinary suit for
libel. They agreed that he would, and accordingly
awarded the damages that had been fixed by the original stipulation.

The second point was whether in writing his account
of the battle of Lake Erie, Cooper had faithfully fulfilled his obligations as an historian. The majority of
the referees decided that he had so done. Mr. Foot dissented to this extent, that Cooper had intended to do so,
but that from error of judgment or from some cause

not impugning the purity of his motives, he had failed in one specified point. This was that the narrative gave the impression that Elliott's conduct in the battle had met with universal approbation, which it had not. The arbitrator added, however, that this was the only particular in which it appeared to him that the historian had failed in fulfilling the high trust he had taken upon himself.

The third point was whether the narrative of the battle of Lake Erie was true or not in its essential facts, and if untrue, in what particulars. The majority decided that it was true. Mr. Foot dissented on the same point, to the same extent, and for the same reason, for which he had dissented from the second.

The fourth point was whether the account of the battle was written in a spirit of impartiality and justice. They all agreed that it was so written.

The fifth point was whether the writer of the criticism, upon which the suit was founded, had faithfully fulfilled the office of a reviewer. If not they were to give the facts upon which their conclusion was based. They unanimously agreed that the writer had not faithfully discharged his obligations as a reviewer; that he had indulged in personal imputations; that he was guilty of misquotations which materially changed the meaning; that his statements were incorrect in several particulars; and that his charge that Cooper had given to Elliott equal credit with Perry in the conduct of the battle was untrue. This last assertion, they add, was made after a careful examination by them of the history itself.

The sixth point was whether the review was true or not in its essential facts; and if untrue, in what particulars. They all agreed that it was untrue, and gave the particulars.

The seventh point was whether the review was written in a spirit of impartiality and justice. The majority decided that it was not so written. Here again Mr. Foot made a partial dissent. He considered the review to have been written under the influence of a wakeful sensibility, inconsiderately and unnecessarily aroused in defense of the reputation of a beloved and deceased friend.

The eighth point was to settle which of the two parties should be required to publish the full text of the decision at his own expense in newspapers published in New York, Washington, and Albany. The referees agreed that this was to be done by the defendant.

Thus ended this suit. For Cooper the result was a great personal triumph. He had had to contend with the prejudices of a nation. For months and years he had been persistently assailed with all the weapons that unscrupulous partisanship or unreasoning family affection could wield. He had been compelled to identify his own cause with that of a man who, in addition to unpopularity with members of his own profession, had drawn upon himself the hostility of a political party. He had been under the necessity of controverting, in some particulars, a generally accepted belief. Against him had been arrayed two of the ablest lawyers of the bar. Naval officers of reputation had on the witness stand criticised his theory of the battle and contradicted his statements. He had been assisted in the conduct of the case by his nephew; but outside of this he had received help from no one. Sympathy with him, there was little; desire for his success, there was less; and the ref-

erees could hardly fail to feel to some extent the influence that pervaded the whole country. In the face of
all these odds he had fought the battle and won it. He
had wrung respect and admiration from a hostile public
sentiment which he had openly and contemptuously defied. Upon the essential matters in dispute the verdict
of three men, of highest rank in their profession and
skilled in the weighing of conflicting evidence, had been
entirely in his favor.

Cooper followed up his victory by a pamphlet which
appeared in August, 1843, entitled, "The Battle of
Lake Erie: or, Answers to Messrs. Burges, Duer, and
Mackenzie." In this he went fully over the ground.
No reply was made to it; there was in fact none to
be made. The popular tradition could best be maintained by silence. Silence at any rate during his life-
time was preserved, and silence in cases where it would
have been creditable to have said something. It certainly affords justification additional to that already
given, for the contemptuous opinion expressed by
Cooper of the American press, that the newspapers
which had been loudest in the denunciation of his history, never so much as alluded to the result of the trial
brought to test authoritatively the fairness and impartiality of the narrative for which he had been condemned.

After reading patiently all that has been written on
both sides of this question, it seems to me that not only
was the verdict of the arbitrators a just one, but that
Cooper was right in the view he took. Still, where
evidence is conflicting there is ample room for difference
of opinion; and in regard to the conduct of Elliott at
Lake Erie the evidence is diametrically opposed. The
only secure method, therefore, of obtaining and main-

taining a comfortable bigotry of belief on the subject is to read carefully the testimony on one side and to despise the other so thoroughly as to refrain from even looking at it. This was then and has since been the course followed by the thick and thin partisans of Perry. But whether the conclusion be right or not at which Cooper arrived, there was never the slightest justification for the gross abuse to which he was subjected. He had everything to gain by falling in with the popular tradition and attacking Elliott. Nothing but lofty integrity and love of truth could have made him take the course he did. If a mistake at all, it was a mistake of judgment. But the charges brought against him were based in most instances upon deliberate misrepresentation of what he had said. This was especially true of the criticisms of Duer and Mackenzie. The perversion of meaning of one of his foot-notes is a striking instance of the unscrupulous nature of these attacks. In this Cooper had spoken of the vulgar opinion which celebrated as an act of special gallantry Perry's passing in an open boat from one ship to another as being the very least of his merits; that the same thing was done in the same engagement by others, including Elliott; that there was personal risk everywhere; and that Perry's real merit was his indomitable resolution not to be conquered, and the manner in which he sought new modes of victory when old ones failed. If this be depreciatory, it is depreciatory to say that greater honor is due to him who manifests the skill and fertility of resource of a commander than to him who exhibits the mere valor of a soldier. But in Duer's review of the " Naval History," and Mackenzie's " Life of Perry," the purport of the note was entirely changed. The concluding portion was dishonestly omitted, and a paragraph that gave to the victor of Lake Erie credit for generalship rather than soldiership was converted into an assertion that the risk he had run was of slight consequence.

This controversy brought in its train another libel suit. To the editor of the "Commercial Advertiser" the result had caused deep mortification. The reviewer also was naturally dissatisfied with a decision which left upon him the stigma of a libeler. He offered, if the case could be brought before a common jury for another trial, to pay double the amount of damages awarded, provided the result was against him. With such an arrangement Mr. Stone declined to have anything to do. He had had, he said, annoyance enough already with the suit. But he was tempted in a moment of vexation to indulge in remarks which implied that Cooper was in a hurry to get the sum awarded, with the object of putting it into Wall Street "for shaving purposes." The insinuation was uncalled for and unjustifiable; and as the editor subsequently admitted that it was only made in jest, it may be imputed to his credit that he had the grace to be ashamed of it. A libel suit, however, followed. It was at first decided in Cooper's favor. It was then carried up to the Court of Errors, and in December, 1845, more than a year after Mr. Stone's death, that tribunal reversed the decision. The result of the trial was hailed with the keenest delight by the Whig press of the state. "The Great Persecutor," as he was sometimes styled, had been finally foiled. "The rights of the press," said one of the newspapers, "are at last triumphant over the tyranny of courts and the vile constructions of the law of libel." The value of the victory, however, was largely lessened by the little respect in which the Court of Errors was held. This tribunal, which consisted in the majority of cases of the Chancellor and of the members of the state Senate, was swept away by the Constitution of 1846. Its influence had gone long before. Cooper was doubtless giving expression to the general feeling as well as venting his own indignation at this particular decision when he spoke of it, as he did a little later, as a "pitiful imitation of the House of Lords' system," by which a body of "small lawyers, country doctors, merchants, farmers," with occasionally a man of ability, were constituted the highest tribunal in the state.

Two other results followed incidentally this controversy about the battle of Lake Erie. One had the nature of comedy, the other partook rather of that of tragedy. Perry, as has been said, was a Rhode Islander, and many of the men he had with him had come from that state. Tristam Burges, in his lecture, had, in many instances, allowed his eloquence to get the better of his sense. In the preface to it, when published, he abandoned the latter altogether. He twice asserted, and gave his reasons for it, that "the fleet and battle of Erie" were to be regarded "as a part of the maritime affairs of Rhode Island." Apparently, however, the whole state took the same view. There seemed to be a feeling prevalent in it that its own reputation lay in destroying the reputation of Perry's second in command. In 1845 Elliott had a medal struck in honor of Cooper. It bore on one side the head of the author surrounded by the words, "The Personification of Honor, Truth, and Justice." At the suggestion of John Quincy Adams copies were sent to the various historical societies of the country. That statesman himself undertook their transmission. Accordingly one was forwarded among the rest to the Rhode Island Society. It reached its destination in March. It threw that body into a tumult of excitement. The trustees reflected upon it anxiously. They referred it to a committee. After prolonged brooding the committee gave birth to a preamble and two resolutions. These were reported to the Society at the meeting of the 10th of September. In one of the resolutions the letter of Adams was embodied, and he was thanked for the care and attention he had displayed in the discharge of the trust committed to him by Commodore Elliott. The second resolution recited substantially that Cooper had not been conducting himself properly in the matter, and had published opinions which the Society could not adopt or sanction. It therefore declined to accept the medal in his honor, and directed the president to transmit it to Adams with the request to return it to Commodore Elliott. Vigorous as this action may now seem, it did not then come up to the level of offended justice. There was to be no tampering with iniquity, even in high places. Elliott was not to succeed in his impudent effort to skulk behind the character of Adams, nor was Adams to escape reproof for the base uses to which he had allowed himself to be put. A motion was accordingly made to strike out the resolution conveying to that statesman the thanks of the Society. It was carried unanimously. The medal was accordingly returned to him with the request that he send it to Elliott with an attested copy of the resolution. Adams's conception of an Historical Society was different from that then entertained in Rhode Island. He clearly thought it no part of their business to be officially engaged in upholding the reputation of favorite

15

sons, or defending the character of heroes. His reply
was curt, not to say tart. " I decline the office," he
wrote, "requested of me by the Historical Society of
Rhode Island, and hold the medal and the copy of the
resolution, which they request me to transmit to Commodore Elliott, to be delivered to any person whom
they, or you by their direction, may authorize to receive them."

Cooper apparently said nothing about this action at
the time. He had before been solemnly warned by the
Providence newspapers not to risk a controversy with
Burges, or, as they more graphically expressed it, not
to " get into the talons of the bald-headed eagle of
Rhode Island." The threatened danger, however, had
not deterred him from exposing the absurdities into
which even eagles fall when they use their pinions for
writing and not for flying. Not even did he have the
fear of the Historical Society itself before his eyes. In
1850 he took occasion to pay his respects to that body.
He was then bringing out a revised edition of his novels.
In the preface to " The Red Rover," he mentioned the
stone tower at Newport, and referred to the way in
which he had been assailed for his irreverence in calling it a mill. He repeated this assertion as to its character. He expressed his belief that the building was more
probably built upon arches to defend grain from mice
than men from savages. " We trust," he added, " this
denial of the accuracy of what may be a favorite local
theory will not draw upon us any new evidence of the
high displeasure of the Rhode Island Historical Society, an institution which displayed such a magnanimous
sense of the right, so much impartiality, and so profound an understanding of the laws of nature and of the

facts of the day, on a former occasion when we incurred its displeasure, that we really dread a second encounter with its philosophy, its historical knowledge, its wit, and its signal love of justice. Little institutions, like little men, very naturally have a desire to get on stilts ; a circumstance that may possibly explain the theory of this extraordinary and very useless fortification. We prefer the truth and common sense to any other mode of reasoning, not having the honor to be an Historical Society at all." No reply, at least no public reply, came from that quarter during his life, to the views he had expressed. It was only when he was unable to defend himself that he was again assailed. In February, 1852, an account of the battle of Lake Erie was delivered before the Rhode Island Historical Society by Usher Parsons, who had been assistant surgeon on board the Lawrence. His testimony had been somewhat severely criticised by Cooper. Now that the latter was in his grave he took occasion to cast imputations upon the motives of the historian, and asperse the honesty of his statements. Parsons added nothing new of moment to the discussion, for what he said was merely a rehash, made in a very bungling way, of the old facts and assertions. But the spirit in which he wrote and the insinuations in which he indulged furnish ample justification for the low opinion which Cooper held of the evidence he had previously given.

With the parting shot in the preface to " The Red Rover," the controversy, on Cooper's part, concluded. He had, however, been concerned in another matter, in which the fortunes of his own work and the fortunes of one of its critics were strangely blended. In 1841 an abridged edition of his " Naval History " was brought out in one volume. The publisher was desirous of having it included in the list of books purchased for the district school libraries of New York. With this object in view he offered it, without Cooper's knowledge, to the Secretary of State, John C. Spencer, who was also superintendent of public instruction. To him was confided, by virtue of his office, the selection of the works which should constitute these libraries. He rejected the proposal with uncomplimentary brevity. He would have nothing to do, he informed the publisher, with so partisan a performance. Soon after this he emphasized his opinion of its partisanship by directing the purchase of Mackenzie's "Life of Perry" — a work which was almost avowedly one-sided. There was a retribution almost poetical in the tragedy that followed; for the same lack of mental balance and judgment that had been exhibited in this biography of Perry was to show itself under circumstances peculiarly harrowing. In October, 1841, Spencer joined the administration of John Tyler as Secretary of War. In December, 1842, Mackenzie, then in command of the United States brig Somers, gave a still further proof of his impartiality by hanging on the high seas Spencer's son, an acting midshipman, for alleged mutiny. It was done without even going through the formality of a trial. It was an act of manslaughter, not committed, indeed, from any feeling of malice, but merely from the same lack of judgment that he had displayed in the literary controversy in which he had been engaged. Mackenzie was brought before a naval court-martial, and succeeded with some difficulty in securing an acquittal. In 1844 the proceedings of the trial were published, and annexed to them was an elaborate review of the case by Cooper. It was written in a calm and temperate tone, but it practically settled the question of the character of the act.

Cooper's interest in the navy led him also to write a series of lives of officers who had been prominent in its history. The first of these appeared originally in "Graham's Magazine" for October, 1842, and the others are scattered through the volumes of that year and the years succeeding. In 1846 they were published in book form. Among them was a life of Perry. In this he took occasion to reaffirm what he had previously said about the battle of Lake Erie. But the injustice which had been done to him did not lead him to treat with injustice the man whose life he was writing, though it was impossible for him to say what would be satisfactory to Perry's partisans without falsifying what he believed to be the truth.

In spite of the numerous attacks made upon it the "Naval History" was successful, as success is measured in technical works of this kind. A second edition, revised and corrected, appeared in April, 1840, and in 1847 a third edition was published. At the time of his death Cooper was projecting a continuation of it, and had gathered together materials for that purpose. The original work ended with the close of the last war with Great Britain. He intended to bring it down to the end of the Mexican War. This was done by another after his death. In 1853 a new edition of the "Naval History" appeared with a continuation prepared by the the Reverend Charles W. McHarg. The matter that Cooper had collected was used, but there was very little in what was added that was of his own composition. Of the original work, it is safe to say, that for the period which it covers it is little likely to be superseded as the standard history of the American navy. Later investigation may show some of the author's assertions to be erroneous. Some of his conclusions may turn out as mistaken as have his prophecies about the use of steam in war vessels. But such defects, assuming that they exist, are more than counterbalanced by advantages which make it a final authority on points that can never again be so fully considered. Many sources of information which were then accessible no longer exist. The men who shared in the scenes described, and who communicated information directly to Cooper, have all passed away. These are losses that can never be replaced, even were it reasonable to expect that the same practical knowledge, the same judicial spirit, and the same power of graphic description could be found united again in the same person.

CHAPTER XI.

1840–1850.

No man could go through the conflicts which Cooper had been carrying on for so many years unharmed or unscarred. For the hostility entertained and expressed toward him in England he cared but little. But though too proud to parade his sufferings, the injustice done him in his own land aroused in his heart an indignation which had in it, however, as much pain as anger. He could not fail to see that he was in a false position, that his motives were misunderstood where even they were not deliberately misrepresented. The generation which had shared in his early triumphs and had gloried in his early fame had largely passed away. From some who survived he had been parted by a separation bitterer than that of death. To the new generation that had come on he appeared only as the captious and censorious critic of his country. His works were read in every civilized country. To many men they had brought all the little knowledge they possessed of America; to certain regions they could almost be said to have first carried its name. But the land which he loved with a passionate fervor seemed largely to have disowned him. It would be vain to deny his sensitiveness to this hostility. Traces of his secret feeling crop out unexpectedly in his later works. They reveal phases of his character which would never be inferred from his acts; they show the existence of sentiments which he would never have directly avowed. "There are men," says the hero of "Afloat and Ashore," "so strong in principle as well as in intellect, I do suppose, that they can be content with the approbation of their own consciences, and who can smile at the praise or censure of the world alike: but I confess to a strong sympathy with the commendation of my fellow-creatures, and a strong distaste for their disapprobation." Especially marked is the reference to himself in the words he puts into the mouth of Columbus in his "Mercedes of Castile." "Genoa," says the navigator, "hath proved but a stern mother to me: and though nought could induce me to raise a hand against her, she hath no longer any claim on my services. . . . One cannot easily hate the land of his birth, but injustice may lead him to cease to love it. The tie is mutual, and when the country ceases to protect person, property, character, and rights, the subject is liberated from all his duties."

It was the attacks connected with the controversy about the "Naval History" that more than anything else embittered Cooper's feelings. He had striven hard to write a full and trustworthy account of the achievements of his country upon the sea. Because he had refused to pervert what he deemed the truth to the gratification of private spite, he had been assailed with a malignity that had hardly stopped short of any species of misrepresentation. Rarely has devotion to the right met with a worse return. The reward of untiring industry, of patriotic zeal, and of conscientious examination of evidence, was little else than calumny and abuse. He felt so keenly the treatment he had received that he regretted having ever written the "Naval History" at all. In a published letter of the early part of 1843 he expressed himself on the matter in words that come clearly from the depths of a wounded spirit. " Were the manuscript of what has been printed," he wrote, " now lying before me unpublished, I certainly should throw it into the fire as an act of prudence to myself and of justice to my children." In his triumphant reply to Burges, Duer, and Mackenzie, while he showed the haughty disdain he felt for the popular clamor which had condemned him without knowledge, he did not seek to hide the bitterness it had caused. " This controversy," he said, " was not of my seeking; for years have I rested under the imputations that these persons have brought against me, and I now strike a blow in behalf of truth, not from any deference to a public opinion that in my opinion has not honesty enough to feel much interest in the exposure of duplicity and artifice, but that my children may point to the facts with just pride that they had a father who dared to stem popular prejudice in order to write truth."

It is in these last lines that Cooper unconsciously revealed the strength which enabled him to go through this roar of hostile criticism and calumny without having his whole nature soured. One great resource he possessed, and its influence cannot be overestimated. In the closest and dearest relations of life with which happiness is connected far more intimately than with the most prosperous series of outward events, he was supremely fortunate. In his own home his lot was favored beyond that of most men. However violent the storm without, there he could always find peace and trust and affection. The regard, indeed, felt for him by the female members of his family, may justly be termed devotion. Towards all women he exhibited deference almost to the point of chivalry. But in the case of those of his own household there was mingled with it a tenderness which called forth in return that ardent attachment which strong natures alone seem capable of inspiring. This deference and tenderness were the more conspicuous by contrast with his opinions. These would fill with wrath unspeakable the advocates of women's rights. Nor was he at all particular about mincing their expression. He sometimes gave utterance to them in the most extreme form. He even made his sentiments more emphatic by putting them into the mouths of his female characters. "There is," says the governess in "The Red Rover," "no peace for our feeble sex but in submission; no happiness but in obedience." In his last novel he denounced furiously the law that gave to the wife control over her own property, and predicted, as a consequence, all sorts of disasters to the family that have never come to pass. All this was eminently characteristic. But like many strong men tenacious of acknowledged superiority he was content with the mere concession. That granted, he would yield to submission infinitely more than recognized equality could have a right to expect or could hope to gain. We may think what we please of his views about women; there can be but one opinion as to his conduct towards them.

A characteristic instance of the wantonness with which Cooper's acts and motives were deliberately misrepresented during this period occurred in 1841. In that year came out a work, which had, in its day, some little notoriety, but has long ago passed to the limbo of forgotten things. It was called "The Glory and Shame of England." The very title shows that this production was maliciously calculated to make the British lion lash his tail with frenzy: and if we can trust its author, Mr. C. Edwards Lester, it met with fierce opposition from British residents in this country and their sympathizers. In an introductory letter addressed to the Reverend J. T. Headley, he told the story of the experiences his agents had undergone in securing subscriptions. In the course of it he made the following allusion to Cooper. "Already," he wrote, "have several educated and highly respectable young men engaged (with unprecedented success) in procuring subscribers for this work been rudely driven from the houses of Englishmen for crossing their threshold with the prospectus. And I blush (but not for myself or my country) to say that one of our celebrated authors, whose partiality for Republicanism has been more than doubted, threatened to kick one of these young men out of his house (castle) if he did not instantly leave it; exclaiming, 'Why have you the impudence to hand me that prospectus? I understand what the GLORY of England means; but as for the SHAME of England, there is no such thing. The shame is all in that base Democracy, which makes you presume to enter a gentleman's house to ask him to subscribe for such a work.'"

This statement was widely copied in the newspapers. But the falsity of the fabrication soon became too apparent for even the journals most hostile to Cooper to endure. They made a vain effort to get from the author a confirmation of his story: but though he did not venture to repeat the lie manfully, he equivocated about it in a sneaking way. The newspapers, feeling, perhaps, that it was undesirable to arm the book agent with new terrors, credited at once the denial the story had re-

ceived, and took back all imputations based upon it, —
a proceeding which ought to have shown Cooper that
they were not so utterly given over to the father of all
evil as he fancied them. But the author of this impudent falsehood never withdrew it, nor did the publishers
of the volume, in which it was contained, disavow it.
The extract given above is taken from an edition which
bears the date of 1845.

It is plain that these calumnious attacks sprang largely
from Cooper's personal unpopularity. It is equally
plain that his personal unpopularity was mainly due to
the censorious tone he had assumed in the criticism of
his country and his countrymen. It may accordingly
be said that, in one sense, he deserved all that he received. He had pursued a certain line of conduct. He
had no reason to complain that it had been followed by
the same results here that would have followed similar
conduct anywhere. In fact, while his censure of England had been far lighter than that of America, the
language used about him in the former country had been
far more vulgar and abusive than that used in the latter.
But there were facts in his career which his countrymen
were bound to bear in mind, but which, on the contrary,
they strove hard to forget, and sometimes to pervert.
He had been the uncompromising defender of his native
land in places where it cost reputation and regard to appear in that light. He was assailed largely by the men
who had toadied to a hostile feeling which he himself
had confronted. His criticism of America was sometimes just, sometimes unjust. It was in a few instances
as full of outrageous misrepresentation as any which he
had resented in others. Even when right, it was often
wrongly delivered. But in no case did it spring from

indifference or dislike. The very loftiness of his aspirations for his country, the very vividness of his conception of what he trusted she was to be, made him far more than ordinarily sensitive to what she was, which fell short of his ideal. Every indignity offered to her he felt as a personal blow; every stain upon her honor as a personal disgrace. He had no fear as to the material greatness of her future. What he could not bear was that the slightest spot should soil the garments of her civilization. It was for her character, her reputation, that he most cared. It is not necessary to maintain that he was as wise as he was patriotic. Had he been in a position where he wielded political power, his impulsive and fiery temperament might very probably have made him an unsafe adviser. His whole idea of foreign policy, as connected with war, may be summed up in the statement that the nation should be as ready to resent a wrong done to ourselves as to repair a wrong done to others. Nothing could be better doctrine in theory. Unfortunately, the nation in all such cases is itself both party and judge, and the question of right becomes, in consequence, a hard one to decide as a matter of fact. Cooper's intense convictions would therefore have been likely to have led the country into war, had he had the control of events, — and war, too, at a time when under the agencies of peace it was daily gathering strength to meet a coming drain upon its resources in a conflict which but few were then far-sighted enough to see would squander wealth as lavishly as it wasted blood. Had it rested with him, it is quite clear that no Ashburton treaty would have been signed. There is a striking passage printed to this day in italics, which he puts into the mouth of Leather-Stocking in the novel of "The

Deerslayer." Its point is made specially prominent when it is remembered that this work was written while the controversy was going on between Great Britain and the United States in regard to the Northeastern boundary. "I can see no great difference," says Leather-Stocking, "atween givin' up territory afore a war, out of a dread of war, or givin' it up after a war, because we can't help it — onless it be that the last is most manful and honorable."

The features of Cooper's personal character, as well as his prejudices and limitations, are always to be kept in mind because they explain much that is defective in his art, and account for much of his unpopularity. Some of them became unpleasantly conspicuous in the writings of his later years. In 1840 he entered upon a new period of creative activity which lasted until 1850. Between and including those years he brought out seventeen works of fiction. Eleven of them were written during the first half of this period ending with 1845, and even these did not constitute the whole of what he then wrote. This fertility is made the more remarkable by the fact that during this same time he was engaged in the special controversy about the battle of Lake Erie, not to speak of his standing quarrel with the press and his running fight of libel suits in which he was not only plaintiff, but did the main work of the prosecution.

It is possible that his unpopularity stirred him to unwonted exertion. There is certainly no question that the years from 1840 to 1845 inclusive, are, as a whole, the supreme creative period of Cooper's career. Its production does not dwarf his early achievement in vigor or interest; but it does often show a far higher mastery of his art. Two of the works then written

mark the culmination of his powers. These were the
Leather-Stocking tales called "The Pathfinder" and
"The Deerslayer." The former appeared on the 14th
of March, 1840, the latter on the 27th of August, 1841.
They complete the circle of these stories; for others
which he contemplated writing he unfortunately never
executed. Still the series was a perfect one as it was
left. The life of Leather-Stocking was now a complete
drama in five acts, beginning with the first war-path in
"The Deerslayer," followed by his career of activity
and of love in "The Last of the Mohicans" and "The
Pathfinder," and his old age and death in "The Pioneers" and "The Prairie."

"The Pathfinder" and "The Deerslayer" stand at
the head of Cooper's novels as artistic creations. There
are others of his works which contain parts as perfect as
are to be found in these, and scenes even more thrilling.
Not one can be compared with either of them as a finished whole. For once, whether from greater care or
happier inspiration, Cooper discarded those features of
his writings in which he had either failed entirely, or
achieved, at the most, slight success. The leading characters belonged to the class which he drew best, so far
as he was a delineator of character at all. Here were
no pasteboard figures like Heywood in "The Last of
the Mohicans," or Middleton in "The Prairie." Here
were no supernumeraries dragged in, in a vain effort to
amuse, as the singing-master in the former of these
same stories, or the naturalist in the latter. Humor,
Cooper certainly had; but it is the humor that gleams
in fitful flashes from the men of earnest purposes and
serious lives, and gives a momentary relief to the stern-
ness and melancholy of their natures. The power of

producing an entire humorous creation he had not at all, and almost the only thing that mars the perfectness of " The Pathfinder " is the occasional effort to make one out of Muir, the character designed to play the part of a villain. But the defects in both these tales are comparatively slight. The plot in each is simple, but it gives plenty of room for the display of those qualities in which Cooper excelled. The scene of the one was laid on Lake Ontario and its shores; the other, on the little lake near which he had made his home; and the whole atmosphere of both is redolent of the beauty and the wildness of nature.

These works were a revelation to the men who had begun to despair of Cooper's ever accomplishing again anything worthy of his early renown. They were pure works of art. No moral was everlastingly perking itself in the reader's face, no labored lecture to prove what was self-evident interrupted the progress of the story. There is scarcely an allusion to any of the events which had checkered the novelist's career. References to contemporary occurrences are so slight that they would pass unheeded by any one whose attention had not been called beforehand to their existence. These works showed what Cooper was capable of when he gave full play to his powers, and did not fancy he was writing a novel when he was indulging in lectures upon manners and customs. " It is beautiful, it is grand," said Balzac to a friend, speaking of " The Pathfinder." " Its interest is tremendous. He surely owed us this masterpiece after the last two or three rhapsodies he has been giving us. You must read it. I know no one in the world, save Walter Scott, who has risen to that grandeur and serenity of colors." " Never," he said in another place, " did the art of writing tread closer upon the art of the pencil. This is the school of study for literary landscape-painters." Cooper himself, if contemporary reports are to be trusted, was at the time in the habit of saying that the palm of merit in his writings lay between this novel and " The Deerslayer." He certainly reckoned them the best of the five stories which have the unity of a common interest by having the same hero, and these five he put at the head of his performances. " If anything from the pen of the writer of these romances," he said, toward the close of his life, " is at all to outlive himself, it is unquestionably the series of ' The Leather-Stocking Tales.' To say this is not to predict a very lasting reputation for the series itself, but simply to express the belief that it will outlast any or all of the works from the same hand."

But at this time no work of his was treated fairly by the American press. His name was rarely mentioned save in censure or derision. Both " The Pathfinder " and " The Deerslayer " on their first appearance were violently assailed. It is giving praise to a good deal of the contemporary criticism passed upon them to call it merely feeble and senseless. Much of it was marked by a malignity which fortunately was as contemptible intellectually as it was morally. Still, neither this hostile criticism nor Cooper's own personal unpopularity hindered the success of the books. He says, to be sure, in the preface to the revised edition of the Leather-Stocking tales which came out towards the end of his life, that probably not one in ten of those who knew all about the three earlier works of the series had any knowledge of the existence of the two last. This assertion seems exaggerated. It certainly struck many with

16

surprise at the time it was made; for both "The Path-finder" and "The Deerslayer" had met with a large sale.

Between the publication of these two novels appeared, on the 24th of November, 1840, "Mercedes of Castile." The subject of this was the first voyage of Columbus. It had several very obvious defects. It was marred by that prolixity of introduction which was a fault that ran through the majority of Cooper's tales. The reader meets with as many discouragements and rebuffs and turnings aside in getting under way as did the great navigator the story celebrates. There was, moreover, an excess of that cheap moralizing, that dwelling upon commonplace truths, which was another of Cooper's be-setting sins. The only effect these discourses have upon the reader is to make him feel that while virtue may be a very good thing, it is an excessively tedious thing. As a novel, "Mercedes of Castile" must be regarded as a failure. On the other hand, as a story of the first voyage of Columbus, told with the special knowledge of a seaman, the accuracy of an historian, and with some-thing of the fervor of a poet, it will always have a pe-culiar interest of its own.

Two sea-stories followed "The Deerslayer." The first of these, entitled "The Two Admirals," was pub-lished in April, 1842, and the second in November of the same year. Cooper was at this time engaged in the hottest of his fight with the American press and people. Publicly and privately he was expressing his contempt for nearly everything and everybody. He, in turn, was undergoing assaults from every quarter. It is, there-fore, a singular illustration of the love of country which burned in him with an intense, even when hidden, flame, that in the midst of his greatest unpopularity he was unwilling to desert his own flag for that of the land to which he was forced to go for material. Yet there was every inducement. He wished to do what had never before been done in fiction. His aim was to describe the evolutions of fleets instead of confining himself to the movements of single vessels. But no American fleet had ever been assembled, no American admiral had ever trod a quarter-deck. In order, therefore, to describe operations on a grand scale he had to have recourse to the history of the mother-country; but he purposely put the scene in "The Two Admirals" in a period when the states were still colonies. This novel takes a very high place among the sea-stories, so long as the action is confined to the water. But it suffers greatly from the carelessness and the incompleteness with which the details are worked out.

In "Wing-and-Wing," which followed it, the fortune of a French privateer is told. The scene is laid in the Mediterranean, and the time is the end of the last century. Though inferior in power to some of his other sea-stories, it is far from being a poor novel; and it was, in fact, one of the author's favorites. But its greatest interest is in the view it gives of a tendency in Cooper's character which was constantly becoming more pronounced. The Puritanic narrowness of the very deep and genuine religious element in his nature was steadily increasing as time went on. In "Precaution" it has been already observed that the doctrine had been laid down by one of the characters that there should be no marriage between Christians and non-Christians. In "Wing-and-Wing" this doctrine was fully carried out. The heroine is a devout Roman Catholic. She loves

devotedly the hero, the captain of the French privateer.
She trusts in his honor; she admires his abilities and
character; she is profoundly affected by the fervor of
the affection he bears to herself. But he is an infidel.
He is too honest and honorable to pretend to believe
and think differently from what he really believes and
thinks. As she cannot convert him, she will not marry
him: and in the end succeeds indirectly, by her refusal,
in bringing about his death. It never seemed to occur
to Cooper that the course of conduct he was holding up
as praiseworthy, in his novels, could have little other
effect in real life than to encourage hypocrisy where it
did not produce misery. The man who, for the sake of
gaining a great prize, changes his religious views is sure
to have his sincerity distrusted by others. That can be
borne. But he is equally certain to feel distrust of himself. He cannot have that perfect confidence in his
own convictions, or even in his own character, that
would be the case had no considerations of personal advantage influenced him in the slightest in the decision
he had made, or the conclusions to which he had come.
Even he who believes in this course of action as something to be quietly adopted might wisely refuse to pro-
claim it loudly as a rule for the conduct of life.

The next important work that followed was " Wyandotte; or the Hutted Knoll." It was published on the
5th of September, 1843. The story, as a whole, was a
tragic one. In spite of the fact that the events occur in
the place and time where some of the author's greatest
successes had been achieved, this novel is inferior to all
his others that deal with the same scenes. Certain man-
ifestations of his feelings and certain traits of character
indicated, rather than expressed, in the tales immediately

preceding, were in this one distinctly revealed. His dislike of the newspapers and the critics has been so often referred to that it needs hardly to be said that in all the writings of this period these offenders were soundly castigated. Especially was this true of the preface. It was there, if anywhere, that Cooper was apt to concentrate all the ill-humor he felt — his wrath against the race and his scorn of the individual. But the two feelings that henceforth became conspicuously noticeable in nearly all his writings were his regard for the Episcopal church and his dislike of New England. They manifest themselves sometimes deliciously, sometimes disagreeably. In the midst of a story remote as possible from the occurrences of modern life, suddenly turn up remarks upon the apostolic origin of bishops, or the desirability of written prayers, and the need of a liturgy. The impropriety of their introduction, from a literary point of view, Cooper never had sufficient delicacy of taste to feel. Less excusable were the attacks he made upon those whose religious views differed from his own. The insults he sometimes offered to possible readers were as needless as they were brutal. In one of his later novels he mentioned " the rowdy religion — half-cant, half-blasphemy, that Cromwell and his associates entailed on so many Englishmen." There is little reason to doubt that under proper conditions Cooper could easily have developed into a sincere, narrow-minded, and ferocious bigot.[1]

[1] Poe wrote a review of *Wyandotte* which appeared in *Graham's Magazine* for November, 1843. As notices of Cooper's novels then went, this may be regarded as a favorable one, though in it the critic took occasion to divide works of fiction into two classes: one of a popular sort which anybody could write, and the other of a kind intrinsically more worthy and artistic, and capable of being produced

Full as marked and even more persistent were his attacks upon New England. There was little specially characteristic of that portion of the country with which he did not find fault. New England cooking of the first class was inferior to that of the second class in the Middle States. The New Yorker of humble life, not of Yankee descent, spoke the language better than thousands of educated men in New England. This dislike kept steadily increasing. As late as 1844, if he sent his heroes to college at all, he sent them to Yale; after that year he transferred them to Princeton. With all this there is constantly seen going on a somewhat amusing struggle between his dislike and the thorough honesty of his nature, which forced him to admit in the men of New England certain characteristics of a high order. Their frugality, their enterprise, their readiness of resource, he could not deny. Still, he continued to imply that these qualities were used pretty generally for selfish ends. In his later works, in consequence, his villains were very apt to be New Englanders. They were not villains of a romantic type. They were mean rather than vicious; crafty rather than bold; given to degrading

only by the few. At the head of the former class he placed Cooper, but had the grace not to include his own name in the latter class which he had created for himself. The reader will be edified to learn from a life of Poe, written by John H. Ingram (2 vols., London, 1880), that the writing of this review was an act of heroic and even desperate hardihood. Poe, it seems, had before valorously depreciated Halleck; but his crowning act of courage is introduced with the statement that "he dared all *published* opinion, and in the very teeth of Cooper's supreme popularity ventured upon saying" the remarks which have already been referred to, and which are quoted in full by the biographer, to whom is also to be given the credit of the italicized word in the foregoing quotation. No small share of the common belief in regard to Cooper's character and career is based upon assertions about as trustworthy as this.

but at the same time cheap excesses. The first of these special representatives of the New England character is the powerful but somewhat unpleasant creation of Ithuel Bolt in "Wing-and-Wing," who finds a fitting sequel to a life passed largely in committing acts of doubtful morality in becoming a deacon in a Congregational church. After him follows a succession of personages who represent nearly every conceivable shade of craft, meanness, and dishonesty that is consistent with the respect of the Puritan community about them, and with a high position in the religious society of which they form a part.

There was, it must be admitted, some justification for Cooper's feelings towards New England on the score of retaliation. He had been criticised from the beginning in that part of the country with a severity that often approached virulence. He had been denied there the possession of qualities which the rest of the world agreed in according him. Cultivated society has always been afflicted with a class too superlatively intellectual to enjoy what everybody else likes. Of these unhappy beings New England has had the misfortune to have perhaps more than her proper share. It was hardly in human nature that the disparagement he received from these should not have influenced his feelings towards the region which had given them birth and consideration.

It is pleasant to turn aside from these scenes and sayings which show the least amiable side of a nature essentially noble, and pass to one of the little incidents that are strikingly characteristic of the man. On board the Sterling, the merchantman on which Cooper's first voyage was made, was a boy younger than himself. His name was Ned Myers. This person had spent his life on the sea. He had belonged to seventy-two crafts, exclusive of prison-ships, transports, and vessels in which he had merely made passages. According to his own calculation he had been twenty-five years out of sight of land. After this long and varied career he had finally landed in that asylum for worn-out mariners, the "Sailors' Snug Harbor." From here, late in 1842, he wrote to Cooper, asking him if he were the one with whom he had served in the Sterling. Cooper, who never forgot a friend, sent him a reply, beginning: "I am your old shipmate, Ned," and told him when and where he could be found in New York. There in a few months they met after an interval of thirty-seven years. Cooper took the battered old hulk of a seaman up to Cooperstown in June, 1843, and entertained him for several weeks. While the two were knocking about the lake, and the latter was telling his adventures, it occurred to the former to put into print the wandering life the sailor had led. Between them the work was done that summer, and in November, 1843, "Ned Myers; or, Life before the Mast" was published. This work has often been falsely spoken of as a novel. It is, on the contrary, a truthful record, so far as dependence can be placed upon the word or the memory of the narrator. "This is literally," said Myers, "my own story, logged by an old shipmate."

In 1842 Cooper had entered into an engagement to write regularly for "Graham's Magazine." This periodical, which had been formed not long before by the union of two others, had rapidly risen to high reputation, and claimed a circulation of thirty thousand copies. In the first four numbers of 1843 Cooper published the shortest of his stories. It was entitled "The Autobiography of a Pocket Handkerchief." For some reason not easy to explain, this has never been included in the regular editions of his novels. In it he made in some measure another effort to reproduce the social life of New York city. The previous failure was repeated. An air of ridiculous unreality is given to this part of the story in which the impossible talk of impossible people is paraded as a genuine representation of what takes place in civilized society. The autobiographical form which he had first adopted in this tale he continued in the two series of "Afloat and Ashore." These appeared respectively in June and in December, 1844. They are essentially one novel, though the second part goes usually in this country under the title of "Miles Wallingford," the name of its hero; and in Europe under that of "Lucy Harding," the name of its heroine.

This work, the first part more particularly, is a delightful story of adventure. As usual there are startling incidents, perilous situations, and hairbreadth escapes enough to furnish sufficient materials for a dozen ordinary fictions. Yet the probabilities are better preserved than in many of Cooper's novels where the events are far fewer, as well as far less striking. But it is interesting, not merely for the incidents it contains, but for the revelation it makes of the man who wrote it. Expressions of personal feeling and opinion turn up unexpectedly everywhere, and make slight but constantly recurring eddies in the stream of the story. Everything is to be found here which he had ever discussed before. The inferiority of the bay of New York to that of Naples; the miserable cooking and gross feeding of New England; the absolute necessity of a liturgy in religious worship; the contempt he felt for the misguided beings who presume to deny the exist-

ence of bishops in the primitive church; his aversion
to paper money; his disdain for the shingle palaces of
the Grecian temple school; his scorn of the idea that
one man is as good as another; these and scores of similar utterances arrest constantly the reader's attention.
But they do not jar upon his feelings as in many other
of his writings. They are essentially different in tone.
There runs through this series a vein of ill-natured amiability or amiable ill-nature — it is hard to say which
phrase is more appropriate — which gives to the whole
what horticulturists call a delicate sub-acid flavor. The
roar of contempt found in previous writings subsided in
these into a sort of prolonged but subdued growl. But
it is a case in which the reader feels that it is eminently
proper that the writer should growl. It is the old man
of sixty-five telling the tale of his early years. His preferences for the past do not irritate us, they entertain us.
It is right that the world about him should seem meaner
and more commonplace than it did in the fever-fit of
youth and love, when it was joy merely to live. The
work, moreover, has another characteristic that gives it
a whimsical attractiveness. It is a tale of the good old
times when New York had still some New York feeling
left; when her old historic names still carried weight
and found universal respect, and her old families still
ruled society with a despotic sway; and especially before the whole state had been overrun by the lank,
angular, loose-jointed, slouching, shrewd, money-wor-
shiping sons of the Puritans, whose restless activity had
triumphed over the slow and steady respectability of the
original settlers. The scene of this story, so far as it
is laid on land, is mainly in the river counties; but in
spite of that fact it is difficult not to think that some

recollections of the writer's own youth were not mingled in certain portions of it. Especially is it a hard
task not to fancy that in the heroine, Lucy Harding, he
was drawing, in some slight particulars at least, the picture of his own wife, and telling the story of his early
love.

The delineation of the New York life of the past
which he had in some measure accomplished in these
volumes, he now continued more fully in certain works
which took up successive periods in the history of the
state. The idea of writing them was suggested by
events that were taking place at the time. The troubles
which arose in certain counties of New York after the
death, in 1839, of Stephen Van Rensselaer, the patroon,
were now culminating in a series of acts of violence and
bloodshed, perpetrated usually by men disguised as Indians. The questions involved had likewise become
subjects of fierce political controversy. Cooper, who
saw in the conduct of the tenants and their supporters
a dangerous invasion of the rights of property, plunged
into the discussion of the matter with all the ardor of his
fiery temperament. He worked himself into the highest state of excitement over the proceedings. It was
his interest in this matter that led him to compose the
three works which are collectively called the Anti-rent
novels. These purport to be the successive records of
the Littlepage family, and each is in the form of an autobiography. They cover a period extending from the
first half of the eighteenth century down to the very
year in which he was writing.

It was about this time that Cooper's reputation
touched the lowest point to which it has ever fallen, so
far, at least, as it depends upon the opinion of critics

and of men of letters. He was now reaping the fruits of the various controversies in which he had been engaged, and of all the hostility which he had succeeded in inspiring. The two anti-rent novels which appeared in 1845 were " Satanstoe," published in June, and " The Chainbearer," published in November. They may have had a large sale. But there is scarcely a review of the period in which they are even mentioned. Even the newspapers contain merely the barest reference to their existence. It is perhaps partly due to this contemporary silence that these two stories are among the least known and least read of Cooper's productions. Moreover, they are constantly misjudged. The tone which pervades the concluding novel of the series is taken as the tone which pervades the two which preceded it. This is an injustice as well as a mistake. In no sense is " Satanstoe," in particular, a political novel. There is no reference to anti-rentism in it save in the preface. Its only connection with the subject is the account it gives of the manner in which the great estates were originally settled. On the other hand it is a picture of colonial life and manners in New York during the middle of the eighteenth century, such as can be found drawn nowhere else so truthfully and so vividly. It takes rank among the very best of Cooper's stories. The characters are, to a certain extent, the same as in " Afloat and Ashore ; " the main difference being, that in the one the events take place principally on land, and in the other on water. Even those majestic first families, whom he had celebrated before, loom up in these pages with renewed and increasing grandeur. But the story is throughout told in a graphic and spirited manner, and as it approaches the end and details the scenes that follow Abercrombie's repulse at Lake George in 1737, it becomes intensely exciting. The villain of the tale is, of course, a New Englander, in this instance a long, ungainly pedagogue from Danbury, Connecticut. He does not, however, blossom out into the full perfection of his rascality until he makes his appearance in " The Chainbearer," the next novel of the series. This tale, though decidedly inferior to " Satanstoe," contains passages of great interest. The description, especially, of the squatter family and the life led by it, is one of Cooper's most powerfully drawn pictures.

It has been the misfortune of this series that the member of it which has attracted most attention is "The Redskins; or, Indian and Injin," which came out in July, 1846. This is one of three or four books which, in a certain way, give one a high idea of Cooper's power in the fact that his reputation has been able to survive them. If he had been anxious to help the antirenters and hurt the patroon, he could hardly have done better than to write this book. As a story it has no merit. The incidents told in it are absurd. It is full, moreover, of the arguments that irritate but do not convince; and is liberally supplied, in addition, with prophecies that have never been realized. Everything that was disagreeable in Cooper's manner and bungling in his art, was conspicuous in this work. His dislikes were not uttered pleasantly, as in " Afloat and Ashore," but with an ill-nature that often bordered upon ferocity. A tone of pretension ran through the whole, a constant reference to what men think who had seen the world, with the implied inference that those who disagreed with the author in opinion had not seen the world. The feeling of the reader is, that if this extravagance and over-statement be the result of travel, men had better stay at home. Nor did Cooper refrain from dragging in everything with which he had found fault before. We are not even spared the everlasting reference to the bays of New York and of Naples. The work is what he himself would have called provincial in the worst sense of that word. Even more than its spirit was its matter extraordinary for a work of fiction. Part of it is little else than a controversial tract on the superiority of Episcopacy; and the temper in which it is written could hardly have been grateful to any but an opponent of that church. "Satanstoe" is full of many of Cooper's likes and dislikes, but there can be no greater contrast conceived than between the tone which pervades that delightful creation, and the boisterous brawling of "The Redskins.

With the publication of this series Cooper's career as a creator of works of imagination practically closed. He wrote several novels afterward, but not one of them did anything to advance his reputation. Some of them tended to lower it. This was not due to failure of power, but to its misdirection. The didactic element in his nature had now gained complete mastery over the artistic. The interest, such as it is, which belongs to his later stories, is rarely a literary interest. Not one of them has the slightest pretension to be termed a work of art. There are, at times, passages in them that thrill us, and scenes that display something of his old skill in description. But these are recollections rather than new creations. Cooper's fame would not have been a whit lessened, if every line he wrote after "The Chainbearer" had never seen the light.

The works that came out during the remaining years

of his life were " The Crater," published October 12, 1847 ; " Jack Tier," published March 21, 1848 ; " The Oak Openings," published August 24 of the same year; " The Sea Lions," published April 10, 1849, and " The Ways of the Hour," published April 10, 1850. Of these " Jack Tier " originally made its appearance in " Graham's Magazine" during the years 1845–1847, under the title of " The Islets of the Gulf," and strictly stands first in the order of time. It shares with " The Crater " the distinction of being one of the two best of these later stories. It may be fair to mention that Bryant saw in it as much spirit, energy, invention, and life-like presentation of objects and events as in anything the author ever wrote. This will seem exaggerated praise when one reads it in connection with " The Red Rover," of which it is in some respects a feeble reflection. It was hard for Cooper to be uninteresting when once fairly launched upon the waves. Without denying the existence in " Jack Tier " of passages of marked power, no small share of it was merely a reproduction of what had been done and better done before. The old woman who is constantly misusing nautical terms is the most palpable imitation of the admiral's widow in " The Red Rover." It is a cheap expedient at best, and must at any time be used with extreme moderation. Above all, it is a device which is abused the very moment it is repeated. As displayed in " Jack Tier," it is simply unendurable. Cooper's silly people, in facts are apt to be silly not only beyond human experience but almost beyond human conception. The tragedy, moreover, with which this novel ends is intended to be terrible, while as a matter of fact it is merely grotesque and absurd. The tale reaches a sudden but necessary conclusion be-

cause nearly all the characters are disposed of at once
by drowning or killing. There is scarcely any one left
to carry on the action of the story.

"The Crater," which in one sense followed and in
another preceded "Jack Tier," has a very special interest to the student of Cooper's character. He had
now lived for so long a time a life remote from the real
clash of conflicting views that he had finally reached
that satisfied state of opinion which thinks the little
circle in which it moves is the proper orbit for the revolution of thought of the whole race. As he advanced
in years he narrowed instead of broadening. The intensity of his faith coupled with his energy of expression makes this fact very conspicuous ; and in "The
Crater" the reader is alternately attracted by the
shrewd and keen remarks of the writer, and repelled
by his illiberality. This novel tells the tale of a ship-
wrecked mariner cast away on a reef not laid down in
any chart and unknown to navigators. This barren
spot he makes bud and blossom as the rose. To the
new Utopia he has created in the bosom of the Pacific
he brings a body of emigrants. Their proceedings are
entertainingly told. But the history of the decline of
the colony from its primitive state of happiness and perfection, which is designed to furnish a warning, tends
instead to fill the irreverent with amusement. While
under the control of its founder and governor, who
combined all the virtues, it is represented as enjoying
peace and prosperity. Demagogism had no control.
The reign of gossip had not begun. The great discovery had not been made that men were merely incidents of newspapers. Care was taken that the children
should not imbibe any false principles, that is, any princi-

ples which the ruling powers thought false. The schools
did not furnish much instruction, but owing to this con-
siderate watchfulness they were innocent if they were
inefficient. Still this ingenious arrangement for stopping
the progress of the human mind could not work forever.
From the start there was a dangerous element, though
in this case the colonists had not come from New England but from the Middle States. Very speedily that
innate depravity of the human heart which does not
like to hear a clergyman read prayers, which looks with
suspicion upon a liturgy, began to manifest itself. This,
however, was kept under control until the arrival of new
colonists. This Eden was then invaded not by one ser-
pent only, but by several. Four of them were clergymen ; one a Presbyterian, one a Methodist, one a Bap-
tist, and one a Quaker. This was too much for the
solitary Episcopalian who had previously been on the
ground, and who is represented as combining a weak
physical constitution with a very strong conception of
his apostolic authority as a divine. It must be conceded
that for a population of about five hundred souls the
supply of spiritual teachers was ample. With them
came also a lawyer and an editor. The seeds of dissolution were at once sown. The colonists became ungrateful, and began to inquire not only into the conduct
of their governor, but even into the title by which he held
some of his lands. He finally left the spot in disgust,
and having first taken the precaution to dispose of his
property at a good price, returned to his native country.
A natural yearning to see the community he had established led the discoverer to revisit, after a few months,
the scene of his trials. He sailed to the spot but he
could not find it. A convulsion of nature similar to

17

that which had raised the reef above the level of the waves had sunk it again out of sight. Ungrateful colonists, clergymen, editor, and lawyer, had all perished.

In June, 1847, Cooper made a trip to the West, and went as far as Detroit. One result of this journey was the novel of "The Oak Openings; or, the Bee-Hunter." This must be looked upon as a decided failure. The desire to lecture his fellow-men on manners had now given place to a desire to edify them; and he was no more successful in the one than he had been in the other. In this instance the issue of the story depends on the course of an Indian who is converted to Christianity by witnessing the way in which a self-denying Methodist missionary meets his death. The whole winding-up is unnatural, and the process of turning the organizing chief of a great warlike confederacy into a Sunday-school hero is only saved from being commonplace by being absurd. Far more singular, however, was the central idea of "The Sea Lions," the story that followed. This is certainly one of the most remarkable conceptions that it ever entered into the mind of a novelist to create. It shows the intense hold religious convictions were taking of Cooper's feelings, and to what extremes of opinion they were carrying him. In "Wing-and-Wing" the hero had been discarded because he was a thorough infidel. But Cooper's sentiments had now moved a long distance beyond this milk-and-water way of dealing with religious differences. In "The Sea Lions" the hero merely denied the divinity of Christ, while he professed to hold him in reverence as the purest and most exalted of men. But if there was any one point on which the heroine was sound and likewise inflexible, it was the doctrine of the Trinity. Whatever else she doubted, she was absolutely sure of the incarnation. She would not unite herself with one who presumed to "set up his own feeble understanding of the nature of the mediation between God and man in opposition to the plainest language of revelation as well as to the prevalent belief of the Church." In this case the hero is converted, apparently by spending a winter in the Antarctic seas. An important agent in effecting this change of belief is a common seaman who improves every occasion to drop into the conversation going on, some unexpected Trinitarian remark. When the master has almost against hope saved his vessel, and in the thankfulness of his heart invokes blessing on the name of God, Stimson is on hand at his elbow to add, "and that of his only and *true* Son." This novel is, indeed, a further but unneeded proof of how little Cooper was able to project himself out of the circle of his own feelings, or to aid any cause which he had near to his heart. He had had much to say about New England cant. Yet in this work he can find no words sufficiently strong to praise what he calls the zealous freedom and Christian earnestness of one of the most offensive canters that the whole range of fiction presents. It would be unjust to deny that when in "The Sea Lions" Cooper abandons his metaphysics and turns to his real business, that he creates a powerful story. One may almost be said at times to feel the cold, the desolation, the darkness, and the gloom of an Antarctic winter confronting and overshadowing the spirit. But there can be little that is more tedious than the dry chaff of theological discussion which is here threshed for us over and over again. Believers in the Trinity had as little reason as believers in Episcopacy to rejoice in Cooper's advocacy of their faith. There was nothing original in his views; there was nothing pointed or forcible in his statement of them. He meant to inculcate a lesson, and the only lesson that can possibly be drawn is the sufficiently absurd one that dwellers in the chilly spiritual clime of Unitarianism can be cured of their faith in that icy creed by being subjected to the horrors of a polar winter. Far more clearly does the novel show the falling-off in his artistic conceptions and the narrowing process his opinions were undergoing. At the rate this latter was taking place it seems probable that had he lived to write another novel on a theme similar to this, his hero would have been compelled to abandon his belief in Presbyterianism, Congregationalism, Methodism, or some other ism before he would be found worthy of being joined in the marriage relation to his Episcopal bride.

The "Ways of the Hour" was the last work that Cooper published. Everything he now wrote was written with a special object. The design of this was to attack trial by jury; but he was not prevented by that fact from discussing several other matters that were uppermost in his mind. The incidents of the story utterly destroyed the effectiveness of the lesson that it was intended to convey. It would be dignifying too much many of the events related in it to say that they are improbabilities: they are simply impossibilities. The "Ways of the Hour" was, however, like the preceding novels, often full of suggestive remarks, on many other points than trial by jury. It showed in numerous instances the working of an acute, vigorous, and aggressive intellect. The good qualities it has need not be denied: only they are not the good qualities that belong to fiction.

The pecuniary profits that his works brought him during this latter period of his life there are, perhaps, no means of ascertaining. Much of the literary activity of his last years was due to necessity rather than to inspiration. He had been concerned for a long time in company with a number of men of business in a series of cotton speculations, and in others connected with Western lands. In both cases the ventures were unprofitable, and the desire of retrieving his losses was one of the causes that led to this constant literary production. There were other circumstances, too, besides his mere unpopularity that had tended to reduce the amount gained from what he wrote. After 1838, the income received from England naturally fell off, in consequence of the change in the law of copyright. The act of Parliament passed in that year provided that no foreign author outside of British dominions should have copyright in those dominions unless the country to which he belonged gave copyright to the English author. No fault can be found with this legislation on the score of justice. The value of anything produced by a citizen of the United States fell at once as a necessary consequence of the want of protection against piracy. The British publisher, not from any motive of mere personal gain, but from an unselfish desire by retaliatory proceedings to bring about a better state of things, went speedily to work to plunder the American author who favored international copyright in order to show his disgust at the conduct of the American publisher who opposed it. As a matter of fact Cooper's novels were from that time published in Great Britain, in cheap form, and sold at a cheap price. Such reprints could not but lower the amount which could be offered for his work. Newspa-

per reports, the correctness of which can neither be
affirmed nor denied, frequently mention that for the
copyright of each of his earlier novels he was in the
habit of receiving a thousand guineas. We know positively that for his later tales, as fast as they were written, Bentley, his London publisher, usually paid him
three hundred pounds each.

In America circumstances of another kind contributed to reduce the profits from his works. Most of them
were published at a price that would have required an
immense sale to make them remunerative at all. It was
about 1840 that two weekly newspapers in New York,
"The New World," and "The Brother Jonathan," had
begun the practice of reprinting in their columns the
writings of the most popular novelists which were then
coming out in England. As soon as these were finished
they were brought out in parts and sold at a small price.
This piracy was so successful that imitators sprang up
everywhere. The large publishing houses were soon
obliged to follow in the wake of the newspaper estab-
lishments. The reign of the so-called "cheap and
nasty" literature began. The productions of the greatest
foreign novelists were sold for a song. The native
writer was subjected to a competition which forced him
at once to lower his price or to go unread. Beginning
with "Wing-and-Wing," the rate at which Cooper's
works were published furnishes a striking commentary
upon the cheap professions of sympathy with letters
current in this country, indicates suggestively the inspir-
iting inducements held out by the law-making power to
enter upon the career of authorship, and shows with disgraceful clearness how utterly the interests of the men
engaged in the creation of literature had been subordi-

nated to the greed of those who traded in it. The barest
recital of the facts makes evident the nature of the encouragement given. "Wing-and-Wing" was published
at twenty-five cents a volume. So were "Wyandotte,"
"The Redskins," "The Crater," "Jack Tier," "The
Oak Openings," and "The Sea Lions." The four volumes of the series "Afloat and Ashore" were published
at thirty-seven and a half cents each; and at the same
rate "Satanstoe" came out, and also "Ned Myers." It
was not till Cooper's last work appeared that the price
went up as high as a dollar and twenty-five cents.
This was in one volume; but it is to be kept in mind,
in considering these prices, that in America his novels
regularly appeared in two.

One further experiment Cooper made in a new field;
and with it the record of his literary life closes. In
the year 1850 he tried the stage. On the 18th of June
a comedy written by him was brought out at Burton's
Theatre, New York. It was entitled, "Upside Down;
or, Philosophy in Petticoats." For the three nights following the 18th it was acted, and was then withdrawn.
It has never been played since, nor has it been published.

All these years he spent his time mainly in his home
at Cooperstown. There, besides the pleasure he found
in the improvement of the extensive grounds about his
house, he gave full vent to that latent passion for wasting
money in agricultural operations, which seems to be one
of the most widely-extended peculiarities of the English
race. On the eastern shore of the lake, about a mile
from the village, he bought a farm of about two hundred
acres which he called the "Châlet." The view from it
was exceedingly beautiful, looking as it did down the

Valley of the Susquehanna. The farm, too, had its picturesque and poetical features; but unhappily it was little adapted to practical agriculture. It stood on a hill-side, the abruptness of which was only occasionally relieved by a few acres of level land. Much of it was still covered with the original forest; and a good deal of the cleared land was full of stumps. To superintend the removal of these latter was one of Cooper's chief relaxations from mental labor. It is a desirable thing to do, but it has never been found pecuniarily profitable in itself. To this place Cooper daily drove in the summer season, and spent two or three hours directing the operations that were going on, finding constantly new ways to spend money, and doubtless pleasing himself occasionally with the fancy that the farm would at some time pay expenses. And in the best sense it did pay expenses. It gave regular diversion to his life; it ministered constantly to his enjoyment of the beautiful in scenery; and it occupied his thoughts with perpetual projects of improvement for which its character furnished unlimited opportunities. He had bought it for pleasure and not for profit; and in that it yielded him a full return for the money invested.

CHAPTER XII.

1850–1851.

COOPER, at the time he published his last novel, was more than sixty years of age; but as yet he showed no traces of physical or intellectual decay. His literary activity remained unabated, though he was now purposing to direct it to other fields than that of fiction. A decided change was likewise taking place in the estimation in which he was held by the public. He had not become popular, to be sure; but he had become less unpopular. There was, moreover, a feeling pretty generally prevalent that he had been hardly used; that in many respects he had been a wronged and persecuted man. The ranks of those who had remained faithful to him during all these years of obloquy were beginning to be largely swelled from the newer generation which had neither part in, nor knowledge of, the bitter controversies in which he had been concerned. His friends were purposing to give a public dinner in his honor in order to show their regard for him as a man, and their appreciation of the credit his writings had brought to his country. Before this project could be carried into effect, the illness had overtaken him which ended in death.

On the other hand time had, in some respect, mollified his own feelings. Many things had occurred to make him more gentle and forbearing. Much of this was certainly due to the increasing strength of his religious convictions, which as has been noticed, steadily deepened during his last years. It is clear from much that appears in his later novels that these had, to some extent, been perverted from their legitimate effect, and had made him at intervals illiberal and even bitter. But they had brought calm to an excitable nature, and healing to a spirit which had been sometimes sorely wounded. In 1851 he carried out a plan long before determined upon. In March of that year he became a communicant in the Episcopal church, and in the following July was confirmed by his brother-in-law, Bishop DeLancey.

In the summer of 1850 he was in New York city. " At this time," says Bryant, " his personal appearance was remarkable. He seemed in perfect health, and in the highest energy and activity of his faculties. I have scarcely seen any man at that period of life on whom his years sat more lightly." But even then the disease which was to destroy him was lurking in his system. In the beginning of April, 1851, he came again to New York partly for medical advice, and his changed appearance struck all his friends with surprise and sorrow. The digestive organs were impaired, the liver was torpid, and a general feebleness had taken the place of the the vigor for which he had previously been distinguished. He remained several weeks in the city and then returned to Cooperstown. That place he never left again. The disease made rapid advances, and at last became a confirmed dropsy. In the latter part of August his old and intimate friend, Dr. Francis, of New York, went up to Cooper's country home to make a full examination of his condition. He found him worse, if anything, than he expected. There was, in fact, little hope of recovery. The physician told him frankly of the danger he was in, and of the possibilities of restoration to health that still existed. Though his own perception of his condition was too clear to make the announcement a shock, it could not have been other than a disappointment. He had many projects still unfulfilled. Plans of new works were in his mind; and one of them on the " Towns of Manhattan," partly written, was at that very time in press. But he met the news as bravely as he had the various troubles of his eventful life. After Dr. Francis' departure the malady steadily increased, and it soon became evident that expectation of recovery must be given up. During all these days he was quiet and cheerful, and his last hours were full of peace and hope. On Sunday, the 14th of September, 1851, at half-past one in the afternoon, he died. Had he lived one day longer he would have been sixty-two years old. In a little more than four months his wife followed him to the grave. They lie side by side in the grounds of Christ's Church at Cooperstown.

His property was found, at his death, to be much impaired in value. Enough was left to insure the family a competency, but it became necessary to give up the mansion where so many years of his life had been passed. The dwelling went, accordingly, into other hands, and it was not a long while after that it burned down. Part of the grounds have since become public property, and that which is not so employed is little better than a waste.

The death of men of letters did not excite at that time the attention which interest or fashion pays to it now. Cooper's relations, too, with many, had been of so strained a nature that it was hardly to be expected that his loss should arouse universal regret. Yet it was felt on all hands that a great man had fallen. On the 25th of September, a few days after his death, a meeting was held in the City Hall, New York, with the intent to make a suitable demonstration of respect to his memory. Washington Irving presided, and a committee of prominent men of letters was appointed to carry into effect the measures for which the gathering had been called. A discourse on the life, genius, and writings of the dead author was fixed upon to be given by his intimate friend, William Cullen Bryant. On the 25th of February, 1852, this address was delivered at Metropolitan Hall before the most cultivated audience the city could boast. With a singular ineptitude, not generally appreciated at the time, Daniel Webster was selected to preside. He had nothing to say, and he said it wretchedly. It was doubtful if he had ever read a single work of the novelist. That, at least, is a natural inference from his speech, which, furthermore, is little else than a collection of dreary platitudes. It was after this fashion that he paid his respects to the man whose memory they had come together to honor. " As far as I am acquainted," he remarked, " with the writings of Mr. Cooper, they uphold good sentiments, sustain good morals, and maintain just taste ; and after saying this I have next to add, that all his writings are truly patriotic and American throughout and throughout." This did not even reach the respectability of commonplace, and the commonplaces to which Webster soared in other parts of his speech did not have the poor merit of being sonorous. Still he looked so majestic and imposing that most of his audience were profoundly impressed by the justness and value of his observations. Any failure, however, on his part in the matter of what he said, was more than made up by the address delivered by Byrant. It is not very long; it contains a few errors of fact, especially in the dates; but it is not only the most eloquent tribute that has been paid to the dead author, it has also remained during all these years the fullest account of the life he lived, and the work he did.

More than sixty years have gone by since Cooper began to write; more than thirty since he ceased to live. If his reputation has not advanced during the period that has passed since his death, it has certainly not receded. Nor does it seem likely to undergo much change in the future. The world has pretty well made up its mind as to the value of his work. The estimate in which it is held will not be materially raised or lowered by anything which criticism can now utter. This will itself be criticised for being too obvious; for it can do little but repeat, with variation of phrase, what has been constantly said and often better said before. There is, however, now a chance of its meeting with fairer consideration. The cloud of depreciation which seems to settle upon the achievement of every man of letters soon after death, it was Cooper's fortune to encounter during life. This was partly due to the literary reaction which had taken place against the form of fiction he adopted, but far more to the personal animosities he aroused. We are now far enough removed from the prejudices and passions of his time to take an impartial view of the man, and to state, without bias for or against him, the conclusions to which the world has very generally come as to his merits and defects as a writer.

At the outset it is to be said that Cooper is one of the people's novelists as opposed to the novelists of highly-cultivated men. This does not imply that he has not been, and is not still, a favorite with many of the latter. The names of those, indeed, who have expressed excessive admiration for his writings far surpass in reputation and even critical ability those who have spoken of him depreciatingly. Still the general statement is true that it is with the masses he has found favor chiefly. The sale of his works has known no abatement since his death. It goes on constantly to an extent that will surprise any one who has not made an examination of this particular point. His tales continue to be read or rather devoured by the uncultivated many. They are often contemptuously criticised by the cultivated few, who sometimes affect to look upon any admiration they may have once had for them as belonging exclusively to the undisciplined taste of childhood.

This state of things may be thought decisive against the permanent reputation of the novelist. The opinion of the cultivated few, it is said, must prevail over that of the uncultivated many. True as this is in certain cases, it is just as untrue in others. It is, in fact, often absurdly false when the general reading public represents the uncultivated many. On matters which come legitimately within the scope of their judgment the verdict of the great mass of men is infinitely more trustworthy than that of any small body of men, no matter how cultivated. Of plenty of that narrow judgment of select circles which mistakes the cackle of its little coterie for the voice of the world, Cooper was made the subject, and sometimes the victim, during his lifetime. There were any number of writers, now never heard of, who were going to outlive him, according to literary prophecies then current,which had everything oracular in their utterance except ambiguity. Especially is this true of the notices of his stories of the sea. As I have turned over the pages of defunct criticism, I have come across the names of several authors whose tales descriptive of ocean life were, according to many contemporary estimates, immensely superior to anything of the kind Cooper had produced or could produce. Some of these writers enjoyed for a time high reputation. Most of them are now as utterly forgotten as the men who celebrated their praises.

But however unfair as a whole may be the estimate of cultivated men in any particular case, their adverse opinion is pretty certain to have a foundation of justice in its details. This is unquestionably true in the present instance. Characteristics there are of Cooper's writings which would and do repel many. Defects exist both in manner and matter. Part of the unfavorable judgment he has received is due to the prevalence of minor faults, disagreeable rather than positively bad. These, in many cases, sprang from the quantity of what he did and the rapidity with which he did it. The amount that Cooper wrote is something that in fairness must always be taken into consideration. He who has crowded into a single volume the experience of a life must concede that he stands at great advantage as regards matters of detail, and especially as regards perfection of form, with him who has manifested incessant literary activity in countless ways. It was the immense quantity that Cooper wrote and the haste and inevitable carelessness which wait upon great production, that are responsible for many of his minor faults. Incongruities in the conception of his tales, as well as in their execution, often make their appearance. Singular blunders can be found which escaped even his own notice in the final revision he gave his works. In " Mercedes of Castile," for instance, the heroine presents her lover on his outward passage with a cross framed of sapphire stones. These, she tells him, are emblems of fidelity. When she comes to inquire about them after his return she speaks of them as turquoise. Again, in " The Deerslayer " three castles of a curious set of chessmen are given in one part of the story to the Indians. Later on, two other castles of the same set make their appearance. This is a singular mistake for Cooper to overlook, for chess was a game of which he was very fond.

In the matter of language this rapidity and carelessness often degenerated into downright slovenliness. It was bad enough to resort to the same expedients and to repeat the same scenes. Still from this charge few prolific novelists can be freed. But in Cooper there were often words and phrases which he worked to death. In " The Wept of Wish-ton-Wish " there is so perpetual a reference to the quiet way in which the younger Heathcote talks and acts that it has finally anything but a quieting effect upon the reader's feelings. In " The Headsman of Berne," " warm " in the sense of " well-to-do," a disagreeable usage at best, occurs again and again, until the feeling of disagreeableness it inspires at first becomes at last positive disgust. This trick of repetition reaches the climax of meaninglessness in " The Ways of the Hour." During the trial scene the judge repeats on every pretext and as a part of almost every speech, the sentence " time is precious ; " and it is about the only point on which he is represented as taking a clear and decided stand.

There were other faults in the matter of language that to some will seem far worse. I confess to feeling little admiration for that grammar-school training which consists in teaching the pupil how much more he knows about our tongue than the great masters who have moulded it; which practically sets up the claim that the only men who are able to write English properly are the men who have never shown any capacity to write it at all ; and which seeks, in a feeble way, to cramp usage by setting up distinctions that never existed, and laying down rules which it requires uncommon ignorance of the language to make or to heed. Still there are lengths to which the most strenuous stickler for freedom of speech does not venture to go. There are prejudices in favor of the exclusive legitimacy of certain constructions that he feels bound to respect. He recognizes, as a general rule, for instance, that when the subject is in the singular it is desirable that the verb should be in the same number. For conventionalities of syntax of this kind Cooper was very apt to exhibit disregard, not to say disdain. He too often passed the bounds that divide liberty from license. It scarcely needs to be asserted that in most of these cases the violation of idiom arose from haste or carelessness. But there were some blunders which can only be imputed to pure unadulterated ignorance. He occasionally used words in senses unknown to past or present use. He sometimes employed grammatical forms that belong to no period in the history of the English language. A curious illustration of a word combining in itself both these errors is *wists*, a verb, in the third person, singular. If this be anything it should be *wist*, the preterite of *wot*, and should have accordingly the meaning "knew." Cooper

18

uses it in fact as a present with the sense of " wishes."
Far worse than occasional errors in the use of words are
errors of construction. His sentences are sometimes involved in the most hopeless way, and the efforts of
grammar to untie the knot by any means known to it
serve only to make conspicuous its own helplessness.

All this is, in itself, of slight importance when set off
against positive merits. But it is constantly forced upon
the reader's attention by the fact that Cooper himself
was exceedingly critical on points of speech. He was
perpetually going out of his way to impart bits of information about words and their uses, and it is rare that
he blunders into correct statement or right inference.
He often, indeed, in these matters carried ignorance of
what he was talking about, and confidence in his own
knowledge of it to the extremest verge of the possible.
He sometimes mistook dialectic or antiquated English for
classical, and laboriously corrected the latter by putting
the former in parentheses by its side. In orthography
and pronunciation he had never got beyond that puerile conception which fancies it a most creditable feature in a word that its sound shall not be suggested by
anything in its spelling. In the case of proper names
this was more than creditable ; it was aristocratic. So
in " The Crater " great care is taken to tell us that the
hero's name, though written Woolston, was pronounced
Wooster ; and that he so continued to sound it in spite
of a miserable Yankee pedagogue who tried hard to
persuade him to follow the spelling. So, again, in " The
Ways of the Hour " we are sedulously informed that
Wilmeter is to be pronounced Wilmington. But absurdities like these belonged not so much to Cooper
as to the good old times of gentlemanly ignorance in

which he lived. In his etymological vagaries, however, he sometimes left his age far behind. In "The Oak Openings" he enters upon the discussion of the word "shanty." He finds the best explanation of its origin is to suppose it a corruption of *chiènté*, a word which he again supposed might exist in Canadian French, and provided it existed there, he further supposed that in that dialect it might mean "dog-kennel." The student of language, much hardened to this sort of work on the part of men of letters, can read with resignation "this plausible derivation," as it is styled. Cooper, however, not content with the simple glory of originating it, actually uses throughout the whole work *chiènté* instead of "shanty." This rivals, if it does not outdo, the linguistic excesses of the sixteenth and seventeenth centuries.

There are imperfections far more serious than these mistakes in language. He rarely attained to beauty of style. The rapidity with which he wrote forbids the idea that he ever strove earnestly for it. Even the essential but minor grace of clearness is sometimes denied him. He had not, in truth, the instincts of the born literary artist. Satisfied with producing the main effect, he was apt to be careless in the consistent working out of details. Plot, in any genuine sense of the word "plot," is to be found in very few of his stories. He seems rarely to have planned all the events beforehand; or, if he did, anything was likely to divert him from his original intention. The incidents often appear to have been suggested as the tale was in process of composition. Hence the constant presence of incongruities with the frequent result of bringing about a bungling and incomplete development. The introduction of certain characters is sometimes so heralded as to lead us to expect from them far more than they actually perform. Thus, in "The Two Admirals," Mr. Thomas Wychecombe is brought in with a fullness of description that justifies the reader in entertaining a rational expectation of finding in him a satisfactory scoundrel, capable, desperate, full of resources, needing the highest display of energy and ability to be overcome. This reasonable anticipation is disappointed. At the very moment when respectable determined villainy is in request, he fades away into a poltroon of the most insignificant type who is not able to hold his own against an ordinary house-steward.

The prolixity of Cooper's introductions is a fault so obvious to every one that it needs here reference merely and not discussion. A similar remark may be made as to his moralizing, which was apt to be cheap and commonplace. He was much disposed to waste his own time and to exhaust the patience of his reader by establishing with great fullness of demonstration and great positiveness of assertion the truth of principles which most of the human race are humbly content to regard as axioms. A greater because even a more constantly recurring fault is the gross improbability to be found in the details of his stories. There is too much fiction in his fiction. We are continually exasperated by the inadequacy of the motive assigned; we are irritated by the unnatural if not ridiculous conduct of the characters. These are perpetually doing unreasonable things, or doing reasonable things at unsuitable times. They take the very path that must lead them into the danger they are seeking to shun. They engage in making love when they ought to be flying for their lives. His heroes, in particular, exhibit a capacity for going to sleep in critical situations, which may not transcend extraordinary human experience, but does ordinary human belief. Nor is improbability always confined to details. It pervades sometimes the central idea of the story. In "The Bravo," for instance, the hero is the most pious of sons, the most faithful of friends, the most devoted of lovers. The part he has to play in the tale is to appear to be a cutthroat of the worst type, without doing a single thing to merit his reputation. It is asking too much of human credulity to believe that a really good man could long sustain the character of a remorseless desperado by merely making faces. This improbability, moreover, is most marked in the tales which are designed to teach a lesson. A double disadvantage is the result. The story is spoiled for the sake of the moral; and the moral is lost by the grossly improbable nature of the story. In the last novel Cooper wrote this is strikingly seen. He who can credit the possibility of the events occurring that are told in "The Ways of the Hour" must give up at the same time his belief in the maxim that truth is stranger than fiction.

It has now become a conventional criticism of Cooper that his characters are conventional. Such a charge can be admitted without seriously disparaging the value of his work. In the kind of fiction to which his writings belong, the persons are necessarily so subordinate to the events that nearly all novelists of this class have been subjected to this same criticism. So regularly is it made, indeed, that Scott when he wrote a review of some of his own tales for the "Quarterly" felt obliged to adopt it in speaking of himself. He describes his heroes as amiable, insipid young men, the sort of pattern people that nobody cares a farthing about. Untrue as this is of many of Scott's creations, it is unquestionably true of the higher characters that Cooper introduces. They are often described in the most laudatory terms; but it is little they do that makes them worthy of the epithets with which they are honored. Their talk is often of a kind not known to human society. One peculiarity is especially noticeable. A stiffness, not to say an appearance of affectation is often given to the conversation by the use of *thou* and *thee*. This was probably a survival in Cooper of the Quakerism of his ancestors; for he sometimes used it in his private letters. But since the action of his stories was in nearly all cases laid in a period in which the second person singular had become obsolete in ordinary speech, an unnatural character is given to the dialogue, which removes it still farther from the language of real life.

His failure in characterization was undoubtedly greatest in the women he drew. Cooper's ardent admirers have always resented this charge. Each one of them points to some single heroine that fulfills the highest requirements that criticism could demand. It seems to me that close study of his writings must confirm the opinion generally entertained. All his utterances show that the theoretical view he had of the rights, the duties, and the abilities of women, were of the most narrow and conventional type. Unhappily it was a limitation of his nature that he could not invest with charm characters with whom he was not in moral and intellectual sympathy. There was, in his eyes, but one praiseworthy type of womanly excellence. It did not lie in his power to represent any other; on one occasion he unconsciously satirized his inability even to conceive of any other. In "Mercedes of Castile" the heroine is thus described by her aunt: " Her very nature," she says, " is made up of religion and female decorum." It is evident that the author fancied that in this commendation he was exhausting praise. These are the sentiments of a man with whom devoutness and deportment have become the culminating conception of the possibilities that lie in the female character. His heroines naturally conformed to his belief. They are usually spoken of as spotless beings. They are made up of retiring sweetness, artlessness, and simplicity. They are timid, shrinking, helpless. They shudder with terror on any decent pretext. But if they fail in higher qualities, they embody in themselves all conceivable combinations of the proprieties and minor morals. They always give utterance to the most unexceptionable sentiments. They always do the extremely correct thing. The dead perfection of their virtues has not the alloy of a single redeeming fault. The reader naturally wearies of these uninterestingly discreet and admirable creatures in fiction as he would in real life. He feels that they would be a good deal more attractive if they were a good deal less angelic. With all their faultlessness, moreover, they do not attain an ideal which is constantly realized by their living, but faulty sisters. They do not show the faith, the devotion, the self-forgetfulness, and self-sacrifice which women exhibit daily without being conscious that they have done anything especially creditable. They experience, so far as their own words and acts furnish evidence of their feelings, a sort of lukewarm emotion which they dignify with the name of love. But they not merely suspect without the slightest provocation, they give up the men to whom they have pledged the devotion of their lives, for reasons for which no one would think of abandoning an ordinary acquaintance. In "The Spy" the heroine distrusts her lover's integrity because another woman does not conceal her fondness for him. In "The Heidenmauer" one of the female characters resigns the man she loves because on one occasion, when heated by wine and maddened by passion, he had done violence to the sacred elements. There was never a woman in real life, whose heart and brain were sound, that conformed her conduct to a model so contemptible. It is just to say of Cooper that as he advanced in years he improved upon this feeble conception. The female characters of his earlier tales are never able to do anything successfully but to faint. In his later ones they are given more strength of mind as well as nobility of character. But at best, the height they reach is little loftier than that of the pattern woman of the regular religious novel. The reader cannot help picturing for all of them the same dreary and rather inane future. He is as sure, as if their career had been actually unrolled before his eyes, of the part they will perform in life. They will all become leading members of Dorcas societies; they will find perpetual delight in carrying to the poor bundles of tracts and packages of tea; they will scour the highways and by-ways for dirty, ragged, hatless, shoeless, and godless children, whom they will hale into the Sunday-school; they will shine with unsurpassed skill in the manufacture of slippers for the rector; they will exhibit a fiery enthusiasm in the decoration and adornment of the church at Christmas and Easter festivals. Far be the thought that would deny praise to the mild raptures and delicate aspirations of gentle natures such as Cooper drew. But in novels, at least, one longs for a ruddier life than flows in the veins of these pale, bleached-out personifications of the proprieties. Women like them may be far more useful members of society than the stormier characters of fiction that are dear to the carnal-minded. They may very possibly be far more agreeable to live with; but they are not usually the women for whom men are willing or anxious to die.

These are imperfections that have led to the undue depreciation of Cooper among many highly cultivated men. Taken by themselves they might seem enough to ruin his reputation beyond redemption. It is a proof of his real greatness that he triumphs over defects which would utterly destroy the fame of a writer of inferior power. It is with novels as with men. There are those with great faults which please us and impress us far more than those in which the component parts are better balanced. Whatever its other demerits, Cooper's best work never sins against the first law of fictitious composition, that the story shall be full of sustained interest. It has power, and power always fascinates, even though accompanied with much that would naturally excite repulsion or dislike. Moreover, poorly as he sometimes told his story, he had a story to tell. The permanence and universality of his reputation are largely due to this fact. In many modern creations full of subtle charm and beauty, the narrative, the material framework of the fiction, has been made so subordinate to the delineation of character and motive, that the reader ceases to feel much interest in what men do in the study which is furnished him of why they do it. In this highly-rarefied air of philosophic analysis, incident and event wither and die. Work of this kind is apt to have within its sphere an unbounded popularity; but its sphere is limited, and can never include a tithe of that vast public for which Cooper wrote and which has always cherished and kept alive his memory, while that of men of perhaps far finer mould has quite faded away.

It is only fair, also, to judge him by his successes and not by his failures; by the work he did best, and not by what he did moderately well. His strength lies in the description of scenes, in the narration of events. In the best of these he has had no superior, and very few equals. The reader will look in vain for the revelation of sentiment, or for the exhibition of passion. The love-story is rarely well done; but the love-story plays a subordinate part in the composition. The moment his imagination is set on fire with the conception of adventure, vividness and power come unbidden to his pen. The pictures he then draws are as real to the mind as if they were actually seen by the eye. It is doubtless due to the fact that these fits of inspiration came to him only in certain kinds of composition, that the excellence of many of his stories lies largely in detached scenes. Still his best works are a moving panorama, in which the mind is no sooner sated with one picture than its place is taken by another equally fitted to fix the attention and to stir the heart. The genuineness of his power, in such cases, is shown by the perfect simplicity of the agencies employed. There is no pomp of words; there is an entire lack of even the attempt at meretricious adornment; there is not the slightest appearance of effort to impress the reader. In his portrayal of these scenes Cooper is like nature, in that he accomplishes his greatest effects with the fewest means. If, as we are sometimes told, these things are easily done, the pertinent question always remains, why are they not done.

Moreover, while in his higher characters he has almost absolutely failed, he has succeeded in drawing a whole group of strongly-marked lower ones. Birch, in "The Spy," Long Tom Coffin and Boltrope in "The Pilot," the squatter in "The Prairie," Cap in "The Pathfinder," and several others there are, any one of which would be enough of itself to furnish a respectable reputation to many a novelist who fancies himself far superior to Cooper as a delineator of character. He had neither the skill nor power to draw the varied figures with which Scott, with all the reckless prodigality of genius, crowded his canvas. Yet in the gorgeous gallery of the great master of romantic fiction, alive with men and women of every rank in life and of every variety of nature, there is, perhaps, no one person who so profoundly impresses the imagination as Cooper's crowning creation, the man of the forests. It is not that Scott could not have done what his follower did, had he so chosen ; only that as a matter of fact he did not. Leather-Stocking is one of the few original characters, perhaps the only great original character, that American fiction has added to the literature of the world.

The more uniform excellence of Cooper, however, lies in the pictures he gives of the life of nature. Forest, ocean, and stream are the things for which he really cares ; and men and women are the accessories, inconvenient and often uncomfortable, that must be endured. Of the former he speaks with a loving particularity that lets nothing escape the attention. Yet minute as are often his descriptions, he did not fall into that too easily besetting sin of the novelist, of overloading his picture with details. To advance the greater he sacrificed the less. Cooper looked at nature with the eye of a painter and not of a photographer. He fills the imagination even more than he does the sight. Hence the permanence of the impression which he leaves upon the mind. His descriptions, too, produce a greater effect at the time and cling longer to the memory because they fall naturally into the narrative, and form a real part in the development of the story; they are not merely dragged in to let the reader know what the writer can do. "If Cooper," said Balzac, "had succeeded in the painting of character to the same extent that he did in the painting of the phenomena of nature, he would have uttered the last word of our art." This author I have quoted several times, because far better even than George Sand, or indeed any who have criticised the American novelist, he seems to me to have seen clearly wherein the latter succeeded and wherein he failed.

To this it is just to add one word which Cooper himself would have regarded as the highest tribute that could be paid to what he did. Whatever else we may say of his writings, their influence is always a healthy influence. Narrow and prejudiced he sometimes was in his opinions; but he hated whatever was mean and low in character. It is with beautiful things and with noble things that he teaches us to sympathize. Here are no incitements to passion, no prurient suggestions of sensual delights. The air which breathes through all his fictions is as pure as that which sweeps the streets of his mountain home. It is as healthy as nature itself. To read one of his best works after many of the novels of the day, is like passing from the heated and stifling atmosphere of crowded rooms to the purity, the freedom, and the boundlessness of the forest.

In these foregoing pages I have attempted to portray

an author who was something more than an author, who in any community would have been a marked man had he never written a word. I have not sought to hide his foibles and his faults, his intolerance and his dogmatism, the irascibility of his temperament, the pugnacity of his nature, the illiberality and injustice of many of his opinions, the unreasonableness as well as the imprudence of the course he often pursued. To his friends and admirers these points will seem to have been insisted upon too strongly. Their feelings may, to a certain extent, be just. Cooper is, indeed, a striking instance of how much more a man loses in the estimation of the world by the exhibition of foibles, than he will by that of vices. In this work one side of the life he lived — the side he presented to the public — is the only one that, owing to circumstances, could be depicted. It does not present the most attractive features of his character. That exclusiveness of temperament which made him misjudged by the many, endeared him only the more to the few who were in a position to see how different he was from what he seemed. In nothing is the essential sweetness of Cooper's nature more clearly shown than in the intense affection he inspired in the immediate circle which surrounded him or that was dependent upon him. He could not fail to feel keenly at times how utterly his character and motives were misapprehended and belied. "As for myself," says the hero of "Miles Wallingford," "I can safely say that in scarce a circumstance of my life, that has brought me the least under the cognizance of the public, have I ever been judged justly. In various instances have I been praised for acts that were either totally without any merit, or at least the particular merit imputed to them;

while I have been even persecuted for deeds that deserved praise."

His faults, in fact, were faults of temper rather than of character. Like the defects of his writings, too, they lay upon the surface, and were seen and read of all men. But granting everything that can be urged against him, impartial consideration must award him an ample excess of the higher virtues. His failings were the failings of a man who possessed in the fullest measure vigor of mind, intensity of conviction, and capability of passion. Disagree with him one could hardly help; one could never fail to respect him. Many of the common charges against him are due to pure ignorance. Of these, perhaps, the most common and the most absolutely baseless is the one which imputes to him excessive literary vanity. Pride, even up to the point of arrogance, he had; but even this was only in a small degree connected with his reputation as an author. In the nearly one hundred volumes he wrote, not a single line can be found which implies that he had an undue opinion of his own powers. On the contrary, there are many that would lead to the conclusion that his appreciation of himself and of his achievement was far lower than even the coldest estimate would form. The prevalent misconception on this point was in part due to his excessive sensitiveness to criticism and his resentment of it when hostile. It was partly due, also, to a certain outspokenness of nature which led him to talk of himself as freely as he would talk of a stranger. But his whole conduct showed the falseness of any such impression. From all the petty tricks to which literary vanity resorts, he was absolutely free. He utterly disdained anything that savored of manœuvring for reputation. He indulged in no devices to revive the decaying attention of the public. He sought no favors from those who were in a position to confer the notoriety which so many mistake for fame. He went, in fact, to the other extreme, and refused an aid that he might with perfect propriety have received. In the early period of his literary career he wrote a good deal for the " New York Patriot," a newspaper edited by his intimate friend, Colonel Gardiner. He objected to the publication in it of a favorable notice, which had been prepared of " The Pioneers," because by the fact of being an occasional contributor he was indirectly connected with the journal. Accordingly the criticism was not inserted. It would not have been possible for him to offer to review his own works, as Scott both offered to do and did of the " Tales of My Landlord," in the " Quarterly." Nor would he have acceded to a request to furnish a review of any production of his own, as Irving did, in the same periodical, of his " Conquest of Granada." No publisher who knew him, even slightly, would have ventured to make him a proposition of the kind. I am expressing no opinion as to the propriety of these particular acts; only that Cooper, constituted as he was, could not for a moment have entertained the thought of doing them.

The fearlessness and the truthfulness of his nature are conspicuous in almost every incident of his career. He fought for a principle as desperately as other men fight for life. The storm of detraction through which he went never once shook the almost haughty independence of his conduct, or swerved him in the slightest from the course he had chosen. The only thing to which he unquestioningly submitted was the truth. His loyalty to that was of a kind almost Quixotic. He was in later years dissatisfied with himself, because, in his novel of " The Pilot," he had put the character of Paul Jones too high. He thought that the hero had been credited in that work with loftier motives than those by which he was actually animated. Feelings such as these formed the groundwork of his character, and made him intolerant of the devious ways of many who were satisfied with conforming to a lower code of morality. There was a royalty in his nature that disdained even the semblance of deceit. With other authors one feels that the man is inferior to his work. With him it is the very reverse. High qualities, such as these, so different from the easy-going virtues of common men, are more than an offset to infirmities of temper, to unfairness of judgment, or to unwisdom of conduct. His life was the best answer to many of the charges brought against his country and his countrymen ; for whatever he may have fancied, the hostility he encountered was due far less to the matter of his criticisms than to their manner. Against the common cant, that in republican governments the tyranny of public sentiment will always bring conduct to the same monotonous level, and opinion to the same subservient uniformity, Democracy can point to this dauntless son who never flinched from any course because it brought odium, who never flattered popular prejudices, and who never truckled to a popular cry. America has had among her representatives of the irritable race of writers many who have shown far more ability to get on pleasantly with their fellows than Cooper. She has had several gifted with higher spiritual insight than he, with broader and juster views of life, with finer ideals of literary art, and, above all, with far greater delicacy of taste. But she counts on the scanty roll of her men of letters the name of no one who acted from purer patriotism or loftier principle. She finds among them all no manlier nature, and no more heroic soul.

19

APPENDIX.

PARTIAL BIBLIOGRAPHY OF COOPER'S WRITINGS.

THE following list embraces the first editions of Cooper's works; articles contributed to magazines; and two or three of the most important communications sent to the newspapers. The titles of his works, as published in England, were sometimes different from the titles used in the United States; and whenever this is the case the former are subjoined. It is also to be remarked that Cooper's works were sometimes published earlier in Europe than they were in America; but the dates given in this biography belong exclusively to the publication of his works in this country. With the exception of No. 45 and of No. 67, all his tales were originally published in two volumes in America; with the exception of No. 45 they were originally published in three volumes in England. First editions of many of his novels are now rarely to be found in libraries; and the titles given have in several cases, in consequence, been taken from contemporary book notices and not from personal examination. The titles are given in the order of publication of the writings.

1. Precaution; a Novel. 2 vols. New York: A. T. Goodrich & Co., 1820.

  The English edition appeared in March, 1821.

2. The Spy; a Tale of the Neutral Ground. By the Author of Precaution. 2 vols. New York: Wiley & Halsted, 1821.

  The English edition appeared in March, 1822.

3. The Pioneers ; or the Sources of the Susquehanna. A Descriptive Tale. By the Author of Precaution. 2 vols. New York : Charles Wiley, 1823.

The English edition appeared in March, 1823.

4. The Pilot; A Tale of the Sea. By the Author of The Pioneers, etc. 2 vols. New York : Charles Wiley, 1823.

The first edition bears the imprint of 1823, but was not actually published until early in January, 1824.

5. Lionel Lincoln; or the Leaguer of Boston. By the Author of The Pioneers, Pilot, etc. 2 vols. New York: Charles Wiley, 1825.

6. The Last of the Mohicans. A Narrative of 1757. By the Author of The Pioneers. 2 vols. Philadelphia: H. C. Carey & I. Lea, 1826.

7. The Prairie; a Tale. By the Author of The Pioneers and The Last of the Mohicans. 2 vols. Philadelphia : Carey, Lea & Carey, 1827.

8. The Red Rover; a Tale. By the Author of The Pilot, etc., etc. 2 vols. Philadelphia : Carey, Lea & Carey, 1828.

9. Notions of the Americans; Picked up by a Travelling Bachelor. 2 vols. Philadelphia: Carey, Lea & Carey, 1828.

10. The Wept of Wish-ton-Wish; a Tale. By the Author of The Pioneers, Prairie, etc., etc. 2 vols. Philadelphia: Carey, Lea & Carey, 1829.

In England this was published under the title of " The Borderers; or the Wept of Wish-ton-Wish." It has also been published with the title of " The Heathcotes."

11. The Water-Witch; or the Skimmer of the Seas. A Tale. By the Author of The Pilot, Red Rover, etc., etc., etc. 2 vols. Philadelphia : Carey & Lea, 1830.

12. The Bravo ; a Tale. By the Author of The Spy, The Red Rover, The Water Witch, etc., etc., etc. 2 vols. Philadelphia : Carey & Lea, 1831.

13. Letter of J. Fenimore Cooper to Gen. Lafayette on the

Expenditure of the United States of America.   50 pp.
Paris: Baudry's Foreign Library, 1831.

14. The Heidenmauer ; or the Benedictines.   A Legend of
the Rhine.   By the Author of The Prairie, Red Rover,
Bravo, etc., etc.   2 vols.   Philadelphia: Carey & Lea,
1832.

15. Letter to the American Public.

Dated Vevay, Canton de Vaud, Oct. 1, 1832; first published in Philadelphia National Gazette, Dec. 6.   The subject is the Expenses' Controversy.   It occupies about two columns.

16. The Headsman; or the Abbaye des Vignerons.   A Tale.
By the Author of The Bravo, etc., etc.   2 vols.   Philadelphia: Carey, Lea & Blanchard, 1833.

17. A Letter to His Countrymen.   By J. Fenimore-Cooper.
116 pp.   New York: John Wiley, 1834.

18. The Monikins; edited by the Author of The Spy.   2
vols.   Philadelphia: Carey, Lea & Blanchard, 1835.

19. Comparative Resources of the American Navy.

In Naval Magazine, vol. i, No. 1, January, 1836, pp.
19–33.

20. Hints on Manning the Navy, etc., etc.

In Naval Magazine, vol. i., No. 2, March, 1836, pp.
176–191.   This was published the following May in pamphlet form by the " Committee of Publication for the Naval Magazine."

21. Sketches of Switzerland.   By an American.   2 vols.
Philadelphia: Carey, Lea & Blanchard, 1836.

The English title was " Excursions in Switzerland."

22. Sketches of Switzerland.   By an American.   Part Second.   2 vols.   Philadelphia : Carey, Lea & Blanchard,
1836.

The English title was " A Residence in France; with an
Excursion up the Rhine, and a Second Visit to Switzerland."

23. Gleanings in Europe.   By an American.   2 vols.   Philadelphia: Carey, Lea & Blanchard, 1837.

This work is devoted to France. Its English title is "Recollections of Europe."

24. Gleanings in Europe. England; by an American. 2 vols. Philadelphia: Carey, Lea & Blanchard, 1837.

This was published in England under the title of "England; with Sketches of Society in the Metropolis."

25. Letter to the Editors of the Knickerbocker. (On the relations between himself and Sir Walter Scott, etc.)

In Knickerbocker Magazine, vol. xi., April, 1838, pp. 380–386.

26. Gleanings in Europe. Italy; by an American. 2 vols. Philadelphia: Carey, Lea & Blanchard, 1838.

Published in England under the title of "Excursions in Italy."

27. The American Democrat; or Hints on the Social and Civic Relations of the United States of America. By J. Fenimore Cooper. Pp. 192. Cooperstown: H. & E. Phinney, 1838.

28. The Chronicles of Cooperstown. Pp. 100. Cooperstown: H. & E. Phinney, 1838.

Published anonymously. Republished at Albany in 1862 with additional notes and details bringing the events down to that year. The republication is entitled "A Condensed History of Cooperstown; with a Biographical Sketch of J. Fenimore Cooper. By Rev. T. S. Livermore, A. M." It is a volume of 276 pages, and contains Bryant's funeral discourse on Cooper, with much other matter. The "Chronicles of Cooperstown" extend from page 9 to page 86 inclusive.

29. Homeward Bound; or the Chase. A Tale of the Sea. By the Author of The Pilot, The Spy, etc. 2 vols. Philadelphia: Carey, Lea & Blanchard, 1838.

30. Review of the "Memoirs of the Life of Sir Walter Scott, Bart. By J. G. Lockhart."

In Knickerbocker Magazine, October, 1838, vol. xii., pp. 349–366.

31. Home as Found. By the Author of Homeward Bound, The Pioneers, etc., etc. 2 vols. Philadelphia: Lea & Blanchard, 1838.

In England published under the title of " Eve Effingham; or Home."

32. The History of the Navy of the United States of America. By J. Fenimore Cooper. 2 vols. Philadelphia: Lea & Blanchard, 1839.

33. Letters in " Cooperstown Freeman's Journal," July 1st and July 8th, 1839.

A reply to the criticism upon his Naval History, or rather upon his account of the battle of Lake Erie, which had appeared in the New York Commercial Advertiser in June, 1839. The first letter occupies two columns, the second more than three.

34. The Pathfinder; or the Inland Sea. By the Author of The Pioneers, Last of the Mohicans, etc. 2 vols. Philadelphia: Lea & Blanchard, 1840.

35. Mercedes of Castile; or the Voyage to Cathay. By the Author of The Bravo, The Last of the Mohicans, etc. 2 vols. Philadelphia: Lea & Blanchard, 1840.

The English title was " Mercedes of Castile. A Romance of the Days of Columbus."

36. History of the Navy of the United States of America. Abridged in one volume. Pp. 447. Philadelphia: Thomas Cowperthwait & Co., 1841.

37. The Deerslayer; or the First War Path. A Tale. By the Author of The Last of the Mohicans, The Pioneers, etc. 2 vols. Philadelphia : Lea & Blanchard, 1841.

38. " Home as Found. Lost Chapter." Preceded by a " Preface," and a " Letter to the Editor." In the " Brother Jonathan" newspaper of January 1, 1842. — Followed by a Letter to the Editor, from Cooper, on " The Effingham Matter," in same paper for February 12, 1842, and by two articles on " The Effingham Controversy," in the numbers for March 26, 1842, and April 9, 1842.

39. The Two Admirals; a Tale. By the Author of The Pilot, Red Rover, Water Witch, Homeward Bound, etc., etc. 2 vols. Philadelphia: Lea & Blanchard, 1842.

40. Edinburgh Review on James' Naval Occurrences and Cooper's Naval History.

In the United States Magazine and Democratic Review, vol. x., for May and June, 1842. First article, pp. 409–435; second article, pp. 515–541.

41. Richard Somers.

In Graham's Magazine for October, 1842.

42. William Bainbridge,

In Graham's Magazine for November, 1842.

43. The Wing-and-Wing; or Le Feu-Follet. A Tale. By the Author of The Pilot, Red Rover, Two Admirals, Homeward Bound, etc., etc. 2 vols. Philadelphia: Lea & Blanchard, 1842.

In England this was published under the title " The Jack o' Lantern (Le Feu-Follet); or the Privateer."

44. Richard Dale.

In Graham's Magazine for December, 1842.

45. Autobiography of a Pocket Handkerchief.

In Graham's Magazine for January, February, March, and April, 1843. It came out in March among the publications of the " Brother Jonathan " newspaper office, and was then entitled " Le Mouchoir; an Autobiographical Romance." The English title was " The French Governess; or the Embroidered Handkerchief."

46. Oliver Hazard Perry.

In Graham's Magazine for May and June, 1843.

47. John Paul Jones.

In Graham's Magazine for July and August, 1843.

48. The Battle of Lake Erie; or Answers to Messrs. Burges, Duer, and Mackenzie. By J. Fenimore Cooper. Pp. 118. Cooperstown: H. & E. Phinney, 1843.

49. Wyandotte; or the Hutted Knoll. A Tale. By the Author of The Pathfinder, Deerslayer, Last of the Mo-

hicans, Pioneers, Prairie, etc., etc. 2 vols. Philadelphia: Lea & Blanchard, 1843.

50. Ned Myers ; or a Life before the Mast. Edited by J. Fenimore Cooper. Pp. 232. Philadelphia: Lea & Blanchard, 1843.

51. John Shaw.
In Graham's Magazine for March, 1844.

52. John Barry.
In Graham's Magazine for June, 1844.

53. Afloat and Ashore ; or the Adventures of Miles Wallingford. By the Author of The Pilot, Red Rover, The Two Admirals, etc. 2 vols. Philadelphia: Published by the Author, 1844.

54. Proceedings of the Naval Court Martial in the Case of Alexander Slidell Mackenzie, a Commander in the Navy of the United States, etc., including the Charges and Specifications of Charges, preferred against him by the Secretary of the Navy. To which is annexed an Elaborate Review. By James Fennimore Cooper. Pp. 344. New York: Henry G. Langley, 1844. (Cooper's review extends from page 263 to page 344 inclusive. The spelling of the name was due to the publisher.)

55. Afloat and Ashore; or the Adventures of Miles Wallingford. By the Author of The Pilot, Red Rover, etc. Vols. 3 & 4. Published for the Author. New York : Burgess, Stringer & Co., 1844.

This second series of Afloat and Ashore goes in this country under the name of " Miles Wallingford." In England it was published as " Lucy Hardinge."

56. John Templer Shubrick.
In Graham's Magazine for December, 1844.

57. Melancthon Taylor Woolsey.
In Graham's Magazine for January, 1845.

58. Edward Preble.
In Graham's Magazine for May and June, 1845.

59. Satanstoe; or the Littlepage Manuscripts. A Tale of

the Colony. 2 vols. New York : Burgess, Stringer & Co., 1845.

60. The Chainbearer; or the Littlepage Manuscripts. Edited by the Author of Satanstoe, Spy, Pathfinder, Two Admirals, etc. 2 vols. New York: Burgess, Stringer & Co, 1846.

61. Lives of Distinguished American Naval Officers. By J. Fenimore Cooper. Author of The Spy, The Pilot, etc. 2 vols. Philadelphia: Carey & Hart, 1846. Also, 2 vols. Auburn : Derby & Jackson, 1846.

Volume I. contains, in the following order : Bainbridge (No. 42), Somers (No. 41), Shaw (No. 51), Shubrick (No. 56), Preble (No. 58).

Volume II. contains : Jones (No. 47), Woolsey (No. 57), Perry (No. 46), and Dale (No. 44); Barry (No. 52) was not included.

62. The Redskins; or Indian and Injin. Being the conclusion of the Littlepage Manuscripts. By the Author of The Pathfinder, Deerslayer, Two Admirals, etc. 2 vols. New York: Burgess & Stringer, 1846.

In England the title of this work was " Ravensnest ; or the Redskins."

63. The Islets of the Gulf; or Rose Budd.

Begun in Graham's Magazine for November, 1846, and continued through every succeeding number until March, 1848, in which month it was concluded. It was published in book form March 21, 1848, by Burgess, Stringer & Co., as " Jack Tier; or the Florida Reefs." In England the title was " Captain Spike; or the Islets of the Gulf."

64. The Crater; or Vulcan's Peak. A Tale of the Pacific. By the Author of Miles Wallingford, The Red Rover, The Pilot, etc., etc. 2 vols. New York: Burgess, Stringer & Co., 1847.

The English title was " Mark's Reef ; or the Crater."

Jack Tier; or the Florida Reefs, 1848. See No. 63.

65. The Oak Openings; or the Bee Hunter. By the Au-

thor of The Pioneers, Last of the Mohicans, Pathfinder, Deerslayer, etc., etc. 2 vols. New York: Burgess, Stringer & Co., 1848.

The English title was " The Bee Hunter; or the Oak Openings."

66. The Sea Lions; or the Lost Sealers. By the Author of The Crater, etc. 2 vols. New York: Stringer & Townsend, 1849.

67. The Ways of the Hour; a Tale. By the Author of The Spy, The Red Rover, etc., etc. 1 vol. New York: G. P. Putnam, 1850.

POSTHUMOUS PUBLICATIONS.

68. Old Ironsides.

In Putnam's Magazine, vol. i., No. v., May, 1853, pp. 473–487; and in No. vi., June, 1853, pp. 593–607.

This is a history of the United States frigate Constitution.

69. Fragments from a Diary of James Fenimore Cooper.

In Putnam's Magazine, new series, vol. i., February, 1868, pp. 167–172; and June, 1868, pp. 730–737.

70. The Battle of Plattsburgh Bay.

In January, 1869, of Putnam's Magazine, vol. iii., new series, pp. 49–59.

A note to this article says that it was prepared as a lecture to be delivered before the New York Historical Society. The records of that Society, however, contain no reference to any lecture delivered by Cooper.

71. The Eclipse.

In Putnam's Magazine, new series, vol. iv., for September, 1869, pp. 352–359. Written about 1831, and gives an account of the eclipse of the sun in June, 1806.

Besides these there are numerous letters written to the newspapers, and in particular the letters written to the Paris journal, the " National," in 1833. During Cooper's life it was frequently said that he was engaged in preparing a work on the Middle States of the Union ; but no trace of such a production was found among his papers. A work of his on " The Towns of Manhattan " was partly finished and in press at the time of his death; but the portion printed was entirely destroyed by fire. Part of the manuscript, however, was recovered. On the 4th of August, 1841, Cooper also delivered an address before the Literary Societies of Hobart College, Geneva, N. Y.; but this he himself burned on the day it was delivered.

A few works have been wrongly attributed to him. One of these is " The Cruise of the Somers; illustrative of the Despotism of the Quarter Deck ; and of the Unmanly Conduct of Commander Mackenzie." New York: 1844. Another is " Elinor Wyllys; or the Young Folk of Longbridge." Philadelphia: 1846. Of this novel Cooper was the nominal editor, and to it he contributed a short preface. A third work, which has been falsely attributed to him, is entitled " The Republic of the United States; its Duties to Itself, and its Responsible Relations to other Countries." New York: 1848.

INDEX.

STANDARD AND POPULAR

Library Books

SELECTED FROM THE CATALOGUE OF

HOUGHTON, MIFFLIN AND CO.

CONSIDER what you have in the smallest chosen library. A company of the wisest and wittiest men that could be picked out of all civil countries, in a thousand years, have set in best order the results of their learning and wisdom. The men themselves were hid and inaccessible, solitary, impatient of interruptions, fenced by etiquette; but the thought which they did not uncover to their bosom friend is here written out in transparent words to us, the strangers of another age. — Ralph Waldo Emerson.

Library Books

OHN ADAMS and Abigail Adams.
Familiar Letters of John Adams and his wife, Abigail Adams, during the Revolution. Crown 8vo, $2.00.

Louis Agassiz.
Methods of Study in Natural History. 16mo, $1.50.
Geological Sketches. 16mo, $1.50.
Geological Sketches. Second Series. 16mo, $1.50.
A Journey in Brazil. Illustrated. 8vo, $5.00.

Thomas Bailey Aldrich.
Story of a Bad Boy. Illustrated. 16mo, $1.50.
Marjorie Daw and Other People. 16mo, $1.50.
Prudence Palfrey. 16mo, $1.50.
The Queen of Sheba. 16mo, $1.50.
The Stillwater Tragedy. $1.50.
Cloth of Gold and Other Poems. 16mo, $1.50.
Flower and Thorn. Later poems. 16mo, $1.25.
Poems. Complete. Illustrated. 8vo, $5.00.

American Men of Letters.
Edited by CHARLES DUDLEY WARNER.
Washington Irving. By Charles Dudley Warner. 16mo, $1.25.
Noah Webster. By Horace E. Scudder. 16mo, $1.25.
Henry D. Thoreau. By Frank B. Sanborn. 16mo, $1.25.
George Ripley. By O. B. Frothingham. 16mo, $1.25.
J. Fenimore Cooper. By Prof. T. R. Lounsbury.
(*In Preparation.*)
Nathaniel Hawthorne. By James Russell Lowell.
N. P. Willis. By Thomas Bailey Aldrich.
William Gilmore Simms. By George W. Cable.
Benjamin Franklin. By T. W. Higginson.
Others to be announced.

American Statesmen.

Edited by JOHN T. MORSE, Jr.

John Quincy Adams. By John T. Morse, Jr. 16mo, $1.25.
Alexander Hamilton. By Henry Cabot Lodge. 16mo, $1.25.
John C. Calhoun. By Dr. H. von Holst. 16mo, $1 25.
Andrew Jackson. By Prof. W. G. Sumner. 16mo, $1.25.
John Randolph. By Henry Adams. 16mo, $1.25.
James Monroe. By Pres. D. C. Gilman. 16mo, $1.25.

(*In Preparation.*)

Daniel Webster. By Henry Cabot Lodge. 16mo, $1.25.
Thomas Jefferson. By John T. Morse, Jr. 16mo, $1.25.
James Madison. By Sidney Howard Gay.
Albert Gallatin. By John Austin Stevens.
Patrick Henry. By Prof. Moses Coit Tyler.
Henry Clay. By Hon. Carl Schurz.

Lives of others are also expected.

Hans Christian Andersen.

Complete Works. 8vo.
1. The Improvisatore ; or, Life in Italy.
2. The Two Baronesses.
3. O. T. ; or, Life in Denmark.
4. Only a Fiddler.
5. In Spain and Portugal.
6. A Poet's Bazaar.
7. Pictures of Travel.
8. The Story of my Life. With Portrait.
9. Wonder Stories told for Children. Ninety-two illustrations.
10. Stories and Tales. Illustrated.

Cloth, per volume, $1.50 ; price of sets in cloth, $15.00.

Francis Bacon.

Works. Collected and edited by Spedding, Ellis, and Heath. In fifteen volumes, crown 8vo, cloth, $33.75.
The same. *Popular Edition.* In two volumes, crown 8vo, with Portraits and Index. Cloth, $5.00.

Bacon's Life.

Life and Times of Bacon. Abridged. By James Spedding. 2 vols. crown 8vo, $5.00.

Björnstjerne Björnson.

Norwegian Novels. 16mo, each $1.00.

Synnöve Solbakken.	A Happy Boy.
Arne.	The Fisher Maiden.
The Bridal March.	Captain Mansana.

Magnhild.

British Poets.

Riverside Edition. In 68 volumes, crown 8vo, cloth, gilt top, per vol. $1.75; the set, 68 volumes, cloth, $100.00.

Akenside and Beattie, 1 vol.	Milton and Marvell, 2 vols
Ballads, 4 vols.	Montgomery, 2 vols.
Burns, 1 vol.	Moore, 3 vols.
Butler, 1 vol.	Pope and Collins, 2 vols.
Byron, 5 vols.	Prior, 1 vol.
Campbell and Falconer, 1 vol.	Scott, 5 vols.
Chatterton, 1 vol.	Shakespeare and Jonson, 1 vol.
Chaucer, 3 vols.	Shelley, 2 vols.
Churchill, Parnell, and Tickell, 2 vols.	Skelton and Donne, 2 vols.
Coleridge and Keats, 2 vols.	Southey, 5 vols.
Cowper, 2 vols.	Spenser, 3 vols.
Dryden, 2 vols.	Swift, 2 vols.
Gay, 1 vol	Thomson, 1 vol.
Goldsmith and Gray, 1 vol.	Watts and White, 1 vol.
Herbert and Vaughan, 1 vol.	Wordsworth, 3 vols.
Herrick, 1 vol.	Wyatt and Surrey, 1 vol.
Hood, 2 vols.	Young, 1 vol.

John Brown, M. D.

Spare Hours. 3 vols. 16mo, each $1.50.

Robert Browning.

Poems and Dramas, etc. 14 vols. $19.50.
Complete Works. New Edition. 7 vols. (*In Press.*)

Wm. C. Bryant.

Translation of Homer. The Iliad. 2 vols. royal 8vo, $9.00. Crown 8vo, $4.50. 1 vol. 12mo, $3.00.
The Odyssey. 2 vols. royal 8vo, $9.00. Crown 8vo, $4.50. 1 vol. 12mo, $3.00.

John Burroughs.

Wake-Robin. Illustrated. 16mo, $1.50.
Winter Sunshine. 16mo, $1.50.
Birds and Poets. 16mo, $1.50.
Locusts and Wild Honey. 16mo, $1.50.
Pepacton, and Other Sketches. 16mo, $1.50.

Thomas Carlyle.

Essays. With Portrait and Index. Four volumes, crown
8vo, $7.50. *Popular Edition.* Two volumes, $3.50.

Alice and Phœbe Cary.

Poems. *Household Edition.* 12mo, $2.00.
Library Edition. Portraits and 24 illustrations. 8vo, $4.00.
Poetical Works, including Memorial by Mary Clemmer.
1 vol. 8vo, $3.50. Full gilt, $4.00.
Ballads for Little Folk. Illustrated. $1.50.

L. Maria Child.

Looking toward Sunset. 4to, $2.50.

James Freeman Clarke.

Ten Great Religions. 8vo, $3.00.
Common Sense in Religion. 12mo, $2.00.
Memorial and Biographical Sketches. 12mo, $2.00.
Exotics. $1.00.

J. Fenimore Cooper.

Works. *Household Edition.* Illustrated. 32 vols. 16mo.
Cloth, per volume, $1.00 ; the set, $32.00.
Globe Edition. Illust'd. 16 vols. $20.00. (*Sold only in sets.*)
Sea Tales. Illustrated. 10 vols. 16mo, $10.00.
Leather Stocking Tales. *Household Edition.* Illustrated
5 vols. $5.00. *Riverside Edition.* 5 vols. $11.25.

Richard H. Dana.

To Cuba and Back. 16mo, $1.25.
Two Years Before the Mast. 16mo, $1.50.

Thomas De Quincey.

Works. *Riverside Edition.* In 12 vols. crown 8vo. Per volume, cloth, $1.50 ; the set, $18.00.
Globe Edition. Six vols. 12mo, $10.00. (*Sold only in sets.*)

Madame De Stael.

Germany.   1 vol. crown 8vo, $2.50.

Charles Dickens.

Works.   *Illustrated Library Edition.*   In 29 volumes, crown
8vo.   Cloth, each, $1.50 ; the set, $43.50.
Globe Edition.   In 15 vols. 12mo.   Cloth, per volume, $1.25 ;
the set, $18.75.

J. Lewis Diman.

The Theistic Argument as Affected by Recent Theories.
8vo, $2.00.
Orations and Essays.   8vo, $2.50.

F. S. Drake.

Dictionary of American Biography.   1 vol. 8vo, cloth, $6.00.

Charles L. Eastlake.

Hints on Household Taste.   Illustrated.   12mo, $3.00.

George Eliot.

The Spanish Gypsy.   16mo, $1.50.

Ralph Waldo Emerson.

Works.   10 vols. 16mo, $1.50 each ; the set, $15.00.
Fireside Edition.   5 vols. 16mo, $10.00.   (*Sold only in sets.*)
"Little Classic" Edition.   9 vols.   Cloth, each, $1.50.
Prose Works.   Complete.   3 vols. 12mo, $7.50.
Parnassus.   *Household Ed.*   12mo, $2.00.   *Library Ed.*, $4.00.

Fénelon.

Adventures of Telemachus.   Crown 8vo, $2.25.

James T. Fields.

Yesterdays with Authors.   12mo, $2.00.   8vo, $3.00.
Underbrush. $1.25.
Ballads and other Verses.   16mo, $1.00.
The Family Library of British Poetry, from Chaucer to the
Present Time (1350–1878).   Royal 8vo.   1,028 pages, with
12 fine steel portraits, $5.00.
Memoirs and Correspondence.   1 vol. 8vo, gilt top, $2.00.

John Fiske.

Myths and Mythmakers.   12mo, $2.00.
Outlines of Cosmic Philosophy.   2 vols. 8vo, $6.00.
The Unseen World, and other Essays.   12mo, $2.00.

Goethe.

Faust.   Metrical   Translation.   By Rev. C. T. Brooks.
16mo, $1.25.
Faust.   Translated into English Verse.   By Bayard Taylor.
2 vols. royal 8vo, $9.00 ; cr. 8vo, $4.50 ; 1 vol. 12mo, $3.00.
Correspondence with a Child.   Portrait of Bettina Brentano.
12mo, $1.50.
Wilhelm Meister.   Translated by Thomas Carlyle.   Portrait of Goethe.   2 vols. 12mo, $3.00.

Bret Harte.

Works.   New complete edition.   5 vols. 12mo, each $2.00.
Poems.   *Household Edition.*   12mo, $2.00.

Nathaniel Hawthorne.

Works.   *"Little Classic" Edition.*   Illustrated. 24 vols.
18mo, each $1.25 ; the set $30.00.
Illustrated Library Edition.   13 vols. 12mo, per vol. $2.00.
Fireside Edition.   Illustrated.   13 vols. 16mo, the set, $21.00.
New Globe Edition.   6 vols. 16mo, illustrated, the set, $10.00.

George S. Hillard.

Six Months in Italy.   12mo, $2.00.

Oliver Wendell Holmes.

Poems.   *Household Edition.*   12mo, $2.00.
Illustrated Library Edition.   Illustrated, full gilt, 8vo, $4.00.
Handy Volume Edition.   2 vols. 18mo, gilt top, $2.50.
The Autocrat of the Breakfast-Table.   18mo, $1.50 ; 12mo,
$2.00.
The Professor at the Breakfast-Table.   12mo, $2.00.
The Poet at the Breakfast-Table.   12mo, $2.00.
Elsie Venner.   12mo, $2.00.
The Guardian Angel.   12mo, $2.00.
Soundings from the Atlantic.   16mo, $1.75.
John Lothrop Motley.   A Memoir.   16mo, $1.50.

W. D. Howells.

Venetian Life. 12mo, $1.50.　　　Italian Journeys. $1.50.
Their Wedding Journey. Illus. 12mo, $1.50 ; 18mo, $1.25.
Suburban Sketches. Illustrated. 12mo, $1.50.
A Chance Acquaintance. Illus. 12mo, $1.50 ; 18mo, $1.25.
A Foregone Conclusion. 12mo, $1.50.
The Lady of the Aroostook. 12mo, $1.50.
The Undiscovered Country. $1.50.　　　Poems. $1.25.
Out of the Question. A Comedy. 18mo, $1.25.
A Counterfeit Presentment. 18mo, $1.25.
Choice Autobiography. Edited by W. D. Howells. 18mo, per vol. $1.25.
I., II. Memoirs of Frederica Sophia Wilhelmina, Margravine of Baireuth.
III. Lord Herbert of Cherbury, and Thomas Ellwood.
IV. Vittorio Alfieri. V. Carlo Goldoni.
VI. Edward Gibbon. VII., VIII. François Marmontel.

Thomas Hughes.

Tom Brown's School-Days at Rugby. $1.00.
Tom Brown at Oxford. 16mo, $1.25.
The Manliness of Christ. 16mo, gilt top, $1.00.

Henry James, Jr.

Passionate Pilgrim and other Tales. $2.00.
Transatlantic Sketches. 12mo, $2.00.
Roderick Hudson. 12mo, $2.00.
The American. 12mo, $2.00.
Watch and Ward. 18mo, $1.25.
The Europeans. 12mo, $1.50.
Confidence. 12mo, $1.50.
The Portrait of a Lady. $2.00.

Mrs. Anna Jameson.

Writings upon Art subjects. 10 vols. 18mo, each $1.50.

Sarah O. Jewett.

Deephaven. 18mo, $1.25.
Old Friends and New. 18mo, $1.25.
Country By-Ways. 18mo, $1.25.
Play-Days. Stories for Children. Sq. 16mo, $1.50.

Rossiter Johnson.

Little Classics. Eighteen handy volumes containing the choicest Stories, Sketches, and short Poems in English literature. Each in one vol. 18mo, $1.00; the set, $18.00 In 9 vols. square 16mo, $13.50. (*Sold in sets only.*)

Samuel Johnson.

Oriental Religions : India, 8vo, $5.00.   China, 8vo, $5.00.

T. Starr King.

Christianity and Humanity. With Portrait. 12mo, $2.00. Substance and Show. 12mo, $2.00.

Lucy Larcom.

Poems. 16mo, $1.25.   An Idyl of Work. 16mo, $1.25. Wild Roses of Cape Ann and other Poems. 16mo, $1.25. Childhood Songs. Illustrated. 12mo, $1.50 ; 16mo, $1.00. Breathings of the Better Life. 18mo, $1.25.

G. P. Lathrop.

A Study of Hawthorne. 18mo, $1.25. An Echo of Passion. 16mo, $1.25.

G. H. Lewes.

The Story of Goethe's Life. Portrait. 12mo, $1.50. Problems of Life and Mind. 5 vols. $14.00.

H. W. Longfellow.

Poems. *Cambridge Edition complete.* Portrait. 4 vols. cr. 8vo, $9.00. 2 vols. $7.00.
Octavo Edition. Portrait and 300 illustrations. $8.00.
Household Edition. Portrait. 12mo, $2.00.
Red-Line Edition. 12 illustrations and Portrait. $2.50.
Diamond Edition. $1.00.
Library Edition. Portrait and 32 illustrations. 8vo, $4.00.
Prose Works. *Cambridge Edition.* 2 vols. cr. 8vo, $4.50.
Hyperion. A Romance. 16mo, $1.50.
Outre-Mer. 16mo, $1.50.   Kavanagh. 16mo, $1.50.
Christus. *Household Edition*, $2.00 ; *Diamond Edition*, $1.00.
Translation of the Divina Commedia of Dante. 3 vols. royal 8vo, $13.50 ; cr. 8vo, $6.00 ; 1 vol. cr. 8vo, $3.00.
Poets and Poetry of Europe. Royal 8vo, $5.00.
In the Harbor. Steel Portrait. 16mo, gilt top, $1.00.

James Russell Lowell.

Poems. *Red-Line Ed.* 16 illustrations and Portrait. $2.50.
Household Edition. Portrait. 12mo, $2.00.
Library Edition. Portrait and 32 illustrations. 8vo, $4.00.
Diamond Edition. $1.00.
Fireside Travels. 16mo, $1.50.
Among my Books. 1st and 2nd Series. 12mo, $2.00 each.
My Study Windows. 12mo, $2.00.

T. B. Macaulay.

England. *New Riverside Edition.* 4 vols., cloth, $5.00.
Essays. Portrait. *New Riverside Edition.* 3 vols., $3.75.
Speeches and Poems. *New Riverside Ed.* 1 vol., $1.25.

Harriet Martineau.

Autobiography. Portraits and illus. 2 vols. 8vo, $6.00.
Household Education. 18mo, $1.25.

Owen Meredith.

Poems. *Household Edition.* Illustrated. 12mo, $2.00.
Library Edition. Portrait and 32 illustrations. 8vo, $4.00.
Shawmut Edition. $1.50.
Lucile. *Red-Line Edition.* 8 illustrations. $2.50.
Diamond Edition. 8 illustrations, $1.00.

Michael de Montaigne.

Complete Works. Portrait. 4 vols. crown 8vo, $7.50.

Rev. T. Mozley.

Reminiscences, chiefly of Oriel College and the Oxford Movement. 2 vols. crown 8vo, $3.00.

E. Mulford.

The Nation. 8vo, $2.50.
The Republic of God. 8vo, $2.00.

D. M. Mulock.

Thirty Years. Poems. 1 vol. 16mo, $1.50.

T. T. Munger.

On the Threshold. 16mo, gilt top, $1.00.

J. A. W. Neander.

History of the Christian Religion and Church, with Index volume, 6 vols. 8vo, $20.00 ; Index alone, $3.00.

C. E. Norton.

Notes of Travel and Study in Italy. 16mo, $1.25.
Translation of Dante's New Life. Royal 8vo, $3.00.

Francis W. Palfrey.

Memoir of William Francis Bartlett. 16mo, $1.50.

James Parton.

Life of Benjamin Franklin. 2 vols. 8vo, $4.00.
Life of Thomas Jefferson. 8vo, $2.00.
Life of Aaron Burr. 2 vols. 8vo, $4.00.
Life of Andrew Jackson. 3 vols. 8vo, $6.00.
Life of Horace Greeley. 8vo, $2.50.
General Butler in New Orleans. 8vo, $2.50.
Humorous Poetry of the English Language. 8vo, $2.00.
Famous Americans of Recent Times. 8vo, $2.00.
Life of Voltaire. 2 vols. 8vo, $6 00.
The French Parnassus. 12mo, $2.00; crown 8vo, $3.50.

Blaise Pascal.

Thoughts, Letters, and Opuscules. Crown 8vo, $2.25.
Provincial Letters. Crown 8vo, $2.25.

E. S. Phelps.

The Gates Ajar. 16mo, $1.50.
Men, Women, and Ghosts. 16mo, $1.50.
Hedged In. 16mo, $1.50.
The Silent Partner. 16mo, $1.50.
The Story of Avis. 16mo, $1.50.
Sealed Orders, and other Stories. 16mo, $1.50.
Friends : A Duet. 16mo, $1.25.
Dr. Zay. 16mo. (*In Press.*)
Poetic Studies. Square 16mo, $1.50.

Adelaide A. Procter.

Poems. *Diamond Edition.* $1.00.
Red-Line Edition. Portrait and 16 illustrations. $2.50.
Favorite Edition. Illustrated. 16mo, $1.50.

Henry Crabb Robinson.

Diary. Crown 8vo, $2.50.

A. P. Russell.

Library Notes. 12mo, $2.00.

John G. Saxe.

Works. Portrait. 16mo, $2.25.
Poems. *Red-Line Edition.* Illustrated. $2.50.
Diamond Edition. 18mo, $1.00.
Household Edition. 12mo, $2.00.

Sir Walter Scott.

Waverley Novels. *Illustrated Library Edition.* In 25 vols.
cr. 8vo, each $1.00 ; the set, $25.00.
Globe Edition. 13 vols. 100 illustrations, $16.25.
Tales of a Grandfather. *Library Edition.* 3 vols. $4.50.
Poems. *Red-Line Edition.* Illustrated. $2.50.
Diamond Edition. 18mo, $1.00.

Horace E. Scudder.

The Bodley Books. 6 vols. Each $1.50.
The Dwellers in Five-Sisters' Court. 16mo, $1.25.
Stories and Romances. $1.25.
Dream Children. Illustrated. 16mo, $1.00.
Seven Little People. Illustrated. 16mo, $1.00.
Stories from my Attic. Illustrated. 16mo, $1.00.
The Children's Book. 4to, 450 pages, $3.50.
Boston Town. Illustrated. 12mo, $1.50.

J. C. Shairp.

Culture and Religion. 16mo, $.125.
Poetic Interpretation of Nature. 16mo, $1.25.
Studies in Poetry and Philosophy. 16mo, $1.50.
Aspects of Poetry. 16mo, $1.50.

Dr. William Smith.

Bible Dictionary. *American Edition.* In four vols. 8vo,
the set, $20.00.

E. C. Stedman.

Poems. *Farringford Edition.* Portrait. 16mo, $2.00.
Victorian Poets. 12mo, $2.00.
Hawthorne, and other Poems. 16mo, $1.25.
Edgar Allan Poe. An Essay. Vellum, 18mo, $1.00.

Harriet Beecher Stowe.

Agnes of Sorrento. 12mo, $1.50.
The Pearl of Orr's Island. 12mo, $1.50.
Uncle Tom's Cabin. *Popular Edition.* 12mo, $2.00.
The Minister's Wooing. 12mo, $1.50.
The May-flower, and other Sketches. 12mo, $1.50.
Nina Gordon. 12mo, $1.50.
Oldtown Folks. 12mo, $1.50.
Sam Lawson's Fireside Stories. Illustrated. $1.50.
Uncle Tom's Cabin. 100 Illustrations. 12mo, full gilt, $3.50.

Bayard Taylor.

Poetical Works. *Household Edition.* 12mo, $2.00.
Dramatic Works. Crown 8vo, $2.25.
The Echo Club, and other Literary Diversions. $1.25.

Alfred Tennyson.

Poems. *Household Ed.* Portrait and 60 illustrations. $2.00.
Illustrated Crown Edition. 48 illustrations. 2 vols. $5.00.
Library Edition. Portrait and 60 illustrations. $4.00.
Red-Line Edition. Portrait and 16 illustrations. $2.50.
Diamond Edition. $1.00.
Shawmut Edition. Illustrated. Crown 8vo, $1.50.
Idylls of the King. Complete. Illustrated. $1.50.

Celia Thaxter.

Among the Isles of Shoals. $1.25.
Poems. $1.50.   Drift-Weed. Poems. $1.50.

Henry D. Thoreau.

Walden. 12mo, $1.50.
A Week on the Concord and Merrimack Rivers. $1.50.
Excursions in Field and Forest. 12mo, $1.50.
The Maine Woods. 12mo, $1.50.
Cape Cod. 12mo, $1.50.
Letters to various Persons. 12mo, $1.50.
A Yankee in Canada. 12mo, $1.50.
Early Spring in Massachusetts. 12mo, $1.50.

George Ticknor.

History of Spanish Literature. 3 vols. 8vo, $10.00.
Life, Letters, and Journals. Portraits. 2 vols. 8vo, $6.00.
Cheaper edition. 2 vols. 12mo, $4.00.

J. T. Trowbridge.

A Home Idyl. $1.25. The Vagabonds. $1.25.
The Emigrant's Story. 16mo, $1.25.

Voltaire.

History of Charles XII. Crown 8vo, $2.25.

Lew Wallace.

The Fair God. 12mo, $1.50.

George E. Waring, Jr.

Whip and Spur. $1.25. A Farmer's Vacation. $3.00.
Village Improvements. Illustrated. 75 cents.
The Bride of the Rhine. Illustrated. $1.50.

Charles Dudley Warner.

My Summer in a Garden. 16mo, $1.00. *Illustrated.* $1.50.
Saunterings. 18mo, $1.25.
Back-Log Studies. Illustrated. $1.50.
Baddeck, and that Sort of Thing. $1.00.
My Winter on the Nile. 12mo, $2.00.
In the Levant. 12mo, $2.00.
Being a Boy. Illustrated. $1.50.
In the Wilderness. 75 cents.

William A. Wheeler.

Dictionary of the Noted Names of Fiction. $2.00.

Edwin P. Whipple.

Works. Critical Essays. 6 vols., $9.00

Richard Grant White.

Every-Day English. 12mo, $2.00.
Words and their Uses. 12mo, $2.00.
England Without and Within. 12mo, $2.00.
Shakespeare's Complete Works. 3 vols. cr. 8vo. (*In Press.*)

Mrs. A. D. T. Whitney.

Faith Gartney's Girlhood. 12mo, $1.50.
Hitherto. 12mo, $1.50.
Patience Strong's Outings. 12mo, $1.50.
The Gayworthys. 12mo, $1.50.

Leslie Goldthwaite. Illustrated. 12mo, $1.50.
We Girls. Illustrated. 12mo, $1.50.
Real Folks. Illustrated. 12mo, $1.50.
The Other Girls. Illustrated. 12mo, $1.50.
Sights and Insights. 2 vols. 12mo, $3.00.
Odd or Even. $1.50.
Boys at Chequasset. $1.50.
Pansies. Square 16mo, $1.50.
Just How. 16mo, $1.00.

John G. Whittier.

Poems. *Household Edition.* Portrait. $2.00.
Cambridge Edition. Portrait. 3 vols. crown 8vo, $6.75.
Red-Line Edition. Portrait. 12 illustrations. $2.50.
Diamond Edition. 18mo, $1.00.
Library Edition. Portrait. 32 illustrations. 8vo, $4.00.
Prose Works. *Cambridge Edition.* 2 vols. $4.50.
John Woolman's Journal. Introduction by Whittier. $1.50.
Child Life in Poetry. Selected by Whittier. Illustrated.
$2.25. Child Life in Prose. $2.25.
Songs of Three Centuries. Selected by J. G. Whittier.
Household Edition. 12mo, $2.00. *Illustrated Library
Edition.* 32 illustrations. $4.00.

Justin Winsor.

Reader's Handbook of the American Revolution. 16mo,
$1.25.

———

*A catalogue containing portraits of many of the above
authors, with a description of their works, will be sent
free, on application, to any address.*

HOUGHTON, MIFFLIN AND COMPANY, BOSTON, MASS.